AFRICAN HISTORICAL DICTIONARIES
Edited by Jon Woronoff

1. *Cameroon,* by Victor T. Le Vine and Roger P. Nye. 1974. *Out of print. See No. 48.*
2. *The Congo,* 2nd ed., by Virginia Thompson and Richard Adloff. 1984. *Out of print. See No. 69.*
3. *Swaziland,* by John J. Grotpeter. 1975.
4. *The Gambia,* 2nd ed., by Harry A. Gailey. 1987.
5. *Botswana,* by Richard P. Stevens. 1975. *Out of print. See No. 70.*
6. *Somalia,* by Margaret F. Castagno. 1975.
7. *Benin (Dahomey),* 2nd ed., by Samuel Decalo. 1987. *Out of print. See No. 61.*
8. *Burundi,* by Warren Weinstein. 1976. *Out of print. See No. 73.*
9. *Togo,* 3rd ed., by Samuel Decalo. 1996.
10. *Lesotho,* by Gordon Haliburton. 1977.
11. *Mali,* 3rd ed., by Pascal James Imperato. 1996.
12. *Sierra Leone,* by Cyril Patrick Foray. 1977.
13. *Chad,* 3rd ed., by Samuel Decalo. 1997.
14. *Upper Volta,* by Daniel Miles McFarland. 1978.
15. *Tanzania,* by Laura S. Kurtz. 1978.
16. *Guinea,* 3rd ed., by Thomas O'Toole with Ibrahima Bah-Lalya. 1995.
17. *Sudan,* by John Voll. 1978. *Out of print. See No. 53.*
18. *Rhodesia/Zimbabwe,* by R. Kent Rasmussen. 1979. *Out of print. See No. 46.*
19. *Zambia,* 2nd ed., by John J. Grotpeter, Brian V. Siegel, and James R. Pletcher. 1998.
20. *Niger,* 3rd ed., by Samuel Decalo. 1997.
21. *Equatorial Guinea,* 3rd ed., by Max Liniger-Goumaz. 2000.
22. *Guinea-Bissau,* 3rd ed., by Richard Lobban and Peter Mendy. 1997.
23. *Senegal,* by Lucie G. Colvin. 1981. *Out of print. See No. 65.*
24. *Morocco,* by William Spencer. 1980. *Out of print. See No. 71.*
25. *Malawi,* by Cynthia A. Crosby. 1980. *Out of print. See No. 54.*
26. *Angola,* by Phyllis Martin. 1980. *Out of print. See No. 52.*

27. *The Central African Republic,* by Pierre Kalck. 1980. *Out of print. See No. 51.*
28. *Algeria,* by Alf Andrew Heggoy. 1981. *Out of print. See No. 66.*
29. *Kenya,* by Bethwell A. Ogot. 1981. *Out of print. See No. 77.*
30. *Gabon,* by David E. Gardinier. 1981. *Out of print. See No. 58.*
31. *Mauritania,* by Alfred G. Gerteiny. 1981. *Out of print. See No. 68.*
32. *Ethiopia,* by Chris Prouty and Eugene Rosenfeld. 1981. *Out of print. See No. 56.*
33. *Libya,* 3rd ed., by Ronald Bruce St John. 1998.
34. *Mauritius,* by Lindsay Riviere. 1982. *Out of print. See No. 49.*
35. *Western Sahara,* by Tony Hodges. 1982. *Out of print. See No. 55.*
36. *Egypt,* by Joan Wucher King. 1984. *Out of print. See No. 67.*
37. *South Africa,* by Christopher Saunders. 1983. *Out of print. See No. 78.*
38. *Liberia,* by D. Elwood Dunn and Svend E. Holsoe. 1985.
39. *Ghana,* by Daniel Miles McFarland. 1985. *Out of print. See No. 78.*
40. *Nigeria,* 2nd ed., by Anthony Oyewole and John Lucas. 2000.
41. *Côte d'Ivoire (The Ivory Coast),* 2nd ed., by Robert J. Mundt. 1995.
42. *Cape Verde,* 2nd ed., by Richard Lobban and Marilyn Halter. 1988. *Out of print. See No. 62.*
43. *Zaire,* by F. Scott Bobb. 1988. *Out of print. See No. 76.*
44. *Botswana,* 2nd ed., by Fred Morton, Andrew Murray, and Jeff Ramsay. 1989. *Out of print. See No. 70.*
45. *Tunisia,* 2nd ed., by Kenneth J. Perkins. 1997.
46. *Zimbabwe,* 3rd ed., by Steven C. Rubert and R. Kent Rasmussen. 1998.
47. *Mozambique,* by Mario Azevedo. 1991.
48. *Cameroon,* 2nd ed., by Mark W. DeLancey and H. Mbella Mokeba. 1990.
49. *Mauritius,* 2nd ed., by Sydney Selvon. 1991.
50. *Madagascar,* by Maureen Covell. 1995.
51. *The Central African Republic,* 2nd ed., by Pierre Kalck; translated by Thomas O'Toole. 1992.
52. *Angola,* 2nd ed., by Susan H. Broadhead. 1992.
53. *Sudan,* 2nd ed., by Carolyn Fluehr-Lobban, Richard A. Lobban, Jr., and John Obert Voll. 1992.
54. *Malawi,* 2nd ed., by Cynthia A. Crosby. 1993.
55. *Western Sahara,* 2nd ed., by Anthony Pazzanita and Tony Hodges. 1994.
56. *Ethiopia and Eritrea,* 2nd ed., by Chris Prouty and Eugene Rosenfeld. 1994.
57. *Namibia,* by John J. Grotpeter. 1994.

58. *Gabon,* 2nd ed., by David E. Gardinier. 1994.
59. *Comoro Islands,* by Martin Ottenheimer and Harriet Ottenheimer. 1994.
60. *Rwanda,* by Learthen Dorsey. 1994.
61. *Benin,* 3rd ed., by Samuel Decalo. 1995.
62. *Republic of Cape Verde,* 3rd ed., by Richard Lobban and Marlene Lopes. 1995.
63. *Ghana,* 2nd ed., by David Owusu-Ansah and Daniel Miles McFarland. 1995.
64. *Uganda,* by M. Louise Pirouet. 1995.
65. *Senegal,* 2nd ed., by Andrew F. Clark and Lucie Colvin Phillips. 1994.
66. *Algeria,* 2nd ed., by Phillip Chiviges Naylor and Alf Andrew Heggoy. 1994.
67. *Egypt,* 2nd ed., by Arthur Goldschmidt, Jr. 1994.
68. *Mauritania,* 2nd ed., by Anthony G. Pazzanita. 1996.
69. *Congo,* 3rd ed., by Samuel Decalo, Virginia Thompson, and Richard Adloff. 1996.
70. *Botswana,* 3rd ed., by Jeff Ramsay, Barry Morton, and Fred Morton. 1996.
71. *Morocco,* 2nd ed., by Thomas K. Park. 1996.
72. *Tanzania,* 2nd ed., by Thomas P. Ofcansky and Rodger Yeager. 1997.
73. *Burundi,* 2nd ed., by Ellen K. Eggers. 1997.
74. *Burkina Faso,* 2nd ed., by Daniel Miles McFarland and Lawrence Rupley. 1998.
75. *Eritrea,* by Tom Killion. 1998.
76. *Democratic Republic of the Congo (Zaire),* by F. Scott Bobb. 1999. (Revised edition of *Historical Dictionary of Zaire*, No. 43)
77. *Kenya,* 2nd ed., by Robert M. Maxon and Thomas P. Ofcansky. 2000.
78. *South Africa,* 2nd ed., by Christopher Saunders and Nicholas Southey. 2000.
79. *The Gambia,* 3rd ed., by Arnold Hughes and Harry A. Gailey. 2000.
80. *Swaziland*, 2nd ed., by Alan R. Booth. 2000.
81. *Republic of Cameroon,* 3rd ed., by Mark W. DeLancey and Mark Dike DeLancey. 2000.
82. *Djibouti*, by Daoud A. Alwan and Yohanis Mibrathu. 2000.
83. *Liberia,* 2nd ed., by C. Elwood Dunn, Amos J. Beyan, and Carl Patrick Burrowes. 2000.

Historical Dictionary
of Djibouti

Daoud A. Alwan
Yohanis Mibrathu

African Historical Dictionaries, No. 82

The Scarecrow Press, Inc.
Lanham, Maryland, and London
2000

SCARECROW PRESS, INC.

Published in the United States of America
by Scarecrow Press, Inc.
4720 Boston Way, Lanham, Maryland 20706
http://www.scarecrowpress.com

4 Pleydell Gardens, Folkestone
Kent CT20 2DN, England

British Library Cataloguing in Publication Information Available

Library of Congress Cataloging-in-Publication Data

Aboubaker, Alwan, Daoud.
    Historical dictionary of Djibouti / Daoud A. Alwan, Yohanis Mibrathu.
       p.   cm. — (African historical dictionaries)
    Includes bibliographical references (p.).
    ISBN 0-8108-3873-7 (cloth : alk. paper)
    1. Djibouti—History—Dictionaries. I. Mibrathu, Yohanis.
    II. Title. III. Series.
    DT411.5 .A34 2000
    967.71′003—dc21   00-040001

Contents

To the memory of Mahamoud Mohamed

Editor's Foreword

If any country in Africa should be in serious trouble, it is the Republic of Djibouti. Small in area by any definition and located at the crossroads of Africa and the Middle East, this country was a vital pawn in the geopolitics of the Cold War era. For decades, long before it became independent, its neighbors have been at war, both internally and with one another. Any of these countries would have been more than happy to absorb Djibouti, had it not been for the permanent presence of a French military base. This installation was created mainly for the port and railroad system, as the country attempted to take advantage of its lead in modern communications to attract foreign investors without much success. After a period of decline, port activities increased in 1998, due to the conflict between Eritrea and Ethiopia, and are now booming; the railroad, unfortunately, remains a poor relation. Amazingly, after a long period of one-party rule, Djibouti finally appears to be somewhat closer to democracy with a four-party system—although so far the results are not promising.

This *Historical Dictionary of Djibouti*, the latest in Scarecrow's African series, presents a rare picture of this unique country, perched on a corner of the Red Sea, largely Muslim, and with a strong Arab influence. For Africans, Middle Easterners, and others interested in a crucial and still strategic part of the world, it is helpful to know more about the Republic of Djibouti—its history, recent politics, economy, society, and culture. This dictionary is one of the very few places where such information is conveniently gathered. And for those whose main or sole language is English, it will be particularly valuable, as illustrated by the heavily French-language bibliography.

This volume was written by Daoud Aboubaker Alwan and Yohanis Mibrathu, both of whom were born and grew up in Djibouti and later attended French universities—the former specializing in history and political science, and the latter studying language and literature in Aix-en-Provence. Both men eventually returned to Djibouti, where Daoud Aboubaker Alwan taught history and worked as a researcher for the Institut Supérieur d'Etude et de Recherche Scientifiques et Technologiques. Yohanis Mibrathu taught English in several schools and worked as a translator for the Chamber of Commerce before moving quite recently to the United States. They obviously know the country very well and are thus able to transmit this knowledge to their readers, many of whom will know nothing about Djibouti before reading this book. This is indeed a worthwhile contribution to a country that recently celebrated twenty years of independence, a country that has been moving slowly but surely into the 21st century.

Jon Woronoff
Series Editor

Reader's Notes

Transliteration

In order not to create confusion in the reader's mind, no specific graphemes have been used for the transcription of local names or terms. We have tried as much as possible to respect the most common spellings, giving the various ones in use when necessary.

Names

Permanent family names do not exist in Djibouti. Individuals are therefore identified by their personal names. Thus, with the name Hussein Ahmed Ali, Hussein is the person's personal name, Ahmed the father's name, and Ali the grandfather's. The use of nicknames to describe their bearers' personality or physical particulars is frequent, especially among the Somali. Therefore, whenever a person is better known by a given nickname, two entries have been made, with the nickname entry cross-referencing to the formal name.

Titles

It is not rare to find names that are followed or preceded by a title. A title such as *hadj*, usually placed before the person's name, indicates that the person has made the pilgrimage to Mecca, whereas the title *sheikh* indicates that its bearer is considered to have a deep knowledge of religion. On the other hand, titles such as *pasha* and *bey* are reminiscent of the Ottoman occupation. These titles are usually placed after the person's personal name and have, in some cases, almost replaced the father's name in everyday use, as is the case in the name Aboubaker Pasha.

Cross-references

Terms printed in bold indicate cross-references.

Acronyms and Abbreviations

AID	Aéroport International de Djibouti
AND	Armée Nationale de Djibouti
BCI-MR	Banque pour le Commerce et l'Industrie-Mer Rouge
BDD	Banque de Développement de Djibouti
BDMO	Banque de Djibouti et du Moyen-Orient
BIS	Banque Indo-Suez
BND	Banque Nationale de Djibouti
CAO	Compagnie de l'Afrique Orientale
CCFAR	Centre Culturel Français Arthur Rimbaud
CCFOM	Caisse Centrale de France et d'Outre-Mer
CDE	Chemin de Fer Djibouto-Ethiopien
CEGED	Centre d'Etudes Géologiques de Djibouti
CES	Collège d'Enseignement Secondaire
CFE	Chemin de Fer Franco–Ethiopien
CFPA	Centre de Formation Professionnelle pour Adultes
CFPEN	Centre de Formation Professionnelle de l'Education Nationale
CFS	Côte Française des Somalis
CICID	Chambre Internationale de Commerce et d'Industrie de Djibouti
CIE	Compagnie Impériale d'Ethiopie
CMAO	Compagnie Maritime d'Afrique Orientale
CRIL	Centre Régional Inter-Linguistique
CRIPEN	Centre de Recherche, d'Information et de Production de l'Education Nationale
DGEN	Direction Générale de l'Education Nationale
DGER	Direction Générale des Etudes et Recherches
DIEST	Défense des Intérêts Economiques et Sociaux du Territoire
DINAS	Direction Nationale de la Statistique
EDD	Electricité de Djibouti
EGTP	Entreprise Générale des Travaux Publics
EPH	Etablissements Publics d'Hydrocarbures

FDLD	Front de Libération de Djibouti
FIDES	Fonds d'Investissement et de Développement Economique et Social
FLCS	Front de Libération de la Côte Somalie
FNS/FNP	Force Nationale de Sécurité / Force Nationale de Police
FRUD	Front pour la Restauration de l'Unité et de la Démocratie
GCF	Groupement Commando des Frontières
IGADD	Inter-Governmental Authority on Drought and Desertification
INAP	Institut National d'Administration Publique
ISERST	Institut Supérieur d'Etudes et de Recherches Scientifiques et Techniques
LEP	Lycée d'Enseignement Professionnel
LIC	Lycée Industriel et Commercial
LPA	Ligue Populaire Africaine
LPAI	Ligue Populaire Africaine pour l'Indépendance
MLCS	Mouvement de Libération de la Côte Somalie
MLD	Mouvement de Libération de Djibouti
MPL	Mouvement Populaire de Libération
MUR	Mouvement d'Union Républicaine
OAU	Organization of African Unity
ONAC	Office National d'Approvisionnement et de Commercialisation
ONARS	Office National d'Assistance aux Réfugiés et aux Sinistrés
ONED	Office National des Eaux de Djibouti
ONTA	Office National du Tourisme et de l'Artisanat
OPT	Office National des Postes et Télécommunications
ORTF	Office de la Radiodiffusion et de la Télévision Française
PAID	Port Autonome International de Djibouti
PAS	Programme d'Ajustement Structurel
PMP	Parti Mouvement Populaire
PND	Parti National Démocratique
PPD	Parti Populaire Djiboutien
PRD	Parti du Renouveau Démocratique
RDA	Rassemblement Démocratique Afar
RDD	République de Djibouti
RPP	Rassemblement Populaire pour le Progrès
RSE	Radio Scolaire et Educative
RTD	Radio Télévision de Djibouti
SEAO	Société d'Etudes d'Afrique Orientale
SID	Société Industrielle de Djibouti
SMI	Service Médical Interentreprise

SOGIK	Société Générale d'Importation du Khat
SRI	Service du Renseignement Intercolonial
STID	Société des Télécommunications Internationales de Djibouti
SUSOC	Student Union of the Somali Coast
TFAI	Territoire Français des Afars et des Issas
UDA	Union Démocratique Afar
UDC	Union pour le Développement de la Culture
UDI	Union Démocratique Issa
UGTD	Union Générale des Travailleurs Djiboutiens
UNECAS	Union Nationale des Etudiants de la Côte Afar et Somalie
UNFD	Union Nationale des Femmes Djiboutiennes
UNHCR	U.N. High Commissioner for Refugees
UNI	Union Nationale pour l'Indépendance

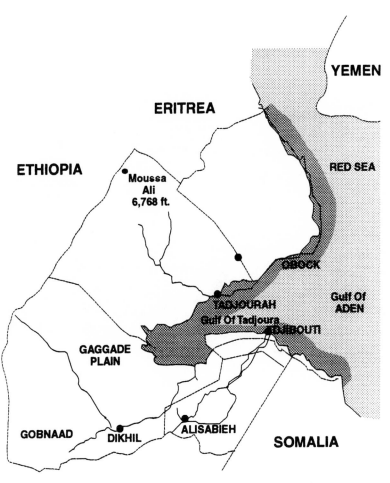

YEMEN

ERITREA

ETHIOPIA

● Moussa
Ali
6,768 ft.

RED SEA

●

OBOCK

Gulf Of
ADEN

TADJOURAH

Gulf Of Tadjoura

DJIBOUTI

GAGGADE
PLAIN

GOBNAAD

● DIKHIL

● ALISABIEH

SOMALIA

Map of the Republic of Djibouti

Chronology

1858   **July 5:** Aboubaker Ibrahim Pasha offers to give up Mount Ras Ali and the Bay of Ouano, on the Gulf of Tadjourah, to France.

1859   **June 4:** Henri Lambert, French consul and trader at Aden, is assassinated by agents of Ali Charmarke, the former *pasha* of Zeila.

1862   **March 4:** France signs a treaty with the Danakil chiefs, giving the French Obock for anchorage and a territory extending from Ras Doumeira (north of the Gulf of Tadjourah) to Ras Ali (to the south). **March 11:** The treaty giving up Obock to France is signed in Paris. **May 20:** France officially takes over Obock.

1869   **November 16:** The Suez Canal is inaugurated.

1874   The Egyptians settle the coastline, from Tadjourah to Berbeira.

1880   The French officially delimit the territory of Obock.

1883   The colony of Obock is officially founded.

1884   **June 24:** Léonce Lagarde is appointed governor of the Protectorat d'Obock et Dépendances.

1885   **March 26:** The first treaty between the French and the Issa chiefs is signed for the transfer of the territory located between the Bay of Ambado and Ras Djibouti.

1887   The city of Djibouti is founded.

1888   **March:** The port of Djibouti is inaugurated.

1889   January 18: A Russian squadron, led by Admiral Atchinoff, anchors at Sagallou. **February:** Admiral Orly shells the fort of Sagallou and dislodges the Russian Cossacks and monks.

1891   April 10: Emperor Menelik of Ethiopia sends a circular letter to the European powers to inform them of his empire's boundaries.

1894   March 9: Emperor Menelik gives the engineer Alfred Ilg a concession to construct a railroad from Djibouti to the Blue Nile via Harar and Entoto.

1896   March 1: The Italians are defeated at Adoua, in northern Ethiopia. **May 20:** The protectorate changes its name to Côte Française des Somalis (CFS). **August 9:** The Compagnie Impériale des Chemins de Fer Ethiopiens (CIE) is created.

1897   July: The construction of the Djibouti–Addis Ababa railroad is started; a series of treaties establishing the boundaries for Ethiopia and neighboring European colonies is signed; a Franco-Ethiopian convention amends the agreements signed in 1885 with the local tribes and establishing the boundaries of a hinterland to the CFS.

**1898   Great Britain conquers Sudan. British Field Marshal H. H. Kitchener settles in Fashoda and will not allow France to establish a physical connection between its western Africa colonies and Djibouti.

**1908   The CIE is liquidated.

1909   April 3: The Compagnie du Chemin de Fer Franco-Ethiopien (CFE) is officially established.

**1913   Emperor Menelik dies and is replaced by Lej Iyasu.

**1916   Haile Selassie eliminates Lej Iyasu and replaces him.

1917   June: The railroad linking Djibouti to Addis Ababa is opened. **August:** The protectorate becomes a colony after a second treaty is signed with Issa elders.

1926   July 12: The *Fontainebleau*, a ship belonging to the Messageries Maritimes, burns and sinks in the port of Djibouti.

1931   Colonial Exhibition is held in Paris.

1932   Work for the port of Djibouti extension is started.

1935   **January 18:** The French administrative officer Bernard is killed at Moraito. **January:** France makes territorial concessions to Italy in Mussolini-Laval agreement; the conflict between Italy and Ethiopia begins; Haile Selassie leaves his country by train via Djibouti and goes into exile in Great Britain.

1938   French troops consisting essentially of Senegalese soldiers arrive in Djibouti following Italian provocation.

1940   The Allied Forces under British command start conquering Somalia, Ethiopia, and Eritrea.

1940   **September:** The Allied Forces impose a blockade on Djibouti as a sanction for its siding with the Vichy government. The blockade will last until January 1942.

1945   **November 9:** A council of representatives is formed.

1946   **December:** The war in Indochina starts.

1949   **March 17:** A new currency, the Djibouti franc, is created. **June:** Violent clashes between the Issa and Gadaboursi communities in the capital city of Djibouti cause the death of 100 people.

1956   **June 23:** The Loi Cadre on the future evolution of the French colonies is enacted. It will be enforced in Djibouti in 1957. **July 26:** Egypt nationalizes the Suez Canal. **September 17:** French General Charles de Gaulle visits Djibouti.

1957   **April 14:** The Conseil des Représentants (Council of Representatives) changes its name to Assemblée Territoriale (Territorial Assembly). **July 22:** The Conseil du Gouvernement (Government Council) is established.

1958   French colonies start moving toward independence.

1960   Following the bankruptcy of the Compagnie des Salines de Djibouti, the working of the salt marshes is stopped.

1962   December 16–31: Port of Djibouti dockworkers go on strike.

1966   August 25–27: French President Charles de Gaulle visits Djibouti. **September 5–15:** The dockworkers go on strike again. **September 13:** Riots erupt in the capital city of Djibouti. Five gendarmerie barracks are set on fire. **September 14:** A checkpoint is set up at the entrance of the city of Djibouti. A curfew is imposed. The import of *khat* is forbidden.

1967   March 19: A referendum on self-determination is organized in Djibouti. The victory of those who support a French presence is followed by riots. The name of the colony, previously called Côte Française des Somalis, is changed to Territoire Français des Afars et des Issas (TFAI). **April 14:** The television station is inaugurated.

1970   January 24: Bomb attack at the Palmier en Zinc café kills 18 people.

1971   April 7: Two prisoners escape from the Tadjourah prison, kidnap the head administrator and his wife, and cross the border to the Somali Republic.

1973   January 15: French President Georges Pompidou visits Djibouti.

1975   March 23: The French ambassador to Somaliland, Jean Gueury, is kidnapped by the Front de Libération de la Côte Somalie (FLCS).

1976   February 3: FLCS hijacks a school bus transporting French students. **December 20:** A bomb explodes at the Mic-Mac bar, killing two people and injuring 16.

1977   March: A roundtable is held in Paris to prepare the French colony for independence. **June 27:** The TFAI becomes independent and takes the name of Republic of Djibouti. **December 15:** Bomb attack at the Palmier en Zinc café. Premier Ahmed Dini Ahmed resigns to protest the repression that ensues.

1977–78   Ethiopia and Somalia go to war. Railroad transport is interrupted for one year.

1981   February: A law allowing for the direct election of the president is enacted. **June:** The first presidential elections are held in Djibouti. Hassan

Gouled, the sole candidate, is elected to a six-year term. **October 24:** The Loi de Mobilisation Nationale, which officially establishes the single-party system, is enacted.

1986   **January:** A bomb explodes at the headquarters of the Rassemblement Populaire pour le Progrès (RPP), killing two people.

1987   **March 18:** A bomb explodes at the Historil, a café mostly frequented by French customers, killing 12 people. **April:** A presidential election is held, and Hassan Gouled is reelected.

1989   **April:** Intercommunity clashes in the city of Djibouti and Tadjourah kill 10 people.

1990   **September 27:** A bomb explodes at the Café de Paris.

1991   **January:** Ali Aref Bourhan and about 100 Afar dissidents are arrested. **February:** Fall of the Syad Barre regime in Somalia. **May:** Fall of the Derg military regime in Ethiopia. **November:** Beginning of an armed conflict between the governmental forces and the Front pour la Restauration de l'Unité et de la Démocratie (FRUD). **December 18:** Eight people are killed and 26 injured in a clash between the security forces and civilians in the neighborhood of Arhiba, populated mostly by Afar.

1992   **September 4:** Djibouti's first constitution is adopted.

1993   **May 7:** Presidential election is held; Hassan Gouled Aptidon is reelected.

1994   **December 26:** A peace agreement is signed at Ab'a with dissident members of FRUD. The demobilization process is initiated.

1996   A crisis within the RPP results in the dismissal from the party—and subsequent imprisonment—of four leading politicians. **November 26:** Mohamed Djama Elabe, leader of the Parti du Renouveau Démocratique (PRD), dies.

1997   **December:** Legislative elections are held. The RPP-FRUD alliance takes all 65 seats in parliament.

1998 **May:** Beginning of the political and military crisis between Ethiopia and Eritrea. The presidential campaign is launched.

1999 **April:** Ismael Omar Guelleh is elected president.

Introduction

As the world prepares to step into the 21st century, the Republic of Djibouti has just celebrated both the 20th anniversary of its existence as an independent state and the centenary of its creation as a French colony. Unity, peace, and equality were the new state's goals upon its emancipation from the tribe-oriented rule of the French colonial system. The nation's 20 years of independence have been relatively peaceful, despite the disruption caused by a three-year armed conflict in the north, but unity and equality still remain a dream the achievement of which is made even more utopian by the serious economic problems the country is still facing.

LAND AND PEOPLE

Situated in the northeast of Africa, at the entrance to the Red Sea, the Republic of Djibouti is a small country covering an area of 23,000 square kilometers (8,800 square miles). Its three neighbors are Eritrea in the north, Ethiopia in the west and south, and Somalia in the southeast.

The climate is mostly hot and semiarid. In the hot season, which lasts from May to September, the mean temperature is 35 degrees Celsius (95 Fahrenheit). From October to April, however, the weather is usually cooler, with a mean temperature of 25 degrees Celsius (77 Fahrenheit). Rainfall is rather scanty: an average of 170 mm (6.7 inches) per year.

The population, estimated at 630,000 with a growth rate of 3.5 percent, consists of two ethnic groups, the Afar and the Somali. The Afar occupy the northern and western parts of the country and the Somali live in the southern part. Both are traditionally nomads and live in territories that extend well past the official frontiers.

The population is more cosmopolitan in the capital city of Djibouti, and includes a Yemeni community as well as some Ethiopians and Indians. The European community (10,000 people) is mostly French military (4,000) and civilian "coopérants," plus small Italian and Greek populations.

Afar and Somali, both of which belong to the Cushitic linguistic group, are the two "identity" languages used in the Republic of Djibouti, and are widely used by the media (radio and television). Arabic and French are the two official languages. French is the language of formal education and, consequently, administration. Arabic, which is spoken by many Djiboutians as a result of the various exchanges with neighboring Arab countries, was introduced in the school curriculum after Djibouti joined the Arab League in 1977.

Islam—whose penetration dates as far back as the eighth century—was proclaimed the state religion in the country's 1992 Constitution, but the political system remains nonconfessional and most non-Muslim communities living in Djibouti have their own places of worship. Formal Islamic education has started to develop, as shown by the opening of numerous schools and institutions that have their own curriculum.

HISTORY

The region that hosts the Republic of Djibouti was once known as the Land of Punt (Land of the Gods). Since antiquity it has been the scene of intense trade among the Somali and Afar nomads living on the arid plains of the coastal zone, the farmers who settled on the Abyssinian highlands, and Indian and Arab merchants from across the sea. It is the abundance in the products exchanged that earned the region its name. The trade routes that crossed the region extended well beyond the limits of the Horn of Africa. Most of the products carried by the caravans reached the Mediterranean via Egypt.

The arrival of the Portuguese in the late 15th century marked the beginning of a new era, one of ceaseless endeavors on the part of the Portuguese, Turks, and Egyptians to control the Indian Ocean and the Red Sea. For most of the 16th century, the Turks remained the masters of the Red Sea whereas the Portuguese controlled the Indian Ocean. Red Sea port activities gradually declined until Napoleon's troops invaded Egypt, sparking renewed interest in the region on the part of the Europeans. By 1839, the British had settled in Aden whereas the French continued to explore the coast. The 1859 assassination of Henry Lambert, a trader and France's consular agent to Aden, and the inquiry that followed finally led to a treaty between France and the Afar chiefs. This treaty, signed in March 1862, gave France the harbor of Obock and a territory extending from Ras Doumeira to Ras Ali. France pretty much ignored its new acquisition, even after the Suez Canal opened in 1869, leaving the Egyptians to settle on the coastline running from Tadjourah to Berbeira in 1874. The signing of a new treaty with the Issa chiefs, in March 1885, created new opportunities for French traders who were trying to penetrate the Ethiopian market. In 1887, the city of Djibouti was founded, soon followed by the inauguration of its port. From then on, the growth of the colony reached cruising speed, with occasional ups and downs.

The name Côte Française des Somalis was adopted in May 1896 to replace the colony's former name, Protectorat d'Obock et Dépendances. The new name, while highlighting the French ownership of this territory in contrast with the other Somali-inhabited colonized territories—namely British Somaliland and Italian Somalia—revealed the nature of the tribe-oriented politics France was creating.

The railroad connecting Djibouti to Addis Ababa, which crossed territory inhabited mostly by the Issa, opened in 1917. Boosted by the opening of the line, the port experienced constant development until the outbreak of World War II. The drastic blockade imposed on the colony from September 1940 to January 1942, as a sanction for its siding with the Vichy government, was one of the most dramatic moments in the country's colonial history.

The postwar years were followed by a new dynamic that was expressed with the creation of a new currency, the Djibouti franc, in March 1949. The outbreak of war in Indochina the following year made France realize the importance of the colony whose port was used as a coaling and fueling station by its navy. Port activities slowed when Egypt nationalized the Suez Canal in July 1956. That year was also marked by General Charles de Gaulle's first visit to the colony and the initiation of the native inhabitants to party politics after the Loi Cadre was enacted and the Conseil du Gouvernement was established.

In the following decades, the growing involvement of the native inhabitants in the colony's evolution led to a movement for independence, which culminated during de Gaulle's second visit in August 1966. The peaceful calls for independence during the presidential parade were met with fierce repression. However, aware that changes were inescapable, the colonial authorities organized a referendum on self-determination in March 1967. As a result, the colony's name was changed to Territoire Français des Afars et des Issas. When, six years later, French President Georges Pompidou decided to visit Djibouti, the subject of independence had become less taboo. The country's independence was finally proclaimed on June 27, 1977.

Hassan Gouled Aptidon took the reins of the new republic and remained its president for more than two decades. Once the euphoria of independence had been spent, the country's citizens realized the challenge before them. Mineral resources were scarce, agriculture almost nonexistent, and the cost of energy was too high to attract potential investors. On the other hand, a strong currency, health care system, and, most of all, the comparative political stability lured economic as well as political refugees from neighboring states. As for France, it became a sort of guarantor of Djibouti's sovereignty by taking an active part in creating the new nation's security and defense system within the framework of a cooperation agreement. Even today, Djibouti remains one of the seven African states bound to France by a defense treaty. However, the limits of French military assistance were revealed in the course of the first armed conflict that the country faced from 1991 to 1994.

Soon after the beginning of the armed conflict, the country adopted its first constitution and opted for a multiparty system. The first presidential elections that were held in April 1999, after the signing of the peace agreement with the Front pour la Restauration de l'Unité et de la Démocratie, gave the country its second president, Ismael Omar Guelleh.

The Dictionary

– A –

ABBAN. While initially a **Somali** word referring to the head of a nomad camp or a caravan, with the arrival of European explorers, travelers, and traders in the middle of the 19th century, this term came to designate a system of protection of people and goods. The Abban at the head of the caravan imposed a tax on all foreigners crossing the territory from the littoral to the hinterland. The functioning of this system is well described in **Alfred Bardey's** *Barr-Adjam*. The creation of the **railroad** line linking **Djibouti** with Addis Ababa in the early 1900s brought about the decline of the Abban system, and a decline of the older ports, such as **Zeila, Tadjourah**, and Berbera, that depended on it.

ABDILLAHI ARDEYEH ABANEH (1935–1992). One of **Mahamoud Harbi**'s companions in the struggle for **independence**. Following the 1958 **referendum** he decided to leave **Djibouti** in order to join Harbi, who was then in exile in **Somalia**. He was a founding member of the **Front de Libération de la Côte Somalie**, and was the movement's first secretary general. His disagreement with the **Somali** government, concerning its concept of the fight for **independence** and its intention to use this struggle to achieve its policy of a Greater Somalia, led him to leave that country. He settled in **Aden, Yemen**, and lived there from 1967 to 1970. From there, he helped the independence movement gain the support of both the Arab League and the **Organization of African Unity**. He served in **Parliament** from 1977 to 1981, when he retired from all political activities.

ABDALLAH MOHAMED KAMIL. Unlike most Djiboutian politicians, Abdallah Mohamed Kamil has a university background. He joined the **Union Démocratique Afar** in 1965 after completing his studies in political science in Paris. In 1967, when the **Afar** political leaders decided

1

to tone down their personal and clan rivalries in order to constitute a sort of *union sacrée,* Abdallah joined the **Rassemblement Démocratique Afar**. The Afar leaders' decision was made within the context of the 1967 **referendum**, which was perceived as a pan-Somali threat.

In April 1974, Abdallah became the first native to be named secretary general of the government, and he gradually started to distance himself from **Ali Aref**. In July 1976, he was elected president of the **Conseil du Gouvernement**, thus becoming the leader of the institutional transition toward **independence**. Consequently, he was one of the major actors at the **roundtable** that was held in Paris in March 1977. He was appointed minister of planning and development in the country's first government. From February to September 1978, he replaced for a brief period Premier **Ahmed Dini**, who had resigned; Abdallah was then replaced by **Barkat Gourad Hamadou**. Abdallah has since aligned himself with the opposition, though behind the political scenes.

Apart from his political activities, Abdallah is a notary public and also a founding member of *Le Pount,* a journal to which he contributed regularly.

ABDI DEEQSI. The creator of **belwo**, an urban poetry genre, was born in the city of Borame, in northwestern Somaliland. Abdi Deeqsi was a lorry driver and mechanic who traveled regularly from **Zeila** and **Djibouti** to Borame and Hargeisa. He acquired the nickname of *Sinimo* (the Somali word for **cinema**) because of his talent at telling and acting out stories and jokes, which made him very popular, particularly among the youth.

On one of his trips, in the mid-1940s, Abdi's lorry broke down in the bush. After several attempts to repair it, he sat down in despair and started reciting the first *belwo*. On his return to Borame, the poem he had improvised was met with success and spread through the country. Abdi resigned from his job and formed a company of artists that started to perform and popularize the new genre. The company was very popular between 1946 and 1948, but disbanded in the early 1950s. Abdi went to live in Djibouti, where he remained until his death on March 19, 1967.

ABDILLAHI DOUALEH WAISS (1947–1977). Better known by the name **Iftine**, Abdillahi Doualeh was one of the earliest native journalists. He completed his secondary studies in Dire Dawa (**Ethiopia**) and partly in **Djibouti**, and started his career in 1970 by writing freelance articles for the official newspaper *Le Réveil de Djibouti* while working as a primary school teacher. Also concerned with the country's **political life**, he was a legislative candidate in local elections in November 1973, but was not elected. A few months later, he created an independent newspaper named *Iftine*, which in **Somali** means "light." This newspaper, which presented articles analyzing Djiboutian society, marked one of the first attempts at independent journalism in Djibouti and was published without interruption until Abdillahi Doualeh's death on August 18, 1977.

ABDOULKADER MOUSSA ALI (1920–1986). A leading political figure of the 1960s, Abdoulkader Moussa got involved in politics after working as a sailor from 1945 to 1952 and as a nurse in public schools. He was elected territorial councilor in 1963 and was eventually appointed minister of agriculture. Though a native of **Obock**, he was one of **Ali Aref's** most fervent supporters. As a member of the **Rassemblement Démocratique Afar**, he became the first **Afar** member of **Parliament** to represent Djibouti at the French National Assembly in 1965.

His political rise coincided with Ali Aref's will to both reunite the traditionally contentious Afar political elite, which was then divided into natives of Obock and natives of **Tadjourah**, and defeat the **Somali** pro-independence coalition. His election to the French National Assembly, together with that of **Barkat Gourad** as senator, blocked the parliamentary debate concerning the evolution of the colony toward independence.

ABDOURAHMAN AHMED HASSAN (?–1990). Also known as **Gaboode**, Abdourahman Ahmed Hassan was a very active union leader in the 1950s. As the secretary of the local branch of the French trade union Force Ouvrière, he took part in the negotiations on the Collective Convention, a body of legislative acts for the protection of workers. In 1957, he was elected councilor to the **Assemblée Territoriale** on the roll of the Union Républicaine, a party led by **Mahamoud Harbi**.

Suspected of communist activities, he was arrested in 1960 and charged with betraying national security. After spending two years in prison, he was paroled and left the country in 1965 to join the **Front de Libération de la Côte Somalie** (FLCS), of which he became the secretary general in 1966. From within FLCS he advocated the liberation and unification of all Somali-inhabited territories to form one independent state. In April 1967, he went to New York to petition the U.N. Decolonization Committee. Abdourahman Ahmed Hassan ended his political activities soon after Djibouti's **independence**. He died in Mogadiscio, Somalia.

ABHE, LAKE (Abbe). Lying at the intersection of the Rift Valley and the **Afar Depression**, in southwestern **Djibouti**, along the border with **Ethiopia**, Lake Abhe ("the rotten lake" in **Afar** language) is a quicksand area scattered with fumaroles. Because it no longer receives water from the **Awash**, a river that originates in Ethiopia, the lake is slowly dying. The lake, which was 160 meters deep 20,000 years ago, is now at an average depth of 12 meters; its total area has gone from 6,000 square kilometers 8,000 years ago to 320 square kilometers in 1972 and 180 square kilometers in 1988. With the planned construction of additional dams in Ethiopia to increase the amount of arable land, the lake is bound to disappear in the coming decades.

ABOUBAKER IBRAHIM CHEHEM (1815–1885). A wealthy and powerful **Afar** merchant, Aboubaker Ibrahim Chehem was pasha (governor) of the city of **Zeila** from 1855 to 1857. When his rival, **Charmarke Ali**, charged him with embezzling money from the customs office, he was arrested and imprisoned for eight months, during which time Charmarke took his place as governor. Thanks to his friend **Henri Lambert**, then consul of **France** in **Aden**, Aboubaker was liberated, after which he proposed to give France the territory extending along the coast from the Bay of Ras Ali, locally known as Raïssali, to **Goubet-el-Kharab**, on the northern shore of the Gulf of **Tadjourah**.

Aboubaker, who had a monopoly on the caravan **trade**, became an Egyptian ally in 1867, after noticing the lack of interest of the French in the territory he had given them and remained so until 1875. He had numerous sons, one of whom, **Bourhan Ibrahim Aboubaker**, became the first notable of the nascent city of **Djibouti**.

ABOUBAKER PASHA. *See* ABOUBAKER IBRAHIM CHEHEM.

ABYSSINIA. The ancient name of **Ethiopia**. *See also* HABBASH.

ACCORDS D'ARTA. A bilateral agreement signed by **Afar** and **Issa** political leaders on September 20, 1963, in the town of **Arta**. The two ethnic groups asserted that they were the exclusive owners of the territory of **Djibouti**. Among the signers of this agreement were **Mohammed**

Kamil, **Hassan Gouled Aptidon**, and **Ali Aref**. The agreement was signed in a context of intense political agitation characterized by ethnic rivalries following the 1958 **referendum**. It was aimed at reassuring the Afar community regarding the danger represented by the growing number of **pan-Somalism** movements advocating the reunification of all Somali-inhabited territories within a single **Somali** state.

ADAÏL (Ada'il, Ad Ali). The name of the **Afar** traditional ruling clan. It is from within this group that all Afar sultans are chosen. The Adaïls, who claim to be the descendants of the legendary **Hadal Mahiss**, were originally natives from south of the Afar land (in northern Djibouti). Their prestige is due to their 12th-century victory over their **Ankala** rivals of the north, in the coastal region of **Eritrea**. The ancient capital of the Adaïls, **Zeila**, was first transferred to the highlands of Harrar, in **Ethiopia**, following the Adaïls' defeat by the Ethiopian army, and then to **Awsa**, in 1597.

ADAL. A 12th-century Muslim kingdom that included the territory of the Republic of Djibouti, northern **Somalia**, and southeastern **Ethiopia**. Its subjects were principally **Somali** and **Afar nomads**. To most Ethiopian highlanders, the term is used to designate all Afar tribes, which has to be considered in the light of the 16th-century wars of **religion** that opposed Christian highlanders to a Muslim coalition.

ADEN. This city in **Yemen**, lying on the northern shore of the eponymous Gulf and at the mouth of the Red Sea, is one of the oldest ports in the region. For centuries, it played an important part in trade relations among Asia, Africa, and Europe. After the British arrived in 1839, Aden became one of the main calling ports on the route to India and Asia, and a coaling station for British ships. Its importance grew after the **Suez Canal** opened in 1869 and an oil refinery was established in 1953. For the developing **port** of **Djibouti**, Aden remained a dangerous rival for decades. The city gained independence from Great Britain in 1967, and the Suez Canal closed shortly after. When the People's Democratic Republic of **Yemen** (Southern Yemen) was established in 1970, Aden became its capital and remained so until the country's unification with the Yemen Arab Republic (Northern Yemen) in 1990. Today, Aden has become a regional capital and its port is no longer a serious threat to the revitalized activities of the port of Djibouti.

ADEN ROBLEH AWALEH (1937–). From 1965 to 1967, while still a law student at the University of Bordeaux, Aden Robleh became the secretary general of the **Union Nationale des Etudiants de la Côte Afar Somali**. In 1968, he dropped out from the university to join the **Front de Libération de la Côte Somalie** (FLCS), of which he became the leader in 1970. As such, he brought the organization to an international scale with his constant efforts to make contact with most liberation movements in Africa.

Aden Robleh personally took part in the kidnapping of Jean Gueury, the French ambassador in Mogadiscio (**Somalia**), on March 23, 1975. This operation was aimed at freeing **Omar Osman Rabeh** and Omar Elmi Khaireh, two FLCS members who had been imprisoned in **France**. Two months later, during the Kampala summit of the **Organization of African Unity** (OAU), Aden Robleh convinced the OAU to accept the **Ligue Populaire Africaine pour l'Indépendance** as one of its members.

Somalian authorities imprisoned Aden Robleh in1976, but he was liberated In 1977. He was shot at and seriously wounded a few days before **independence**, while the FLCS was getting ready to integrate the future national **army**. Although he was still in a hospital in France, he was appointed minister of the port in the republic's first government. On October 2, 1978, he became minister of transport, commerce, and tourism but had to resign in March 1983 because of his political differences with President **Hassan Gouled**. In 1986, soon after he had been sentenced to life imprisonment, he secretly left the country and went into exile in **Ethiopia**, where he lived for six years. When an amnesty law was passed, he returned to participate in the 1992 legislative elections with his newly created party, the **Parti National Démocratique** (PND). Although he was suspected of being involved in the September 27, 1990, bomb blast (*see also* CRIMINAL ATTACKS) that targeted European customers at the Café de Paris, Aden Robleh is still at the head of one of the only four legal political parties.

ADMINISTRATIVE ORGANIZATION. The administrative organization of the Republic of Djibouti, inherited from colonial times, consists of territorial units called **districts**, each bearing the name of its main locality: **Djibouti, Dikhil, Ali Sabieh, Obock,** and **Tadjourah.** Due to its size, the district of Djibouti has been subdivided into five **arrondissements** and two administrative posts, Arta-Wéa and Damerjog. At the head of each district is a **Commissaire de la République**, appointed by the Council of Ministers to represent the **president.** Outside the capital city of Djibouti, all the existing public administration services are centralized in the commissaire's office. However, in many cases it is the central authority based in the capital city that makes the final decisions. Decentralization has been set as a priority goal in the 1992 **Constitution**.

Because administrative agents are recruited mostly on a tribal basis, they tend to consider themselves to be untouchables as long as their protector is in office. Because of this, faithfulness to the protector is better rewarded in terms of promotion than job effectiveness or competence. On the other hand, unfaithfulness is sanctioned by disgrace or even lawsuits. In a nutshell, malfunction and embezzlement are stimulated by the prevailing latitudinarianism.

ADOUA (Adwa, Adua, Adowa). A small northern Ethiopian town (once the capital of the province of Tigray) that was the scene of a battle between Italian colonial troops and Ethiopian resistors in March 1896. This battle, which the resistors won, is regarded as the symbol of Africans' resistance to having their continent partitioned by European colonial powers at the end of the 19th century. In the wake of this victory, **France**, Italy, and Great Britain (which occupied, respectively, French Somaliland, **Eritrea** and Somalia, and British Somaliland) started negotiating their respective boundaries and limits of influence with the Ethiopian empire. The current **borders** between the states in the Horn of Africa are a legacy of the Battle of Adoua.

ADOY MARA. The **Afar** are divided into two main groups: the Adoy Mara (the "whites") and the **Assay Mara** (the "reds"). Many interpretations have been given as to the meaning of this dichotomy. While some people believe this reflects a social divide—the "whites" being the commoners and the "reds" the nobles—others try to explain it in terms of geographical settlement. The Adoy Mara are generally settled along the shore of the Red Sea, whereas the Assay Mara live in the Ethiopian hinterland.

AFAMBO, LAKE. Situated to the north of **Lake Abhe** and supplied by the waters of the **Awash** River, Lake Afambo was the site of a border-control station on the caravan route from **Awsa** to **Djibouti**. The lake was strategically important because it enabled control of the western border and more particularly that of the **Hanle** plain, a zone of pastureland of crucial importance to the **Afar nomads**. Although **Ethiopia** started claiming the area in 1945, the lake remained part of the colony until a treaty, signed January 16, 1954, transferred it to Ethiopia in exchange for **Mount Moussa Ali**. This transaction, which actually concerned a territory of about 7,500 square kilometers, was not approved by the native politicians, and from 1954 through the 1960s the issue remained a heated one in **Parliament**.

AFAR. The Afar are a mainly nomadic people whose total number is estimated at about 2 million living in a triangle-shaped area between **Djibouti**, **Ethiopia**, and **Eritrea**. Their traditional sociopolitical organization is based on a sophisticated hierarchical system with a **sultan** at its head. The four sultanates are Aoussa (**Awsa**) in Ethiopia, Baylul in Eritrea, **Rahaita** straddling Eritrea and Djibouti, and **Tadjourah** in the Republic of Djibouti. The two main groups that make up this ethnic entity are the **Adoy Mara** and the **Assay Mara**.

The Afar are mainly concentrated in northern Djibouti, although they are also present in the region of **Dikhil**, in the southwestern border area. Since **independence** in 1977, this community's representation in the political apparatus has been more formal than effective. The frustration engendered by this situation was, to some extent, at the origin of the **armed conflict** that convulsed the country from August 1991 to December 1994.

AFAR DEPRESSION. The Afar Depression, which extends over three countries—**Ethiopia, Eritrea**, and **Djibouti**—is a zone situated below sea level and scattered with **salt** lakes and volcanoes. It is an area where the continental crust is particularly thin. The tectonic, seismic, and volcanic activities that take place there are expected to bring about the total separation of the Horn of Africa from the rest of the continent in millions of years, thus giving birth to a new body of water that has already been named the Eritrean Ocean.

AGRICULTURE. Agriculture is almost nonexistent in Djibouti, mostly because the population largely consists of **nomads** who have become settled only recently. Also, scanty rainfall makes it difficult to grow anything but certain fruits and vegetables. These account for 2 percent of the gross domestic product. In recent years, however, a growing number of small-scale farming projects have developed with the contribution of underpaid labor consisting of Ethiopian farmers who had left their country for various reasons. *See also* AMBOULI.

AHMED ABDALLAH. Also known as **Dimis,** this native of the village of As-Eyla, in the district of **Dikhil,** is a founding member of the **Mouvement Populaire de Libération,** which he later left to side with **Ahmed Dini.** He was appointed minister of culture in the independent state's first government but resigned a few month later. The transcription of the **Afar** language he and **Jamaleddin Abdulkader Reedo** elaborated in 1976 remains the most widely used one to date. Both men have also published a number of studies on Afar language and customs.

AHMED BOURHAN OMAR. *See* MOUVEMENT DE LIBERATION DE DJIBOUTI.

AHMED DINI AHMED (1930–). Ahmed Dini is a native of **Obock** who appeared on the political scene in 1958, when he was elected to **Parliament.** In May 1959, he was elected vice president of the **Conseil du Gouvernement** to replace **Hassan Gouled.** Given his disagreement with **Ali Aref,** he went through a rather eventful period in the 1960s, sometimes in government, sometimes in the opposition. The final break occurred in 1970, when he was dismissed from his office as minister of the interior by Ali Aref, whom he had accused of having too much liking for the French administration. From then on, he led the Ligue pour l'Avenir et l'Ordre, which, in 1972, merged with **Hassan Gouled**'s Union Populaire Africaine to give birth to the **Ligue Populaire Africaine pour l'Indépendance** (LPAI).

As the secretary general of the LPAI, Ahmed Dini played a crucial role in the emancipation of the country from French colonial rule. In July 1977, after the colony achieved **independence,** he became prime minister. However, he resigned a few months later, disappointed by the limitations of his power (the president was also the head of government) and in reaction to the violent repression against the **Afar** community that followed the **Palmier en Zinc** bomb blast. *See* CRIMINAL ATTACKS.

Ahme Dini attempted to organize a parliamentary opposition before he created the **Parti Populaire Djiboutien,** a short-lived opposition party that was immediately made illegal. He was imprisoned from September to January 1982. After his release, he retired from the political scene for 10 years. In 1992, in the midst of the war against the government, he joined the **Front pour la Restauration de l'Unité et de la Démocratie** (*see also* ARMED CONFLICTS) as president, and has been living in exile ever since.

AHMED GOUMANEH ROBLEH. A native of the small town of **Ali Sabieh**, Ahmed Goumaneh was the faithful friend and lieutenant of **Mahamoud Harbi**, on whose roll he was elected to **Parliament** on June 23, 1957. He left the colony in the 1960s to join the **Mouvement de Libération de la Côte Somalie** and was eventually appointed vice president of the National Assembly of the **Republic of Somalia**.

AHMED HASSAN LIBAN (1921–). Better known as **Gohad**, Ahmed Hassan Liban is an active politician who started his career in 1957, when he was elected to **Parliament** on **Mahamoud Harbi**'s roll and became minister of the interior. However, he was imprisoned in October 1958 when a meeting in which he was participating turned into a clash between the pro-independence militants and the supporters of French colonization. In September 1966, he was imprisoned again for taking part in the riots that were organized during French President Charles de Gaulle's visit to **Djibouti**.

Ahmed Hassan retired from political activities in 1966 until 1970, when he was elected to the **Assemblée Territoriale** on **Ali Aref**'s roll. This did not prevent him from joining the parliamentary revolt against the latter in 1976. After **independence**, he held a number of ministerial posts: labor from 1978 to 1981; public health, 1981–1982; and agriculture and rural development, 1982–1986. He has been a member of the politburo of the **Rassemblement Populaire pour le Progrès** since March 1982.

AHMED SALEH. Ahmed Salah became **Djibouti**'s first world-famous athlete when he won the first world marathon in 1985 at Hiroshima, Japan. His career had started long before that, however, in his hometown of **Ali Sabieh**, where he took part in most of the competitions organized by the local garrison. His first victory outside Djibouti was in Abidjan, Côte d'Ivoire, in 1978. Although he had become the emblem of Djibouti's athletics, Ahmed Salah never had the attention he deserved and was handicapped by the lack of efficient coaching.

AHMEDIYA. An Islamist order that was established in Saudi Arabia, in the Mecca region, between the late 18th century and early 19th century by Sayid Ahmad Ibn Idriss Al Fasi (1760–1837). This order, which was concerned with religious reform, gradually spread over the Arabian Peninsula and beyond to the Horn of Africa (**Djibouti, Ethiopia, Somalia,** and Sudan). *See also* ORDERS.

AIR DJIBOUTI. Founded by Bernard Astraud de Robiglio in 1963, this local airline was originally a private company that focused its efforts on developing regional flights. The company grew rapidly and started serving **Ethiopia** and **Yemen**, in addition to the domestic lines.

Following the country's **independence**, Air Djibouti was turned into a national airline with long-distance flights toward **France**. The chaos that characterized the company's management led to its gradual decline. It went bankrupt and ceased all activities toward the end of 1990. *See also* CIVIL AVIATION.

ALI ABLISS. The legendary **Afar** chief of the Able clan. He gave his daughter in marriage to **Hadal Mahiss**, thus inaugurating the emergence of the sultanate system in the social and political structure of the Afar.

ALI AREF BOURHAN (1934–). Ali Aref, a native of Tadjourah, was elected to the **Assemblée Territoriale** in 1957. Three years later, he was appointed vice president of the **Conseil du Gouvernement**, replacing **Ahmed Dini**. A fervent supporter of General Charles de Gaulle, he campaigned for the latter during the 1965 French presidential elections. However, following the violent demonstrations that were organized during President de Gaulle's visit to **Djibouti** in August 1966, Ali Aref had to resign. On November 5, 1966, **Mohamed Kamil** became the new vice president of the Conseil du Gouvernement for a short period. On April 27, 1967, Ali Aref was again elected and kept this position until July 1976. Although he opposed **independence**, he decided to change his party's name to **Union Nationale pour l'Indépendance** when he was confronted by a parliamentary opposition led by **Barkat Gourad Hamadou**. He nevertheless had to resign on the eve of Djibouti's independence, and thereafter became the main figure of the political opposition.

After a long period of retirement from **political life**, during which time he was involved in business, Ali Aref was accused of plotting against the government and imprisoned in January 1991, a few months before the outbreak of the **armed conflict** in the north. Since being released from prison, he has again retired from political involvement.

ALI BAHDON BOUH. Both a sailor and a tradesman, Ali Bahdon helped to introduce a species of tree known as *Conocarpus,* or "Somali laurel," which today lines most of the capital city's main avenues.

ALI CHARMARKE SALEH (1775–1861). A trader of **Somali** origin, Ali Charmarke became the chief of customs authority in **Zeila** in 1841. The city was then under the political control of the **Ottomans**, whose representative was the **pasha** of Hodeida in **Yemen**. In 1857, keen competition between Ali Charmarke and his rival, **Aboubaker Ibrahim Chehem**, ensued after the agreement for the management of the city's customs services expired. Aboubaker Ibrahim finally succeeded in obtaining the contract.

The two men's mutual hatred led them to seek political alliances in order to support them in their race for commercial hegemony on the African shores of the Gulf of Aden, between **Tadjourah** and Zeila. Ali Charmarke supported a British presence in **Aden** and was regarded as a protégé of the British crown in exchange for his assistance to British subjects and to Royal Navy ships calling at Zeila. Thus, the end of Charmarke's might coincided with the emergence of French interests in the area. Considered to be the main instigator of **Henri Lambert**'s murder, he was arrested by Ottoman authorities in Yemen and handed over to the French navy to be judged in Constantinople. However, Charmarke died May 25, 1861, during the journey.

ALI FARAH AHMED, Captain (1914–1975). Also known as **Hirad**, Ali Farah was the first native high-ranking officer in the **Djibouti**-based French army. As a teenager, he started his career in the **militia**, and in 1941 enrolled in the Forces Françaises Libres as a sergeant. He fought in Lebanon, **Egypt**, Turkey, and Algeria before returning to **Djibouti** to retire.

ALI SABIEH. This small town, 94 kilometers southeast of the capital city, is located 700 meters above sea level in a sedimentary massif whose culminating peak is Mount Arreh (1,200 meters). The town emerged in the early 20th century when the **railroad** linking **Djibouti** to Addis Ababa was constructed, and still is the main station in the Djibouti-Dire Dawa section of the line. Due to its proximity to the Ethiopian border it is also a major stop for caravans and travelers. These characteristics, added to the construction in 1982 of an all-weather road to the capital city, have contributed to the development of the town that today has about 12,000 residents, mostly **Issa**.

Ali Sabieh is the capital of the **district** that bears its name. Consequently, it hosts all the public facilities: dispensary, primary, secondary and technical schools, and telecommunication and postal services.

AMBADO. Located at about 10 kilometers to the west of the capital city, the Bay of Ambado is the site where the **Issa** chiefs signed the March 26, 1885, treaty giving **France** the right to anchor at what was to become the **port** of **Djibouti**. The Ambado treaty is the first international agreement signed by the Issa with a colonial power. Today, the site hosts one of the most attractive beaches in the outskirts of the capital city. *See also* TREATIES.

AMBOULI. This seasonal river flows west when it crosses the capital city, **Djibouti**. The river bed marks the separation line between the old town in the low plains and the new suburb of **Balbala**. Originally used by the **nomads** as a water point—particularly during the hot season—it was the capital city's first water reservoir and thus played a part in the choice of Djibouti as a harbor for the French navy. The two banks of the river, which constitute a zone of small-scale agriculture and farming, form a sort of green belt. The first Muslim cemetery, established in an area bought by **Hamoudi Ahmed**, extends into part of the neighborhood now known by the same name, Ambouli.

AMOLLE. Derived from the name of an **Afar** clan, *amolle* is the word used to designate the rectangular **salt** bars, used as **currency** by the **nomads** of the eastern lowlands in their exchanges with the highland populations of **Ethiopia**. These salt bars are extracted from the reserves made up by the salt lakes of the **Afar Depression**, located between **Eritrea**, Ethiopia, and the Republic of **Djibouti**, and transported by camel following age-old caravan tracks. Although this traditional salt trade is still maintained, the significance of the salt currency has long been made obsolete by the introduction of modern currency.

ANKALA (Ankali). The name of an **Afar** clan that once settled along the northern coast of **Djibouti** and southern **Eritrea**. Originally the Ankala constituted the leading political and military structure of the Afar. Toward the 12th century they were defeated by the Islamic sultanate of the **Adaïl**, mostly based between the Gulf of **Tadjourah** and the eastern escarpments of the Ethiopian rangeland. Subsequently, the Ankala were totally Islamized and integrated in the Adaïl nobility. What is left of the Ankala kingdom is now located in the region of Tiho, in Eritrea.

ARCHAEOLOGY. Despite the discoveries made by Georges Revoil in 1882 and Félix Jousseaume in 1885, no serious archaeological research was undertaken in **Djibouti** until 1928–1929, when one of the pioneers, Brother Pierre Teilhard de Chardin, conducted a mission in association with P. Lamare. The second research mission, carried out by Reverend Henri Breuil and H. Wernert in 1932, resulted in the discovery of items dating back to the Late Stone Age.

After a long interruption, scientific missions renewed their interest in the region in the 1970s and the 1980s. In the meantime, however, most of the sites, which were generally located in southern Djibouti and more particularly in the plains of **Hanle** and **Gobaad**, had been plundered by private collectors.

Among the significant discoveries made by the archaeologists were the skeleton of an elephant 1.3 million to 1.6 million years old in the plain of Gobaad, and the skeleton of a girl, dating from the third millennium, on the sites of Assa Koma and Assa Ragid in the Gobaad plain in southwestern Djibouti. Because there is no national museum in Djibouti, most of the findings are exhibited in museums in **France**.

ARDOUKOBA. This 40-meter-high volcano was born in November 1978 in the **Lake Assal** area. Its eruption, which opened an enormous fault between Lake Assal and the Bay of **Goubet-el-Kharab**, is a testimony to the intense seismic activity in the region.

ARHIBA. This expression, which means "welcome" in the **Afar** language, is also the name of a housing project inaugurated in 1970 to accommodate the Afar dockers working at the **port** of **Djibouti**. Owing to the housing problems that accompanied the rapid urbanization of the capital city, and in the absence of a long-term housing policy, the neighborhood quickly turned into an overpopulated ghetto. Arhiba was the scene of bloodshed on December 18, 1991, during an **armed conflict** between the **Front pour la Restauration de l'Unité et de la Démocratie** and the government. The bloodshed was caused by the security forces.

ARMED CONFLICTS. The expression "armed conflicts" is used here to designate confrontations between the government's military forces and guerrillas in the postindependence period. All the rebellions that took place in the postindependence period had two points in common: first, they essentially involved politically frustrated **Afar** youth; second, the rebels used **Ethiopia** as a rear-base, because this neighboring country allowed them to establish political and sometimes military structures within its territory.

The Republic of **Djibouti** experienced its first such conflict in 1979 when the **Mouvement Populaire de Libération** (MPL) went underground after the government ordered it disbanded. This rebellion took place in the context of the Cold War, when countries in the Horn of Africa were involved in the East-West conflict. It was motivated by competition for the control of the state apparatus by a group of Afar youth who believed their community had been barred from participating in the political institutions. The conflicts ended in 1981 when an amnesty law was enacted as a result of a political rapprochement between Ethiopia and Djibouti. Many of MPL members returned to Djibouti and some of them are now in the political system.

Some of the rebels who remained in Ethiopia resumed the struggle under the name of **Front pour la Restauration de l'Unité et de la Démocratie** (FRUD). The three-year armed conflict—which started in August 1991, a few months after the Ethiopian military government collapsed—coincided with an unprecedented social, economic, and political crisis in Djibouti. About 12,000 men were mobilized to reinforce the government's army, which aggravated the country's economic situation. The conflict resulted in the isolation of the northern region, which had become the main battlefield, from the rest of the country. A peace agreement between the conflicting parties, signed December 26, 1994, at Ab'a, brought to light the dissension existing within the FRUD. When the FRUD's military wing decided to lay down arms, the rebels were integrated in the governmental army, and their leaders were given high positions within the state apparatus. However, not all the rebels agreed to the treaty. They remained in exile in order to carry on the struggle, with **Ahmed Dini** at their head; some were extradited by Ethiopian authorities and imprisoned in Djibouti.

ARMS. Due to its strategic location at the crossroads of Africa and the Arabian peninsula, **Djibouti** has from the early days been a transit point for the **trade** in arms for rebels in neighboring countries. The weapons were generally imported from **France**, Belgium, Great Britain, Germany, and other European countries, and gave many French traders and adventurers an opportunity to make easy money. French colonial authorities occasionally made attempts to control the trade, but the efforts were more for show rather than an enforcement of international regulations.

Generally speaking, the numerous conflicts that regularly shake the subregion, combined with the practical difficulties encountered in controlling the **borders**, make the elimination of this trade an almost impossible task.

ARMY. Djibouti's national army—Armée Nationale de Djibouti (AND)—was set up quickly a few weeks before **independence** day, June 6, 1977, and was placed under the command of the head of the new state. The army counted only 1,500 men at the time but it was considerably developed during the **armed conflict** between the government and the **Front pour la Restauration de l'Unité et de la Démocratie**.

Due to the absence of native senior officers serving in the French army before independence, the new army was placed under the technical supervision of French army officers serving as technical advisers within the framework of **cooperation** with **France**. In its early days, the AND had little military equipment aside from the few automatic weapons brought by the **Front de Libération de la Côte Somalie** (FLCS) guerrillas who joined the new army.

Given the AND's lack of technical capability to protect the territory in a context of regional instability, an agreement was signed with France, making that country responsible for Djibouti's defense. Over the years, Djibouti's army has benefited from material and financial support of various countries such as **Egypt**, Saudi Arabia, Morocco, and the United States. Currently, the amount allocated to defense represents the largest single entry in the country's budget.

ARRONDISSEMENT. This term designates the smallest unit in the **administrative organization** of the capital city. The unit's role is mainly concerned with law and order, hygiene, and general administration. The head officer is a representative of the city mayor and is assisted by a **caadi** and a *chef de quartier,* or neighborhood chief. This administrative form, which was originally motivated by a desire to control the population, has enabled permanent contacts to be established between citizens and the administration. The city of **Djibouti** counts five arrondissements today.

ARTA. This small town of 4,000 is located 30 kilometers from **Djibouti**, overlooking the Gulf of **Tadjourah** at an altitude of 750 meters above sea level, in the Ougoul Massifs. Its rise is linked to the 1946 construction of a housing estate, where most of the companies of the time came to settle. Due to its almost permanently cool and dry weather, Arta became a summer resort frequented by the French military and the

Djiboutian political elite, many of whom own a second home there. Arta, which is administratively attached to the District of Djibouti, hosts a catering training center and a geophysics observatory.

ASSA JOG. A **Somali** term that means "the people from the red land" and that was initially used to designate the natives of a region extending along the **railroad** line between **Ali Sabieh** and Aichaa (in **Ethiopia**). The **Issa** subclans that make up this population have been profoundly influenced by the advent of the railroad. Their way of life has been transformed to such a great extent that they have even given the name Assa Jog to one of the trains crossing their territory. Today, the expression essentially refers to natives of Ali Sabieh.

ASSAL, LAKE. Situated in the center of the country, Lake Assal is a **salt** lake lying 153 meters under sea level—making it the lowest point on the African continent—and covering an area of 50 square kilometers. Its salt bank, which is two meters deep and extends to an area of about 180 square kilometers, has long been the **nomads**' main source of currency in the shape of salt bars called **amolle**. Although Emperor Menelik of **Ethiopia** granted a concession to the Société du Lac Assal, established by **Léon Chefneux**, the company was never able to operate because the French government refused to issue them a license.

Lake Assal is one of the country's potential geothermal energy sources, although these remain untapped to this day. Six thousand years ago, the lake covered an area of 1,100 square kilometers, from the northwest to the center of the country. The rapid decrease of its depth contributed to the increase of its salinity, caused by the infiltration of seawater into the craters of the lake.

ASSAY MARA. *See* ADOY MARA.

ASSEMBLÉE CONSTITUANTE. *See* ASSEMBLEE NATIONALE.

ASSEMBLÉE NATIONALE. The first parliamentary institution of the Republic of **Djibouti**. Its legislative body has been renewed four times since its establishment. The initial Assembly was established shortly before **independence** on May 8, 1977. Then called **Assemblée Constituante**, it was created to be a transitional chamber with the task of drawing up the **constitution**, which it never did. In fact, the Assembly changed the electoral procedures in order to cut short all form of legislative opposition and impose the rule of one party, the **Rassemblement Populaire pour le Progrès** (RPP). The elections of May 21, 1982, resulted in a partial (one-third) renewal of the legislative body.

The second Assembly lasted from May 1982 to May 1987, and worked to homogenize the legislative body.

During the third Assembly, from May 1987 to September 1992, the first Constitution of the Republic of Djibouti was enacted subsequent to a **referendum**. The elections that were due to take place in May 1992 were postponed to December 18. For the first time, two parties were to be in competition, the RPP and the **Parti du Renouveau Démocratique** (PRD); a third group, the **Parti National Démocratique** (PND), decided to boycott the elections. Unsurprisingly, the RPP won all 65 Assembly seats. A few months later, on May 7, 1993, the first pluralist presidential elections were organized with the participation of three parties (RPP, PRD, and PND) and two independent candidates, Mohamed Moussa Ali (also called "Turtur") and Ahmed Ibrahim. The outgoing **president**, **Hassan Gouled**, received more than 60 percent of the valid votes.

After legislative elections on December 19, 1997, a new Assembly was established in which, for the first time since **independence**, a party other than the Rassemblement Populaire pour le Progrès (RPP) was represented. The **Front pour la Restauration de l'Unité et de la Démocratie**, which entered a coalition with the RPP following the signing of a peace agreement, now holds a few seats in Parliament.

The Assemblée Nationale is the only organ invested with legislative power. Some of its other functions consist of examining the budget and approving the nomination of executives. It cannot dissolve the government, but it can be dissolved by the head of state only.

ASSEMBLÉE TERRITORIALE. The Assemblée Territoriale was a local parliament set up in June 1957 to replace the **Conseil Représentatif**. It was the consequence of the decentralization policy conducted by Paris by means of the **Loi Cadre**. Its role, which consisted of electing the **Conseil du Gouvernement** and drawing up the budget, was actually very limited because the governor (**gouverneur**) could veto decisions it made. The Assemblée Territoriale disbanded in November 1968 when the **Chambre des Députés** was created, subsequent to the modification of the colony's status.

ATCHINOFF. A Cossack officer who was at the head of the expedition that landed at **Sagallou** in 1889. Atchinoff, a rebellious character known for his ambitions, had created a separatist movement in the Caucasus. In a disguised attempt to get rid of him, the czar sent him to the Red Sea on an adventurous and risky mission.

AWASH. The name of both a river and a region in **Ethiopia**. The region of Awash hosts the leading **Afar sultanate** of **Awsa**, which has its seat in the administrative center of Asaïta.

AWDAL. The **Somali** word for **Adal**. This name was officially given to the northernmost region of **Somalia** bordering **Djibouti**. Today, it is mainly populated by **Issa** and **Gadaboursi nomads**. The capital of Awdal is the once prosperous port of **Zeila**.

AWSA (Aoussa, Aussa). An oasis and marshland situated in the **Afar Depression** along the **Awash** River. Also called Kalo by the **Afar**, it is their most fertile region and the base of their most important **sultanate**. The sultanate of Awsa settled in the eponymous area after it withdrew from the Harrar region, due to intense Oromo raids and the **Adaïl** defeat by the Ethiopian state in the middle of the 16th century. The **Walasma**, the then-ruling family, was overthrown in 1769 by the Aïdahiso, the group of the present **sultan**, Ali Mira. The descendants of the Walasma are now known by the name of Kabirto and have enormous moral ascendancy on the sultan.

– B –

BAB EL MANDEB. An Arabic term meaning "the door of laments." Bab el Mandeb is a strait between the coasts of **Yemen** and northern **Djibouti** that separates the Red Sea from the Gulf of **Aden**. It is one of the spots where the African and Asian continents are the closest to each other. The still heavy French military presence, despite the end of the Cold War, bears witness to the strategic importance of this strait, which is a key position on one of the main oil routes.

BADA WEIN (Bara Wein). Bada Wein (or Grand Bara) and Bada Yer (Petit Bara) are vast arid plains formed by ancient lakes now dry. They are situated in the center of the country and mark the delimitation between the sedimentary and volcanic formations. During the rainy season, these clay plains change into water reservoirs and pastures.

BALBALA. Perched on the basaltic plateau, dominating the old town to the south, **Djibouti**'s southern suburb is said to derive its name from the blinking (*bal-bal* in **Somali** language) of the lighthouse standing at its doors.

It was in the wake of the 1966 riots that the colonial administration decided to erect a checkpoint at the entrance of the capital city to prevent "subversive elements" from entering the town. The massive rush of migrants, either from the hinterland or from the neighboring countries, together with the informal establishment of a precarious cattle-market and a caravan halt, gave birth to a permanent settlement. Police raids within the capital city itself and subsequent arrests and deportations contributed to a population increase in the area along the checkpoint. As a result, this area became a gigantic shantytown.

Soon after **independence** the checkpoint was removed, thus bringing about the changing of Balbala into a residential area. Today, Balbala counts four primary schools, the country's most modern secondary school, and the second biggest hospital. It has lost its negative image and been integrated into the urban development scheme of Djibouti. Its population has been estimated at more than 80,000.

BANKS. The first bank to settle in **Djibouti**, in January 1908, was the **Banque de l'Indochine**, now called Banque Indo-Suez (BIS). As soon as it was opened, the Banque de l'Indochine played a crucial role in the colony's economic development. Not only did it finance the construction of the **railroad** but it also issued the colony's **currency**.

In 1954, the Banque Nationale pour le Commerce et l'Industrie (now called Banque pour le Commerce et l'Industrie-Mer Rouge [BCI-MR])—a subsidiary of the Banque Nationale de Paris—opened a branch in Djibouti. The Banque de l'Indochine lost its monopoly, but ever since the two banks have had the lion's share in the country's financial activities.

Despite its early presence in the colony's financial sector, the Commercial Bank of Ethiopia has been hindered by the rigidity of its administrative organization, particularly during the 18 years of Derg rule (*see also* ETHIOPIA). As for the British Bank of the Middle East, the branch it opened in 1975 had to close in 1986 after failing to adapt itself to the market.

The postindependence years were marked by the opening of a number of short-lived Arab banks, such as the Gulf Trust Bank, the Banque de Djibouti et du Moyen-Orient, and the Banque Al Baraka. The Gulf

Trust Bank never really started its operation; Al Baraka was liquidated in 1999; and the Banque de Djibouti et du Moyen-Orient remains in an ambiguous legal status.

Set up in 1982, the Caisse de Développement de Djibouti, whose name was changed in 1992 to Banque de Développement de Djibouti, is essentially concerned with financing development projects. The Banque Nationale de Djibouti, which has had a formal status since independence, is in charge of issuing the country's currency as well as defining its monetary policy.

BANOYTA. An **Afar** term designating the successor of the **dardar**. As the sultanic office is shared between two dynastic families, the Bourhanto and the Dinite, the *banoyta* cannot be chosen from the same family as the reigning *dardar*.

BANQUE DE L'INDOCHINE. Known today as the Banque Indo-Suez (BIS), the Banque de l'Indochine opened its first branch in **Djibouti** on January 6, 1908. The bank was opened to finance the construction of the Addis Ababa–Djibouti **railroad**, which was to turn the new **port** into the outlet of Ethiopian trade. This decision, which was demanded by the French government, occurred when the **Compagnie Impériale d'Ethiopie** (CIE) was facing serious financial difficulties. The role of the Banque de l'Indochine therefore consisted of bringing the necessary funds and taking over the concession, which it did when the CIE officially went bankrupt. With the development of the railroad, the bank gained increasing clout, reaching its peak in the late 1930s, at the time of the railroad boom. The bank also financed **salt** exports as well as **imports** of coffee, wax, and hides.

Apart from its role as a trade bank, the Banque de l'Indochine was also in charge of issuing the country's **currency**. The opening in 1954 of the Banque Nationale pour le Commerce et l'Industrie (now called Banque pour le Commerce et l'Industrie-Mer Rouge [BCI-MR])—a subsidiary of the Banque Nationale de Paris—coincided with the monetary reform that followed the creation of the **franc Djibouti** in 1949, and put an end to the monopoly of the Banque de l'Indochine.

Nowadays, despite the presence of other foreign and national **banks**, most of the country's financial activities are under the control of the BIS and BCI-MR, which employ a considerable part of the population in the tertiary sector.

BANYANS. A community of Indian merchants, originating from the province of Gujrat, who established themselves on the Red Sea coastal area as early as the 17th century. The Banyans moved to **Djibouti** following the decline of the port of **Zeila** and started working as retailers and craftsmen. Most of the Banyans still living in Djibouti are either barbers or moneychangers, but the word has now come to designate any member of the Indian or Pakistani communities.

BARDEY, ALFRED (1854–1934). A French trader in coffee and hides, and native of Lyon, **France**, Bardey arrived in **Aden, Yemen**, in May 1880 and opened a coffee trading company to supply the company his family owned in Lyon. Discouraged by the fierce competition he met in Aden, he decided to open an agency in Harrar, **Ethiopia**, and hired **Arthur Rimbaud** with the intention of settling him as his agent there. As a member of the Société de Géographie Commerciale, Bardey wrote several articles about the region that were published in this association's journal. His travelog, titled *Barr Adjam,* describes the last hours of Egyptian presence in Harrar before the city was taken by Menelik's army.

BARKAT GOURAD HAMADOU (1930–). Barkat Gourad has been prime minister of the Republic of **Djibouti** since September 1978 and first vice president of the **Rassemblement Populaire pour le Progrès** since its creation in March 1979. He has been part of Djibouti's political scene since November 1958 when he was first elected as a representative to the **Assemblée Territoriale**. From June 1960 to 1975, he held various positions under the leadership of **Ali Aref**, whose fall he provoked in early 1976 as head of a parliamentary insurrection.

BATAILLON SOMALI. A corps of 1,700 voluntarily enrolled soldiers, established in May 1916 at the height of World War I. The battalion was mainly composed of **Somali nomads**, mostly natives of **Djibouti**, northern **Somalia**, and **Ethiopia**. It took part in most of the battles around Verdun, in **France**, and more particularly in the most deadly fight to take place over the famous Chemin des Dames, which remained under their control from August to October 1917. From May to June 1918, these soldiers distinguished themselves by defending Mont de Choisy, thus barring the road from German troops heading to Paris. As a testimony to their bravery they received a total of more than 1,200 individual and six collective decorations.

BELWO. A poetic genre that was born in the town of Borame, in northwestern **Somalia**, in the mid-1940s. This essentially urban genre is the immediate predecessor of the **heelo**. It is essentially concerned with love themes and is recited to the accompaniment of drums. The *belwo* is also characterized by the fact that it can be recited by both men and women, something rather rare in **Somali** society. Its invention has been attributed to **Abdi Deeqsi** (a.k.a. **Sinimo**).

BENDER JEDID. Bender Jedid ("the new port" in Arabic) is the name still used for *Quartier 1* and *Quartier 2,* two of the capital city's neighborhoods mainly inhabited by the natives. These are in fact the most ancient and most cosmopolitan urban settlements in the city. *See also* QUARTIERS.

BENDER SALAAM. Now known as *Quartier 4,* Bender Salaam is a neighborhood that started to be developed in the 1920s as a southern extension of the capital city.

BERNARD, ALBERT (1910–1935). A French colonial administrator who arrived in **Djibouti** in 1934, after completing his studies at the Ecole Coloniale in Paris. He was one of the pioneers of French administration settlement in southwestern Djibouti, which was then an insecure border area. Bernard was killed January 17, 1935, at **Moraito** during the punitive expedition he had launched against a party of **Assay Mara** warriors, who had just rustled cattle from the **Issa** and **Debne nomads** who were settled in that area.

BESSE, ANTONIN (?–1951). Antonin Besse, nicknamed "the king of the Red Sea," was one of the major economic operators in the region during the first half of the 20th century. However, despite his considerable financial means, Besse, who had established his business in **Aden**, never really succeeded in setting foot in **Djibouti** until 1949, when he founded an oil company, the Société des Pétroles Somalis.

BEY. This title was given to a high-ranking military or civil officer in the **Ottoman empire**. The term was also sometimes used to distinguish the head of a wealthy family from the nobility.

BLOCKADE. The pro-Italian policy of the French colonial authorities in the territory of Djibouti during World War II led the British to take a series of sanctions. The most dramatic form of the sanctions, as far as the consequences on the population and the garrison, was the blockade (*blocus* in French) that lasted from September 18, 1940, to January 15, 1942. This blockade enabled the British, who were established in neighboring **Yemen** and northern **Somalia**, to control sea and land **transport** or movement. Toward the end of March 1941, with the liberation of **Ethiopia** by British troops, the blockade became so tight that the colony suffered an unprecedented famine. In addition to the physical hardships imposed by the blockade, the atmosphere of terror installed by **Pierre Nouailhetas**, then governor (**gouverneur**) of the colony, rendered the ordeal even more unbearable.

The departure of most merchants and the resulting economic stagnation gave the capital city's streets a dreary look. Malnutrition-linked diseases caused havoc among the native population and more particularly among women and children, who represented 70 percent of the victims. The blockade ended with the surrender of the pro-**Vichy** authorities to the alliance of British and Gaullist French forces.

BORDERS. The territory of the Republic of **Djibouti**, which spreads over 23,000 square kilometers, was delimited along with the reinforcement of the French colonial presence. Its present configuration is the result of a series of **treaties** that started with the cession of a coal storage point to **France** by the **Afar sultans** at **Obock**, and ended with the November 1954 border arrangements with **Ethiopia**.

The border with **Somalia** was agreed upon on February 2, 1888, during the British colonial rule in northern Somalia, which was then known as British Somaliland. Today, the main crossing points on this border are **Loyada**, on the east, facing the Gulf of Aden, and Jallelo and Guistir, on the southeast.

The border with Ethiopia, which runs from the west of the Republic of Djibouti down to the south, is by far the longest. It was delineated by successive treaties, the first of which was signed March 20, 1897, following the Ethiopian victory over Italian colonial aspirations at Adwa (**Adoua**). The main negotiators were, on the French side, **Léonce Lagarde**, then governor (**gouverneur**) of the French colony, and, on the Ethiopian side, Ras Mekonnen, Emperor Haile Selassie's father and then governor of the Ethiopian province of Harrar. Following the end of World

War II, on September 5, 1945, France and Ethiopia signed a protocol on drawing the frontier that was finally delimited on November 2, 1954 (*see also* AFAMBO).

The border with the Italian colony of **Eritrea**, to the north of the Republic of Djibouti, was delineated by the protocols of January 1900 and July 1901.

BOURHAN BEY. *See* BOURHAN IBRAHIM ABOUBAKER.

BOURHAN IBRAHIM ABOUBAKER. Better known as **Bourhan Bey**, he was one of the sons of **Aboubaker Pasha** and the first notable to move from **Zeila** to settle on the present site of **Djibouti** in 1885, as soon as the **borders** between the French colony and British Somaliland were delimited. Two years later, with the transfer of the colonial administration from **Obock** to Djibouti, he was appointed as the first village chief. As such, he convinced some of his friends, such as **Hadj Dideh**, to move to the emerging city with their fellow countrymen in order to boost its development. The house that he first lived in—on the site of what was, until the late 1920s, the natural **port** of Djibouti called *Quai au bois*—was given to the Ethiopian government to house its embassy.

BOUTRES. Rangy wooden vessels mostly used by **Yemenite** seamen to travel and engage in **trade** in an area extending from the Red Sea to the Indian Ocean. The *boutres,* which were widely used in **Djibouti** until the late 1940s, played an important part during the **blockade** imposed by the British from 1940 to 1942. The coming of more modern means of transport caused their decline simultaneously with that of ancient coastal cities such as **Zeila** and **Tadjourah**.

BURAMBUR. *See* POETRY.

– C –

CAADI. An Arabic term designating a judge in Muslim societies. The caadi, who is at the head of the **Sharia**, is appointed by the government to deal with social affairs concerning the Muslims. The court in which he presides settles litigation relative to inheritance, divorces, and other family conflicts. *See also* JUDICIAL SYSTEM.

CARMII. A local word describing the 18-month **blockade** imposed on **Djibouti** (then a French colony) by the British during World War II as a sanction for its collaboration with the Italian fascist forces occupying most of the Horn of Africa. The term is said to be derived from the name of a sorghum usually reserved for cattle and that the population consumed during the dearth caused by the blockade.

CATHOLIC MISSION. In 1885, two Capucin priests sent by the Lord Bishop of Harrar opened a school and an orphanage in **Obock**. Three years later the Lord Bishop of Harrar himself, accompanied by three sisters from the Franciscaines de Calais order, arrived in Obock, and they were soon joined by another two sisters. They opened a girls' school and an orphanage but they also started working at the hospital.

The mission was transferred to **Djibouti** in 1896 where it gradually developed. Until October 1922, the only schools in French Somaliland were those of the Catholic Mission. In 1914, the Catholic Mission, which had been under the authority of the Harrar Vicar, became an apostolic prefecture. In 1955, Pope Pius XII introduced ecclesiastical hierarchy in Francophone Africa, thus placing the Djibouti diocese under the direct authority of the Holy See.

CENTRE DE RECHERCHE D'INFORMATION ET DE PRODUC-TION DE L'EDUCATION NATIONALE (CRIPEN). This institution, founded in 1988, delivers information concerning **education** and conducts applied research in pedagogy, producing pedagogical material and planning curricula. One of the most significant actions of the CRIPEN is certainly the creation, in 1989, of the Educational Radio (Radio Scolaire et Educative), which has since been broadcasting educational programs twice a week. CRIPEN is currently working on an educational television project. The institution also publishes a quarterly bulletin, *Le Bulletin de l'Education Nationale*.

CERCLE. A term inherited from colonial times and used to designate the largest administrative unit. The division of the territory into *cercles* was initiated in March 1949. It is paradoxical that **Obock**, which was the original location of the colony, became a *cercle* only in 1965. After **independence**, the term *cercle* was replaced by **district**.

CHAILLEY, MARCEL (1910–1962). Marcel Chailley was a French military officer who was stationed in the colony from 1935 to 1937. Posted to **Tadjourah**, Sismo, and **Djibouti**, he took advantage of his stays in northern Djibouti to write on the local population's customs and social organization. Many of the articles he published, mostly in the quarterly journal *Le Pount*, are still used to study this part of the country.

CHAMBER OF COMMERCE. The International Chamber of Commerce and Industry of Djibouti, formed in 1912 and reorganized by the March 24, 1947, decree as the Chamber of Commerce of Djibouti, was, in its early years, a forum for concert, aiming to develop business. It gradually evolved to take a more active part in making decisions affecting the economy.

During World War II, the Chamber of Commerce stood as a bastion hostile to the **Vichy** government. As such it played a major role in the negotiations that led to the liberation of the colony from Vichy rule.

The Chamber of Commerce was renamed Chambre Internationale de Commerce et d'Industrie de Djibouti (CICID) in 1978, one year after Djibouti's **independence**. Today, the CICID is a multiprofessional public institution with a goal to focus on all economic activities and is a privileged partner to both the major economic operators and the public authorities.

The CICID has traditionally been under the control of a class of wealthy merchants who initially had close ties to the **railroad**, and who could influence the **political life** as well as the economic one. Its present chairman, **Said Ali Coubèche**, has held this position since June 1957, and is one of the leading public figures in the country.

CICID derives its income from a levy attached to the cost of business licenses, and also from the earnings of its training department and the bonded warehouses that are under its control. It publishes a quarterly magazine, *Djib-Eco,* and a monthly bulletin, *Djib-Import.*

CHAMBRE DES DÉPUTÉS. The Chambre des Députés was formed in July 1967, when the **Côte Française des Somalis** changed its name to **Territoire Français des Afars et des Issas**. It was a **parliament** whose 32 members were elected by the local population, in accordance with electoral laws based on an ethnic quota and geographic distribution. The first assembly was elected on November 17, 1968, thus putting an end to the **Assemblée Territoriale**. Its main tasks consisted of drawing up the budget, dealing with social problems, and electing members of the **Conseil du Gouvernement**.

When the colony gained **independence** in 1977, the Chambre des Députés was replaced by a transitional legislative body called **Assemblée Constituante**. *See also* ASSEMBLÉE NATIONALE.

CHAPON-BAISSAC. Governor (**gouverneur**) of the colony from May 1924 to 1934, Chapon-Baissac was at the origin of the colonial penetration into the hinterland. His governorship was marked by the creation of the **cercle** of **Tadjourah** in May 1927, that of **Dikhil** in 1928, and the construction of the colony's first medical dispensary. Deeply concerned with the image of **France** that was given to the colonized populations, he fought against the slackening of moral standards within the society of the French colonizers.

CHEFNEUX, LÉON (1853–1927). Léon Chefneux was a French trader who landed at **Obock** in 1878, in the same period as **Paul Soleillet**. Both were arms traders who wanted to deal with **Ethiopia**. Chefneux succeeded in making contact with Emperor Menelik and soon became his main **arms** supplier. Once he was received in Menelik's court, Chefneux, who had also been trained as an engineer, helped talk the emperor into building a **railroad** to link the town of Ankober to the Red Sea coast. His goal was to put an end to the **Abban**-controlled monopoly on caravan trade. He had previously succeeded, in 1886, in obtaining from Menelik a concession to exploit the **salt** of **Lake Assal**. Menelik consented to the railroad being constructed, and gave the job to Chefneux and to the Swiss engineer Alfred Ilg, who thereafter became one of the emperor's closest advisers and as such contributed to the modernization of the railroad.

CHEMIN DE FER DJIBOUTO-ETHIOPIEN (CDE). The **railroad** line linking **Djibouti** with Addis Ababa had been operated by the **Chemin de Fer Franco-Ethiopien** since 1909. However, following Djibouti's **independence** in June 1977 and in the context of the **Ogaden War**, the company vanished without even going into liquidation. It is only in March 1981, two years after the end of the conflict, that a new company, the Chemin de Fer Djibouto-Ethiopien, was created. Although a considerable section of the line had been damaged, the necessary repairs were made and traffic resumed, putting an end to the dramatic shortage in agricultural products.

CHEMIN DE FER FRANCO-ETHIOPIEN (CFE). The Chemin de Fer

Franco-Ethiopien was established in Addis Ababa in July 1909, to carry through the works initiated by the **Compagnie Impériale d'Ethiopie** (CIE). Financed by the newly established **Banque de l'Indochine**, now called Banque Indo-Suez (BIS), the company succeeded in having the works completed by 1915. The **railroad** line started operating two years later. For more than 60 years, the company, chaired by **Charles Michel-Côte** from the 1920s to 1959, remained the mainspring of the colony's economic development. However, the company closed in 1977, without even filing for bankruptcy.

CINEMA. The history of cinema in **Djibouti** is closely linked to that of the **Gleyzes**, the family that introduced the invention to this part of the world. The Gleyzes opened movie theaters in **Ethiopia** and in Djibouti in the 1920s, at a time when the capital city was being developed. To some extent, the introduction of cinema influenced the way of life for the newly urbanized population. The theaters became a place where the colonizers and the colonized could observe each other in a relaxed atmosphere.

With the development of the movie industry, more and more theaters were opened (Eden in 1934, Olympia in 1939, Le Paris in 1965, Al Hilal in 1975). In the 1970s, the capital city counted five movie theaters, and each district had its own. In that period, a few local attempts at filmmaking were carried out with the participation of local actors. One of these was *Burta Djinka,* a film in **Somali** that was made by G. Borg in 1972.

When these theaters weren't showing films, they hosted political meetings and musical shows. The invasion of the market by videotapes, combined with the theater-owners' lack of innovation, led to fewer people attending movies in the 1980s, and the gradual closing down of almost all the theaters.

CIVIL AVIATION. The development of **Djibouti** as a French military base on the eve of World War II led to the establishment of a military airfield at **Ambouli**, five kilometers from the city. This airfield, which consisted of three runways used by the military, was improved in 1949 to receive bigger planes. At the same time, work began on a civil aerodrome that opened in 1950. Until 1958, this civil aerodrome remained under the technical management of the Ministry of Public Works.

The Civil Aviation Authority was officially established in December 1961. In 1963, a new aerodrome was constructed and **Air Djibouti** was created. Between 1963 and 1964, several efforts were made to improve the infrastructures: workshops were built, and the runway was extended.

In 1973, the civil aerodrome was placed under private management before being extended and modernized two years later. This upgrading was completed with the inauguration of a new terminal in 1976.

CLOTHING. In the absence of weaving traditions in the pastoral way of life, the **nomads** living in **Djibouti** traded for cotton fabrics from people living in the Ethiopian highlands. Thus, the traditional clothes, which consist of a loincloth worn by men as well as women (although in a different way), were made using this material. Toward the end of the 19th century, merchants from the coast started importing an inexpensive fabric called *abu jadid* from Japan. Very quickly, this new product became popular and replaced to a large extent the material imported from **Ethiopia**. Increasing **trade** with the Arabian Peninsula and Asia introduced new articles, gradually influencing the population's clothing habits. The national dress for women now consists of a colorful and almost transparent gown called *dirre,* worn over an underskirt called *gogera*; the hair and shoulders are usually covered with a shawl. As for men, the loincloths they now wear are imported from countries such as Malaysia and Indonesia.

CLUBS. Officially described as social and cultural associations within the country's various communities, the clubs were, in fact, a disguised way to attract electors and, at a time when **political parties** were not authorized, served as platforms from which political ideas could be expressed. The first such clubs to be established were the Club de la Jeunesse Arabe (*see also* YEMENITES) that was founded in 1937 and the Club de la Jeunesse Somali et Dankali, which **Mahamoud Harbi** founded in 1946. In 1949, in the wake of the ethnic clashes that took place in the capital city, the clubs were banned. They reopened a few years later but under stricter control from the administration.

COMMISSAIRE DE LA RÉPUBLIQUE. The title borne by the head of a **district**, the commissaire is, in fact, a civil servant appointed by the Council of Ministers. Under the authority of the Ministry of the Interior, the commissaire's main function consists of representing the central government in the territory of the district he administers. He is therefore responsible for making known and executing laws enacted by the government. Since he is also responsible for keeping law and order, he is the chief of the National Police Force. In addition, the commissaire is also a registrar and as such is authorized to officiate in civil marriages. As the person responsible for the district, he executes the budget allocated to his services by the government, is in charge of matters relative to urbanization, and can intervene in cases of litigation referred to the customary courts. *See also* ADMINISTRATIVE ORGANIZATION; JUDICIAL SYSTEM.

COMPAGNIE DE L'AFRIQUE ORIENTALE (CAO). Established in 1890 by a retired navy officer, marquis de L'Enferna, the Compagnie de l'Afrique Orientale was a maritime company located in **Obock** that engaged in trade with **Ethiopia**. The company left Obock to settle in the nascent **port** of **Djibouti** in 1896. In exchange for the concession that was received from the colonial administration, the company agreed to transport free of charge the administrative mail in the area. Then, from 1908 on, the CAO was entrusted with both the colony's bonded warehouses and the depot of **arms** and ammunitions to be exported to Ethiopia. The company left the region in 1955, leaving the market to the **Compagnie Maritime d'Afrique Orientale** (CMAO).

COMPAGNIE DES SALINES DU MIDI ET DE DJIBOUTI. This company was established in **Djibouti** in 1899 to extract **salt** from the coastal plains of the capital city. From 1912 to 1956, the company exported salt all over the world, but mainly to **Ethiopia** and Japan. The federation of Ethiopia and **Eritrea** in 1952 led to the decline of the Ethiopian salt imports from Djibouti to the advantage of the newly acquired Eritrean port of Assab. The salt industry in Assab was far more developed and cost effective than its Djiboutian competitor. This brought about the bankruptcy of the Compagnie des Salines.

COMPAGNIE IMPÉRIALE D'ETHIOPIE (CIE). The idea of establishing a **railroad** that would link **Ethiopia** to **Djibouti** dates back to 1889, although it wasn't until 1896 that a Swiss engineer, Alfred Ilg, and **Léon Chefneux** set up a private company chiefly financed by British capital. The company's first scheme was to build a railroad that would go through the Ethiopian city of Harar. Construction began in 1897 but was interrupted in 1902 when the line reached the Ethiopian town of Dire Dawa. The company then filed for bankruptcy in February 1907 and was liquidated a year later. After a period of transition, the remaining phase of the project was carried out by the **Chemin de Fer Franco-Ethiopien** (CFE).

COMPAGNIE MARITIME D'AFRIQUE ORIENTALE (CMAO). Established in October 1919, the Compagnie Maritime d'Afrique Orientale was one of the largest companies to operate in the colony at its origins and played an important part in most of the decisions that were made concerning its management. With the development of the **port**, the company's headquarters were transferred to **Djibouti** in 1924, and, in 1938, a sister company, the Société des Pétroles de Djibouti, was opened. It was installed on the Plateau du Marabout and was entrusted with the supply of fuel to all the ships berthing at the port of Djibouti.

CONSEIL DU GOUVERNEMENT. One of the changes brought by the enactment of the 1956 **Loi Cadre** was the establishment of the Conseil du Gouvernement. This council, which was elected by the **Assemblée Territoriale** and consisted of six to eight members and a president, constituted the executive of the colony. Until the 1960s, its president was the head of the colony, a French government officer appointed by the Council of Ministers of France, whereas its vice president was the native candidate who had gathered the majority of the votes. The Conseil du Gouvernement had limited powers.

CONSEIL REPRÉSENTATIF. Set up on November 9, 1945, the Conseil Représentatif was an assembly elected for four years and consisted of two constituencies: one for the Europeans and the other for the natives. Until August 1950, each constituency comprised 10 members, six of whom had to be elected whereas the remaining four were appointed by the governor (**gouverneur**). A new law enacted August 19, 1950, brought the number of councilors to 25: 13 natives and 12 French. The council's main role consisted of drawing up the budget. All council decisions had to be submitted for the governor's approval, leaving this council little authority. In 1957, the Conseil Représentatif was replaced by the **Assemblée Territoriale**.

CONSTITUTION. Until 1992, no constitution as such existed but the country did have a body of assorted laws establishing the sovereignty of the Republic of **Djibouti** and the main principles of government. The most important among these were Act LR/77-001, of June 27, 1977 (known as Constitutional Act Number 1), and Act LR/77-002 of June 27, 1977 (known as Constitutional Act Number 2). Djibouti's first constitution was submitted and adopted in September 1992 in a context of **armed conflict** opposing an **Afar** front to the government. The constitution's goal was to introduce a form of limited multiparty system (only four parties are authorized) after 15 years of one-party rule.

Although the 1992 Constitution guaranties the independence of the judiciary, legislative, and executive powers, the judicial process is often influenced by political considerations, and the powers of the **president** are unlimited. In addition, even though freedom of speech, **religion**, and peaceful assembly are recognized for all citizens, censorship, both straightforward and disguised, remains common practice.

COOPERATION, FRENCH. The emancipation of the colony from French rule on June 27, 1977, was accompanied by the signing with **France** of a set of cooperation treaties aimed at guaranteeing the economic viability and the military defense of the newly independent state. Concretely, this cooperation was in the form of technical assistance to various ministries and financial support in many fields. Thus the organization of the Djiboutian **army** was entrusted to French military advisers, and until the 1980s the Armée Nationale Djiboutienne received financial support from the French government.

In the field of **education**, the French Ministry of Cooperation provided most of the secondary school teachers until they could be replaced by Djiboutian staff trained in French universities. As the number of scholarships granted to Djiboutian students decreased, a new policy consisting in the establishment of local postsecondary institutions was adopted.

In addition to defense and education, the French mission of cooperation allocates to the Republic of Djibouti financial support for several other projects, such as the upgrading of the **railroad** infrastructure. Some of the funds are given directly by France, while some is given via the European Union.

CÔTE FRANÇAISE DES SOMALIS (CFS). Côte Française des Somalis was the name of the French colony of **Djibouti** between 1896 and 1967. This name, which was given by the May 20, 1896, decree organizing the colony's administration, was chosen to emphasize the French ownership of this territory in contrast with the other **Somali**-inhabited colonized territories, namely British Somaliland and Italian Somalia. On August 28, 1898, another decree dealing with the administrative organization of the colony was signed. The French colony's name was changed once more, following the 1967 **referendum**, and became the **Territoire Français des Afars et des Issas.**

COUBÈCHE, SAID ALI. The son of a wealthy and influential family of merchants of **Yemenite** descent, Said Ali Coubèche took an active part in the colony's **political life** from the late 1940s to the late 1950s. He was elected vice president of the **Conseil Représentatif** in March 1946 and represented the **Côte Française des Somalis** at the Assemblée de l'Union Française in November 1947.

In 1953, he gave up his seat as adviser at the French Assembly and retired from political activities until 1957, when he was again elected Conseiller Territorial in **Mahamoud Harbi**'s roll. However, when in September 28, 1958, a **referendum** for self-determination was organized, he left Harbi and joined **Hassan Gouled** as an opponent of **independence**. Coubèche has been the president of the **Chamber of Commerce** of Djibouti since June 1957.

CRIMINAL ATTACKS. The political history of Djibouti is studded with a series of deadly criminal attacks that started in the 1930s, when voluntary organizations such as the Club Arabe and the Club Somali et Dankali (*see also* CLUBS) first emerged. These organizations were very political in nature, and often resorted to violence to settle their antagonisms. It is in this atmosphere that Abdallah Coubèche, a prominent member of the Club Arabe, was assassinated in 1937. Many other assassination attempts aimed at political figures were organized in the following years.

The bomb attacks that followed the 1967 **referendum** were more related to the struggle for **independence**. On January 24, 1970, a bomb blast devastated the **Palmier en Zinc**—a bar with a French clientele—killing 18 people. On December 5, 1975, a grenade was thrown at **Ali Aref**'s car and killed his bodyguard. A year later, on December 20, 1976, the Mic-Mac bar was hit by a bomb blast that killed two people and injured 16. This bombing was condemned by the pro-independence organizations.

In the postindependence period, terrorist attacks were used to protest government policy. Hardly six months after the independence celebrations, on December 15, 1977, the terrace of the Palmier en Zinc was again blown up by a bomb. This prompted a wave of arrests in the **Afar** community. Outraged by the brutality and repression that occurred under the supervision of the minister of the interior, and mostly aimed at the Afar neighborhood of **Arhiba**, Premier **Ahmed Dini** and four other Afar ministers resigned.

On January 14, 1986, the **Rassemblement Populaire pour le Progrès** headquarters were the target of a bomb attack that caused no casualties. On March 18, 1987, in the excited atmosphere that preceded the legislative and presidential **elections**, a bomb exploded at the Historil Café, killing 11 people and injuring more than 40. **Aden Robleh**'s opposition party was officially accused of the attack. On the eve of the Gulf War, on September 27, 1990, a bomb exploded at the Café de Paris, killing a child.

CURRENCY. Djibouti's economy is based on the strength of its currency, the **franc Djibouti**, which is freely convertible and at a fixed parity with the U.S. dollar. This currency came into existence in 1949 as part of a vast scheme to make **Djibouti** a tax-free **trade** zone.

– D –

DANCE. In **Afar** and **Somali** traditional societies, major social events are often accompanied by singing and dancing. Tapped out by hand clapping and foot stomping, traditional dances are usually adjunct to either war chants or love songs. Although these dances are still occasionally performed during wedding ceremonies or in cultural shows, the rapid urbanization of the population is inexorably working against their perpetuation. *See also* MUSIC.

DANKALI. Although the name has often been used to designate all the **Afar**, the Dankali were originally an Afar clan that settled along the coast of **Eritrea** where they were in contact with the Arab seamen and traders from **Yemen**.

DARDAR. Mostly used in the **sultanates** of **Tadjourah** and **Rahaita**, this title refers to the man who is at the head of the sultanate. Although the function is hereditary, there is a sharing of power between two dynastic families, the Bourhanto and the Dinite. Thus, if the *dardar* is a member of the Dinito dynasty, then the **banoyta** has to be a Bourhanto. The *dardar* is assisted by a council of notables. *See also* SULTAN.

DAY FOREST. A primary era forest located in the **Goda** Mountains, in northern Djibouti, 1,700 meters above sea level. Because of the endangered species it shelters, the Day Forest is a protected area; however, uncontrolled woodcutting and overgrazing are damaging the ecosystem at a frightening rate. *See also* FLORA.

DEBNE. The name of an **Afar** clanic federation regrouping the Ankali, the Ayrolasso, the Harkamela, and the Garayssa, and now settled in an area that extends from the region of **Gobaad** in southwestern **Djibouti** to the Obno, a river in southeastern **Ethiopia**. Originally, the Debne, who are named after an eponymous river, were settled in the Mabla Mountains, in the region of **Tadjourah**. In the early 19th century, the federation, headed by **Sultan** Loîta Ibrahim, migrated to the south.

DEUXIÈME BUREAU. This is a branch of the Service du Renseignement Intercolonial (SRI), the French colonial intelligence agency created by the Front Populaire government in the 1930s. The SRI consisted of two departments: the Section d'Etudes, which was created in 1935 and dealt with civil intelligence; and the Deuxième Bureau, concerned with military intelligence. The Deuxième Bureau was in turn divided into eight sectors; sector 4, which was based in **Djibouti**, had to deal with Italian East Africa, British East Africa, Arabia, and the Persian Gulf. In reaction to the Italian fascist menace in the Horn of Africa, the SRI was reorganized to follow the situation, support Ethiopian high-ranking dignitaries in exile, and provide the internal resistance with material assistance, notably arms. At the end of World War II, civil and military intelligence were separated again.

DIA (Diya). Derived from Arabic, this term refers to a procedure of blood compensation in **Heer** or **Somali** traditional law. The *dia* is usually paid or received collectively by members of groups that have entered into this sort of contract. The compensation to be paid is calculated according to a preestablished rate based on the seriousness of the wrong caused and the sex of the victim. Despite the existence of an official **judicial system**, the *dia* is still widely practiced in rural as well as urban centers.

DIKHIL. Although the **sultanate** of **Gobaad** had been placed under the protection of the French as early as January 2, 1885, with the signing of a treaty between **Sultan Houmed Loita** and then-Governor **Léonce Lagarde**, it was only in 1927 that the colonial administration decided to establish an administrative post. A fort was built to host a company of 10 men headed by Commandant Rossat. This fort was actually intended to serve as a base for colonial penetration into the territory's hinterland. When Captain **Alphonse Lippmann** took over, the administrative post gradually developed and was turned into a **district** that comprised the present districts of Dikhil and **Ali Sabieh**. During the Italian invasion of **Ethiopia** in 1936, the administrative post was reinforced by the arrival of a detachment of *tirailleurs sénégalais*.

The construction in 1973 of the road that leads to Ethiopia via Dikhil and the later establishment of an electric plant supplying the whole region, were instrumental in the development of this cosmopolitan city. Among other things, Dikhil is a major center in the cattle **trade** with Ethiopia.

The particularity of this district resides in the fact that it is a crossroads between the **Afar** and **Issa** grazing areas. It is thus an example of pastureland sharing between two otherwise antagonist communities. *See also* MANDAYTOU.

DIMIS. *See* AHMED ABDALLAH.

DINI AHMED ABOUBAKER. In 1839 and again in 1842, Dini Ahmed Aboubaker, one of **Aboubaker Pasha**'s nephews, accompanied Rochet d'Héricourt, **France**'s official envoy to **Abyssinia**, in his two journeys through the **Afar** territories and assisted him as an interpreter. Later in Paris, in the name of the **sultans** of **Tadjourah** and **Rahaita**, he signed the treaty of March 11, 1862, ceding to France the territory extending from Ras **Doumeira** to **Goubet-el-Kharab**.

DINKARA. A pair of timbales made of copper and covered with steer skin. The *dinkara,* which is the symbol of the **sultan**'s power, is made on the day of his enthronement and destroyed at his death. *Dinkara* is also the name of the dance executed in the honor of the sultan.

DISTRICT. A term referring to the country's largest administrative unit. There are five districts, each bearing the name of its main town: **Djibouti**, **Ali Sabieh**, **Dikhil**, **Obock**, and **Tadjourah.** Each district is administered by a **Commissaire de la République**, a sort of governor appointed by the head of the state. This partly reflects the centralized character of the administrative and political apparatus. Each district is in turn divided into administrative zones called "postes administratifs." In terms of area, the district of Djibouti is the smallest but the population of the capital city itself represents two-thirds of the country's total. The peculiarity of the capital city resides in its being divided into areas called **arrondissements**, which have under their control smaller housing zones called **quartiers**. The other four districts are mainly rural pastoral areas whose populations maintain close links with the neighboring countries.

DJAMA ALI MOUSSA (1910–1963). Djama Ali also known as **Zeila'i**, was a major political figure from the mid-1940s to the late 1950s, and was appointed by the local legislative body in December 1946 as a representative of **Djibouti** to the Conseil de la République in **France**. The period in which he was active politically was characterized by both the prominent position held by the **Gadaboursi** community in the social and **political life** of the city, and the alliance between the leaders of the Arab and Gadaboursi communities to hold the front of the political stage. Djama Ali's successive elections led to the exacerbation of urban violence and the outburst of the most violent ethnic clashes between the **Issa** and Gadaboursi communities in June 1949. His death in November 1963 coincided with the rise in power of both the **Afar** and Issa leaders, whose episodic alliances and antagonism have since fueled the country's political history. The Afar and Issa entered into these alliances when the Gadaboursi and the Arabs, who outnumbered the Afar and Issa in the city of Djibouti, dominated political life.

DJAMA YOUSSOUF MAHAMOUD (? –1996). Djama Youssouf, better known as Djama Maître, started his career as a primary school teacher in 1934 in the district of **Dikhil**. However, being a learned man at a time when few natives had access to formal education, he quickly became a notable in Dikhil and also served as a registrar to help the local administration. For a long time, he was remembered for encouraging the school canteen system that was later extended to all the primary schools outside the capital city. This system attracted the children of the **nomads** who were reticent about schooling. Djama ended his career as an educational adviser to the schools of the capital city. He died on July 6, 1996.

DJIBOUTI (Jibuti, Gabouti). Many explanations have been given as to the origin of the name Djibouti, which results from the transcription in French of a local word or expression. To the **Somali**, the name comes from the expression *jab buti,* which can be translated as the place where the ogress was defeated, a reference to the hard climatic conditions of the area. According to the **Afar**, the name is derived from the word *gabod,* meaning tray, which is a reference to the geomorphology of the site.

France's decision in 1885 to settle on the site of what is now Djibouti was motivated by ease of accessibility. Effectively, the seawaters were quite deep and groundwaters were not too far from the shore, thus making it easy for the calling vessels to make provisions. However, the choice of Djibouti was also an attempt to escape from the rule of the **Abban** system in the **trade** with **Ethiopia**. The **port** of Djibouti became an outlet to the new trade route French traders were trying to open. Their endeavors were rewarded when the **railroad** linking Djibouti with Addis Ababa was inaugurated in 1917, boosting the port's activities. It is around these two poles, the port and the railroad, that the new city developed until the outbreak of World War II. The international conflict transformed the colony, but more particularly its capital, into a military base. This function has since been a major part of its raison d'être.

After the country achieved **independence** in 1977, a number of diplomatic representations and international organization offices were established in the capital city. Most of U.N. major agencies, such as the U.N. Development Program, the High Commissioner for Refugees, the World Food Program, and the UNICEF, still operate from Djibouti. The concentration of almost all administrative authorities, health centers, and other international organizations in the capital city may be one of the reasons why the development of other towns has been rather slow.

From its early days, the capital city has been populated by a mosaic of peoples from the region: **Yemenites**, Indians, **Greeks**, Armenians, and Sudanese, to mention but a few. The growth of the population, which has been estimated at 300,000 people, is regularly boosted by the inflow of immigrants from neighboring countries.

DJIBOUTI, LE. The owners of the **Entreprise Générale des Travaux Publics** (EGTP), the company entrusted with the construction of the **railroad**, began publishing this newspaper on February 4, 1899. The newspaper closed in October 1903, soon after the company had stopped its activities. What followed was a long period of lethargy as far as the written press was concerned, until the creation of *Le Réveil de Djibouti* in 1943.

DOCKERS. The colonial economy, which organized itself around **port** activities and the **salt** industry, was instrumental in the growth of cheap labor, composed of workers coming from the neighboring ports of **Aden**, Hodeida, **Zeila**, and Berbera. This rush of new labor in turn contributed to the city's development.

Port workers were divided into two groups: those who loaded the ships with coal and those who loaded and unloaded other products onto and from ships. As the jobs were highly coveted, they were used as lures by the various political organizations to recruit their rank and file. When the port workers became aware of their strength, they started using it to claim social benefits. Strikes were often used as a weapon in this struggle.

Following the 1962 dock strikes, **Ali Aref** started replacing the **Somali** port workers, who seemed more inclined to make claims and to protest, with **Afar** laborers.

DOUMEIRA. An island located to the north of the Republic of **Djibouti**, at the entrance of the **Bab el Mandeb** strait. This island, which constitutes a strategic position for the control of the Red Sea, was given up to Italy in 1935, before being taken back by **France** in November 1943.

DRAMA. Drama and **music** are closely linked to one another and strengthened with urbanization. Artists and their works do not belong to a country but to a culture. Thus, **Somali** artists, playwrights, composers, and singers in the Horn of Africa have an audience that extends from **Somalia** to **Ethiopia**, **Djibouti**, and Kenya. This phenomenon was emphasized by the creation and development of local radio stations in the 1950s (*see also* RADIO). In addition, the creation of a Somali department at the BBC in 1957 was crucial. The founding of a number of cultural organizations also played a significant part.

Dramatic themes mainly focus on antagonisms, such as bush life versus urban life, and on tradition, prejudices, the struggle against colonialism, and so on. These themes are related to the social and political preoccupation of the time. However, to evade censorship, most playwrights hid political messages under descriptions of everyday life.

The creation in 1979 of a national band, which immediately became the exalter of the one-party system, opened an era of standardization, accentuated by the fact that, in the absence of copyrights, most playwrights and composers had to join the national band in order to survive. At the same time, the publication of Hassan Cheik Moumin's *Leopard among Women* in 1979 (translated into English by Professor Andrewjeski) was instrumental in the passage of Somali drama from the oral tradition to its written form.

DURRA. The local name of sorghum, which the **nomads** include in their daily diet, mainly in the shape of pancakes. This cereal has been at the core of the **trade** exchanges between the nomads of the littoral and the farmers of the Ethiopian highlands. The nomads supplied the latter with **salt** and imported products such as sugar, rice, and tea in exchange for *durra*. In the wake of the crisis that shook the pastoral economy in the late 1940s, most herders began growing the cereals they used to buy from farmers.

– E –

ECOLE FRANCO-ISLAMIQUE. *See* NAJAH AL ISLAMIYA.

ECONOMY. The Djiboutian economy, which is essentially **trade-** and service-oriented, depends on the condition of the country's infrastructure. It is a paradox that the **railroad**, which was in a way at the origin of the country's development, is today the least developed, although much used, means of **transport**. Most goods forwarded to or from **Ethiopia**, notably fresh fruits and vegetables, are transported by rail.

Since its early days, the **port** has functioned as one of Ethiopia's main outlets and access to the Gulf of Aden. This contributed to its early development. When the **Suez Canal** was closed (1967–1975), the port lost most of its activity and, despite the intensive upgrading of its equipment, never really recovered until the outbreak of the conflict between **Eritrea** and Ethiopia in May 1998.

The modernization of the airport (*see also* CIVIL AVIATION), which took place in the 1970s, was a logical consequence of **Djibouti**'s position as a strategic base for the French armed forces. It has brought about the establishment of new links beyond the regional limits.

The parity of the **franc Djibouti** with the U.S. dollar, combined with the **currency**'s free convertibility and the absence of exchange controls, has worked as an incentive to foreign **banks** and firms. However, due to the deep crisis Djibouti is going through, many of these businesses have already closed, putting into question Djibouti's aspirations to becoming a major financial center in the region. Its strong dependence on these service infrastructures, which are tributary to political stability in the area, makes the Djiboutian economy structurally fragile.

High production costs and political uncertainties have been major obstacles to the creation of industries, despite the existence of a tax-free zone and modern infrastructures. One of the few industrial production units, Eau de Tadjourah, a mineral-water-bottling factory that was established in 1985, was destroyed during the 1991–1994 conflict that opposed the north-based guerrillas being in the government. As for the dairy plant (Laiterie de Djibouti), and the short-lived fodder-mill production unit, they symbolize the failure of the young republic's industrialization policy that is dependent on foreign aid.

The scarcity of surface water, the poverty in arable land, and the predominantly pastoral tradition of the population explain the absence of a significant agricultural sector. The only attempt to develop a large-scale farming unit was a financial disaster. On the other hand, the few small-scale farming cooperatives that have settled along the beds of some of the main seasonal rivers have been ignored by the numerous agricultural development schemes.

Whether it is practiced by the **nomads** along the age-old caravan tracks or by the **shershari** flying as far as Indonesia, trade, in its various forms, has always been a dominant activity among the local population. Despite the present economic difficulties, it remains one of the government's main sources of income and a large portion of the population's means of subsistence. *See also* AGRICULTURE; INDUSTRY; PROGRAMME D'AJUSTEMENT STRUCTUREL; SALT.

EDUCATION. The origins of the formal education system date back to 1885 with the formation of an official structure entrusted with the mission of giving minimum education to the natives. The first schools to open their doors in the capital city were a boys' school and a girls' school run by French missionaries (Frères de St. Gabriel and Franciscaines de Calais), and exclusively opened to the children of European settlers. After a failed attempt in 1906, the colonial administration finally entrusted a Alliance Française committee with the task of organizing the education of the native peoples, who were increasingly needed by foreign employers. This committee held a monopoly on education in the colony up to the beginning of World War I. Between 1915 and 1922, the debate on the educational system opposing secular schools and confessional schools placed a cloud over the growing needs of an ever increasing and urbanizing native population. The present educational system's foundations began in 1922 with the victory of the partisans of a free public and nonconfessional school.

Today's educational system, with the exception of a few private schools, is under state control. The curriculum and directives are prepared by the Ministry of Education, under the supervision of French technical assistance. Due to the absence of reliable data and to the inadequacy of the administrative structure in a country with growing needs in terms of education, the government has been unable to develop a true education policy. The Ministry of Education budget has been cut regularly over the past decade and the survival of the educational apparatus is now closely related to the funds provided by money-lending institutions, such as the World Bank and the African Development Bank. This is aggravated by a substantial reduction of **France**'s financial and human assistance to the sector (*see also* COOPERATION, FRENCH).

This crisis of the educational system is all the more serious as Djibouti, the only Francophone enclave in this part of the world, finds it difficult to adapt to and find perspectives in the regional environment. Moreover, as can be seen from the table below, most of the educational infrastructure is concentrated in the capital city.

	Capital city	Districts
Primary schools	30	27
Junior secondary	4	4
High schools	1	0
Vocational	1	1

Until the late 1980s, students who had passed their *baccalauréat* (12th grade) were granted scholarships, either by the French Ministry of Cooperation or by the Djiboutian Ministry of Education, to pursue higher studies abroad, most of the time in France. However, due to the soaring number of applicants for these scholarships and a change in France's policy, the number of scholarships has become insufficient. Although Djiboutian students still register at French universities, fewer do so every year. The creation of postsecondary two-year studies and a university embryo in cooperation with French universities has opened a new, although limited, alternative for some of the 300 students or so who complete their secondary studies at the country's only high school.

Formal education, however, concerns only a small portion of the population (the literacy rate in 1990 was 48 percent). Parallel to that type of education, there is an unofficial religious education system. A considerable number of Koranic schools are in charge of the religious education of the population, mainly in lower-class urban and rural areas.

EGYPT. The relations between the Horn of Africa and Egypt originated in the ancient times of **Punt**. However, it was chiefly during the second half of the 19th century, when Egypt freed itself from **Ottoman** rule under the reign of Khedive Ismaïl, that Egyptians came to occupy all the ports on the African coastline of the Gulf of Aden previously controlled by the Turks. In 1867, urged by **Aboubaker Pasha**, who had noticed that the French showed little desire to settle on the territory conceded to them through the 1862 Treaty, the governor general of Egyptian Sudan raised the Egyptian flag in **Tadjourah**, despite the presence of the French in the region. In 1875, the garrison of Tadjourah was reinforced and a tax officer came to settle there. Egypt's plan was to launch from Tadjourah a conquest of both the **Awsa** sultanate and the kingdom of Shoa in **Ethiopia**. *See also* MUNZINGER EXPEDITION.

ELABE, MOHAMED DJAMA (1940–1996). Elabe, who was born into a family of wealthy merchants, was elected in 1973 to **Parliament**, representing the district of **Dikhil**, his native town. This was the beginning of a long political career that ended at his death. In the pre-independence era, he was a faithful supporter of **Ali Aref** until 1976, when he joined the parliamentary opposition led by **Barkat Gourad**. After **independence**, he was entrusted with various ministries until he resigned from his office as minister of public health to protest the violence perpetrated by security forces December 18, 1991, in the **Afar** neighborhood of **Arhiba**, and to express his disagreement with the government's policy concerning the **armed conflict** taking place in northern **Djibouti**. Soon after resigning, Elabe created the **Parti du Renouveau Démocratique** (PRD), an opposition party of which he was the candidate during the presidential elections of May 1993. Until his brutal death on November 26, 1996, Elabe preserved both the positive aura that he had acquired in the public opinion through his sense of moderation and the liking of the French authorities.

ELECTIONS. A by-product of the enactment of the **Loi Cadre** in 1956, the electoral principle was introduced with the establishment of the colony's first **parliament**, the **Assemblée Territoriale**, whose members were elected in a universal suffrage, two-round majority list system, with a single constituency vote. These elections, which took place June 23, 1957, ended in victory for the **Mouvement d'Union Républicaine** (MUR), with **Mahamoud Harbi** at its head, over the Défense des Intérêts Economiques et Sociaux du Territoire (DIEST), led by **Hassan Gouled**. The following year, the colony started participating in all the elections concerning the French Republic. This undoubtedly contributed to the maturation of the native political elite.

Since independence, legislative elections have been held every five years to renew the **Assemblée Nationale**. The first ones were organized May 21, 1982, shortly after the enactment of the **Loi de Mobilisation Nationale** that installed the single-party system. As a result, one-third of the legislative body was renewed.

The legislative elections of December 18, 1992, marked the inauguration of the multiparty system adopted by the government in the aftermath of the 1990 summit of La Baule, in **France**. Despite the participation of the **Parti du Renouveau Démocratique** (PRD), all 65 seats were won by the **Rassemblement Populaire pour le Progrès** (RPP). This absolute majority lasted until the December 19, 1997, legislative elections, when the **Front pour la Restauration de l'Unité et de la Démocratie** (FRUD) obtained a few seats.

Presidential elections are held every six years. This was made possible after the enactment, in February 1981, of a new electoral law allowing for the direct election of the president. However, prior to the adoption of the 1992 **Constitution**, only the members of the RPP could theoretically run for a presidential mandate. Thus, until the 1993 elections, **Hassan Gouled Aptidon** was the sole candidate each time. In the 1993 elections, the late **Mohamed Djamah Elabe**, the leader of the PRD, decided to challenge Hassan Gouled but was defeated. The latest elections, which were held in 1999, were officially open to all four authorized parties. However, they resulted again in the victory of a representative of the RPP, **Ismael Omar Guelleh**.

ELECTRIC POWER. Alfonso Repicci, a private entrepreneur, was the first to produce and supply electric energy in Djibouti, starting in 1906. The colonial administration bought the facilities in 1939 from Repicci, and placed them under public management. In 1954, a new plant was built in the northern part of the city of **Djibouti**, in the vicinity of the **port**, followed by the formal creation in 1961 of Electricité de Djibouti (EDD), a public company that produced and supplied electric power to the whole country. The present plant, located in the southeastern part of the city, was built in 1975 to meet the growing city's increasing demand for electricity.

Today, the EDD is overwhelmed by management problems as well as booming demand. Apart from the main plant in the capital city, there are two smaller units, one in **Tadjourah**, and the other in **Dikhil**.

ENTREPRISE GÉNÉRALE DES TRAVAUX PUBLICS (EGTP). Also called Société Duparchy & Vigouroux, the names of its two owners, the

EGTP was established in **France** in 1898. It was entrusted with the construction of the Djibouti–Addis Ababa **railroad**, but disappeared in 1902 with the bankruptcy of the **Compagnie Impériale d'Ethiopie** (CIE). However, it contributed to the urbanization of the capital city by installing the colony's first water-supply system and building the first hospital, among other things. The EGTP also published a leaflet called *Le Djibouti*.

ERITREA. This northernmost neighbor state achieved independence in 1993 following a referendum that was organized at the end of a two-year transitional period. Eritrea then established diplomatic relations with the Republic of **Djibouti** and signed a treaty of friendship and cooperation in 1994. However, following the outbreak of a military conflict with **Ethiopia** in 1998, the relations between Djibouti and Eritrea deteriorated and were interrupted.

ETHIOPIA. The Republic of **Djibouti** emerged as an independent state at a time when Ethiopia was going through one of its most violent periods. The collapse of the feudal empire in 1974 was followed by the dictatorial rule of a military regime, the Derg. Although Ethiopia was among the first countries to officially recognize the newly independent Republic of Djibouti in 1977, the relations between the two states have seen ups and downs, including, from 1977 to 1981, a period characterized by mutual suspicion. Djibouti accused its neighbor of supporting the **Front de Libération de Djibouti** (FDLD), an armed front based in Ethiopia, and Ethiopia, in turn, was not satisfied with Djibouti's obedience to the Arab League, which supported the Eritrean liberation movements as well as the invasion of **Ogaden** by **Somalia**. The Republic of Djibouti, however, was more concerned with remaining neutral during this conflict.

From 1981 until its downfall in 1991, Ethiopia's military regime changed its course. As a consequence, the offices of the **Mouvement Populaire de Libération** (MPL) were closed and the relations between the two countries became friendlier. **Hassan Gouled**'s official visit in 1981 to Ethiopia, and Colonel Menguistu Haile Mariam's visit to Djibouti, indicated that closer ties were developing. Later, the establishment of the **Inter-Governmental Authority on Drought and Desertification** (IGADD) in 1986 was an attempt at extending this cooperation to the other states in the region. The military regime's downfall was accompanied by the massive exodus of some 60,000 soldiers escaping from the Eritrean battlefront. This once more raised the **refugee** issue, which had long been present in the relations between the two states.

The advent of a new regime in Ethiopia in 1991 led to a further consolidation of cooperation with the signing of a number of agreements and the setting up of joint committees to focus on joint issues, particularly in the **transport** sector. In its search for alternatives to the port of Assab in **Eritrea**, Ethiopia started using the transport infrastructures of the Republic of Djibouti, notably the **port**.

– F –

FAUNA. Despite the apparent aridity of the environment, **Djibouti**'s fauna is represented by a variety of indigenous species. The sea fauna is particularly rich and attracts hosts of international visitors to diving sites such as Ras Syan and the Sept-Frères islands (also called Sawabi). Land fauna consists essentially of various sorts of gazelles, and scavengers such as jackals and hyenas. Djibouti is also a haven for several bird species such as flamingoes, pelicans, herons, and a number of passerines. However, intensive woodcutting, overgrazing, fishing, and picking are contributing to the degradation of the ecosystem. This, combined with the absence of an effective conservation program, is gradually leading to the extinction of a wide range of species.

FERRY, ROBERT (1920–1997). Robert Ferry arrived in Djibouti in 1946 as an officer of the French army in the context of intense social and cultural activities that followed the end of the **blockade**. He left the country in 1947 but came back twice—from 1955 to 1958 and from 1960 to 1963—before leaving the army and settling as a teacher in the country's only high school. He was later appointed head of the Service de Statistiques et de Documentation, which was to become the Direction Nationale de la Statistique in 1982.

Ferry was actively involved in scientific research concerning Djibouti, and founded the **Société d'Etude de l'Afrique Orientale** (SEAO), which published the quarterly journal *Le Pount*, and later participated in the creation of the Centre d'Etudes Géologiques et de Développement. In 1978, this branch of the French Bureau de Recherches Géologiques et Minières became the **Institut d'Etudes et de Recherches Scientifiques et Techniques** (ISERST).

Ferry, who ended his career as a technical adviser at ISERST, continued to show interest in the region long after he left Djibouti in 1982. He belonged to a category of colonial administrators who originated from a military environment, and who developed a particular interest in the study of various aspects of the country in which they worked. Among these were Edouard Chedeville, Henri Labroussse, and **Marcel Chailley**. Their works remain essential tools for the study of Djibouti and its region.

FIIMA. Among the **Afar**, men and women are usually organized into solidarity groups called *fiima*. The members of a *fiima* have to give assistance to one another in any situation, more particularly in organizing wedding and death ceremonies. They cannot disobey the decisions made by the *fiima* and may be punished if they infringe the rules, although they cannot be expelled. Each *fiima* is identified by its personal name, which may correspond to particular events or characteristics related to the generation it gathers. *Fiima* membership can be based on ascription at birth, which is the commonest way, or by appointment by elders for a specific mission. The leader of the first category is called *ebo; the leader of the second category is called fiima-abba.*

FLAG. Djibouti's flag, which was established on Independence Day, consists of two equal green and blue horizontal bands with a white isosceles triangle based on the hoist side, at the center of which is a red five-pointed star.

FLEURIOT DE LANGLES, ALPHONSE, Admiral. The admiral headed the French fleet in the 1860s, with the mission of keeping watch on the maritime routes of the Indian Ocean, from the eastern littoral of Africa to the western shores of India. He took the lead in exploring the coast, with the goal of establishing a French naval base. He supervised the official settlement of the French in **Obock** and began looking for a better anchorage site for French ships to the south of the Gulf of **Tadjourah**. This led to the establishment of the French on the present site of the city of **Djibouti**. Fleuriot de Langles also conducted the inquiries into the circumstances surrounding **Henri Lambert**'s death.

FLORA. Given the poor quality of the soil and the semi-arid nature of the climate, with an annual rainfall of 100 to 200 mm (four to eight inches), Djibouti's flora consists essentially of species that have adapted to drought conditions. In terms of quantity, the flora is poor; it is interesting, however, because it hosts a number of rare species. In the coastal plains and, generally speaking, at sea level, the vegetation consists of varieties of acacia (*acacia mellifera, acacia asak,* and *acacia tortilis*), palm trees (*hyphaenea thebaica*), and bushes of *salvadora persica.* More vegetation can be found at higher altitudes, rainfall being somewhat greater, particularly in the regions of mounts **Goda** and Mabla. One of the most interesting sites is the **Day Forest,** where endangered species such as *juniperus procera, buxus hildebranti, livistonia carinensis,* and *dracaena ombet* can be seen. Although it is officially a protected area, the forest is slowly dying because of intensive woodcutting and overgrazing.

FONDS D'INVESTISSEMENT ET DE DÉVELOPPEMENT ECONO-MIQUE ET SOCIAL (FIDES). Established on April 30, 1946, the Fonds d'Investissement et de Développement Economique et Social was a funding institution whose mission was to financially support the economic take-off of the French overseas territories. It derived its budget from the Caisse Centrale de France et d'Outre-Mer (CCFOM), which was later renamed Caisse Centrale de Coopération Economique. The projects it funded in **Djibouti** between 1947 and 1952 were concerned with extending the **port**, upgrading the airport, constructing roads, and developing the health and **education** systems. These projects had a considerable impact on the evolution of the colony in the sense that they created temporary employment, thus encouraging the immigration of labor from the neighboring countries.

FONTAINEBLEAU. This French steamboat, which belonged to the **Société des Messageries Maritimes**, linked **Djibouti** to **France** and Asia. It was destroyed by fire and sank in Djibouti waters in July 1926. Its wreck was used to build the first quay of Djibouti's **port**.

FOOD. Traditionally, food habits are rooted in the pastoral way of life that has long characterized the living environment of most of the country's population. The consumption of products derived from cattle breeding, which provided the **nomads** with the food necessary for their subsistence, was supplemented with cereals, such as **durra,** imported from the Ethiopian highlands. Products such as tea, sugar, rice, and dates were imported from the Indian subcontinent and the Arabian Peninsula via the ancient ports of **Tadjourah** and **Zeila**. These products are still at the root of the food habits in both rural and urban areas.

At the end of the **blockade** imposed on Djibouti during World War II, vegetables and fruit started being regularly imported from **Ethiopia** by train. This was at the origin of a profound and positive change in the population's food habits, although it resulted in an increased dependency on Ethiopia. This change in food habits also provoked a change in the nature of trade, which evolved from a barter system to a monetarized one.

Although the country has a more than 300-kilometer-long coastline on the shores of one of the wealthiest seas in terms of seafood, only people living in the coastal cities of Tadjourah and **Obock** include fish in their daily diet. The hinterland's nomadic populations derive their rations of animal proteins from camel meat. Ritual ceremonies reserved to men, such as *buulo* among the **Somali** and *dasiga* among the **Afar**, provide this opportunity in times of abundance. Camel meat is otherwise preserved according to ancestral techniques (*see also* MUQMAD) and makes up the nomads' reserves in proteins during their transhumance.

FRANC DJIBOUTI. The December 25, 1945, decree issued by **France** set the new parity between the currencies of French territories and that of their colonizer. Thus were born the franc CFA and the franc CFP. The franc Djibouti, which was created March 17, 1949, had the peculiarity of belonging to the dollar zone instead of the franc zone, mostly because its geographic location put **Djibouti** at the intersection of lively **trade** exchanges between Africa and Asia. In addition, the **currency** was created during intense political negotiations conducted by the French government's representatives to Ethiopian imperial authorities. The goal was to harmonize trade exchanges between the two countries and create opportunities for Djibouti to benefit from the postwar economic boom. Among the chief promoters of creating this new currency, and creating the **port**'s free zone, was P.H. Siriex, then governor (**gouverneur**) of the colony.

FRANCE. France, which first colonized Djibouti, has played a crucial role in the country's historical development, from the early days through the creation of the modern state and its organization. This was manifested, among other things, by the constant military presence of France and its participation in the economic life.

France's settlement in what is now the Republic of Djibouti owes a lot to the initiative of individuals, including government agents, traders, and adventurers. The rivalry between France and Great Britain flowed through a series of historical events, including the assassination of **Henri Lambert** in June 1859; the acquisition of **Obock** and the territory extending from **Ras Doumeira** to Ras Ali in 1862; and the beginning of more than a century of colonial presence that extended beyond the Gulf of **Tadjourah** and led to the founding of the city of **Djibouti** in 1887. The mixed feelings the French politicians had about the usefulness of this tiny acquisition were at the origin of a number of debates in the French National Assembly, and the successive changes that were made to the colony's name reflected to some extent the relationship between the colonizers and the natives.

General Charles de Gaulle's two visits to Djibouti—one as president of France— marked crucial moments in the development of this relationship. The first one, in September 1956, took place soon after the enactment of the June 1956 **Loi Cadre**. The second, in August 1966, is remembered for the massacre that followed when the pro-independence movements protested during the presidential parade. When, seven years later, French President Georges Pompidou made an official visit to Djibouti, **independence** had become a less taboo issue.

Immediately after the country's independence in June 1977, France became a sort of guarantor of Djibouti's sovereignty, taking an active part in the new nation's security and defense systems within the framework of a **cooperation** agreement. Djibouti remains one of the seven African states bound to France by a defense treaty. However, the limits of French military assistance were revealed in the course of the first **armed conflict** that the country faced, from 1991 to 1994. Nonetheless, to this day, France remains Djibouti's first partner in many fields, whether economic or military.

FRONT DE LIBERATION DE DJIBOUTI (FDLD). Arising in 1979 from the merge of the two **Afar** opposition parties, **Union Nationale pour l'Indépendance** (UNI) and **Mouvement Populaire de Libération** (MPL), the FDLD used **Ethiopia** as a rear-base to organize an armed struggle that included a number of spectacular actions. Among these were the assault on the Khor Angar garrison in northern **Djibouti** and the kidnapping of a French teacher in Yoboki, in the region of **Dikhil**. From 1981 on, with the political rapprochement between the Ethiopian and Djiboutian governments, most of the organization's members returned to Djibouti, taking advantage of the amnesty granted by the government. Those who decided to remain in exile had to stop all their guerrilla activities for a time. In 1991, with Mohamed Adoyta at their head, they formed a coalition with three other movements to create the **Front pour la Restauration de l'Unité et de la Démocratie** (FRUD). The **armed conflict** that ensued lasted three years, from 1991 to 1994.

FRONT DE LIBÉRATION DE LA CÔTE SOMALIE (FLCS). Created by **Mahamoud Harbi** in July 1959, following his defeat concerning the 1958 **referendum** for self-determination, the Front de Libération de la Côte Somalie remained the main armed liberation front until the country gained **independence**. Although it was founded in **Aden (Yemen)**, the FLCS moved its head office to Mogadiscio (**Somalia**) and used this country as its rear-base as early as 1960.

The FLCS became particularly active after the 1967 referendum, organizing several actions against the French presence. A number of **Somali** youth, who had been disappointed by the result of the vote, joined in the efforts. When **Aden Robleh** was chosen as its president in 1969, the front turned more radical, but it succeeded in gaining international recognition and began to represent those seeking independence when dealing with the main international organizations combating colonization, such as the **Organization of African Unity**, the Arab League, and the Non-Aligned Movement.

In 1974, the FLCS decided to coordinate its activities with the **Ligue Populaire Africaine pour l'Indépendance** (LPAI), a legal pro-independence organization headed by **Hassan Gouled**. In early 1975, the two leaders signed a secret agreement that made provisions for three ministries (Defense, Interior, and Foreign Affairs) to be granted to the FLCS after independence. However, an assassination attempt was made on Aden Robleh on the eve of independence and, although he survived his injuries, the agreement was put aside. As for the FLCS freedom fighters, they were integrated into the newly created national **army**.

Some of the FLCS's most spectacular actions include kidnapping an administrative officer in **Tadjourah** in 1971 (*see also* DOMINIQUE PONCHARDIER), kidnapping the French ambassador to Somalia in March 1975, and hijacking a school bus transporting French children in February 1976.

FRONT POUR LA RESTAURATION DE L'UNITÉ ET DE LA DÉMOCRATIE (FRUD). Established in 1991, in the context of a deteriorating economic situation, the Front pour la Restauration de l'Unité et de la Démocratie was an armed front consisting mostly of **Afar** youth.

The numerous setbacks it inflicted on governmental forces in the early days of the **armed conflict** pushed the government into mobilizing and sending thousands of young people to northern **Djibouti**, where the fighting was taking place. Although a dissident branch led by **Ahmed Dini Ahmed** refused to negotiate and continued to fight the government, most of the FRUD guerrilla actions stopped after a peace agreement was signed December 26, 1994, in Ab'a. During the cabinet reshuffle of June 8, 1995, two of FRUD leaders, Ali Mohamed Daoud and Ougoure Kiffle, were appointed ministers. Two years later, FRUD became a conventional political party and entered a coalition with the **Rassemblement Populaire pour le Progrès** (RPP).

– G –

GABAY. This is a form of **poetry** in **Somali** oral **literature** that is generally composed to convey political messages or important tribal decisions.

GABODE. A geographical term used to designate the coastal zone that lies to the east of the capital city of **Djibouti**. Because the country's only civil prison was built on this site, the name has now become a synonym for penitentiary.

GABOODE. *See* ABDOURAHMAN AHMED HASSAN.

GAD. An **Afar** term used to designate **poetry** in general. The genre includes very subtle subdivisions based on whether the poems can be sung or danced to, the themes they deal with, or the circumstances in which they can be declaimed.

GADABOURSI. One of the **Somali** clans belonging to the Deer group. The Gadaboursi, who live mainly in northwest Somalia and between Harrar and Jijiga in **Ethiopia**, also constitute an important part of the capital city's population.

GALAFI. A small village on the border with **Ethiopia**. Since 1975, it has been served by an all-weather road, the main land link between **Djibouti**, Ethiopia, and **Eritrea**. Used by thousands of merchants every year, this road is a sort of spare wheel to the Djibouto-Ethiopian **trade** that is otherwise carried out via the **railroad**. It proved its usefulness in 1978, during the **Ogaden War**, when the **railroad** connection was interrupted.

GALILEH (Guelilé). *See* BORDERS.

GAMES. Urbanization, together with the advent of secular **education**, has brought about the disappearance of most traditional games. However, some of the games are still played, particularly in rural areas, the most common of which are the *dabuda* within the **Afar** community, and the *sah* (a sort of draughts game) within the **Somali** community. Other games, particularly among the Afar, are more physical and can be considered sports; they are usually ball games such as *fareyta, laloyta,* and *radoyta.*

GANDE. The name of both the council of elders and its members in **Issa** traditional law. The *Gande* consisted of 44 members chosen for their wisdom and knowledge of the **heer** to represent the 44 clans making up the Issa confederation. Although its role consisted of preserving the spirit of the original text and protecting it from any alterations, the *Gande* had the right to amend the *heer*. It also exerted a control on the **ogaz**, whom it could even depose. The institution disappeared in the late 1940s, essentially because it refused to compromise with the modern Ethiopian state.

GEOLOGY. It is during the Tertiary Period that great tectonic movements induced the creation of the Rift Valley, which extends from western Asia to southern Africa, and set in motion the volcanic activity that took place later. At the beginning of the Miocene Epoch, these tectonic movements, which nearly separated Africa from Arabia, led to the creation of the Gulf of Aden and the emergence of a network of faults. The Republic of **Djibouti**, because it is located at the heart of this network of faults, is subject to regular seismic activity. This was manifested in November 1978 with the eruption of **Ardoukoba**, a new volcano located in the **Lake Assal** region, and the subsequent opening of another large fault. Due to the facility with which its geological phenomena can be observed, this region, the lowest point in the African continent (153 meters below sea level) has attracted both experienced and lay observers for many years.

GEOTHERMAL ENERGY. The first attempts at exploring the geothermal potential occurred in 1973, when French research missions started exploring the region of **Lake Assal**, the most promising area in terms of geothermal energy. Since then, many other attempts have been made to put geothermal energy to use in various parts of the country, particularly in the **Hanle**. To this day, however, none of these projects, funded by international lending agencies such as the World Bank, has come about.

GLEYZES, THE. A family of French pioneers who were among the first to introduce the **cinema** in **Ethiopia** and **Djibouti**. Georges Gleyze arrived in Djibouti in 1898 to work as an engineer on the **railroad** construction site. Once the railroad was completed, he devoted his time to his passion for movies. He opened his first movie theater in Djibouti in the 1920s and a second one, Olympia, in 1934. After his death, his son Edouard—better known as Coco—took over and opened two more theaters, Le Paris in 1965 and Eden in 1972. Edouard, who in 1973 made the first film featuring Djiboutian actors, *Bourta Djinka,* is a major contributor to the introduction of the seventh art in Djibouti's cultural landscape. Today, with the advent of the videotape culture, all the theaters owned by the Gleyzes have closed.

GOBAAD. This depression plain is located in southwestern **Djibouti**, where the Ethiopian rift and the **Afar Depression** meet. This plain, the extension of the **Awash** Valley in **Ethiopia**, is rich in interesting paleontological and archeological sites (*see also* ARCHAEOLOGY). Gobaad, which is also the fief of the **Debne**, constitutes a zone of contact between the **Afar** and **Issa nomads**.

GODA. A mountain range lying in northern Djibouti. The Goda, whose highest peak measures 1,750 meters, is the site of the **Day Forest**.

GOHAD. *See* AHMED HASSAN LIBAN.

GOUBET-EL-KHARAB. Sunk at the extremity of the Gulf of **Tadjourah**, Goubet-el-Kharab is a bay whose bottlenecked entrance has probably favored the conservation of rare marine species. This, and the strange-shaped volcano that lies in its middle, have certainly contributed to creating a number of superstitions as to its **fauna**. The extinct volcano marks the bay as located in the prolongation of the Rift Valley. *See also* GEOLOGY.

GOUVERNEUR (Governor). The title was borne by the principal representatives of the French government in the colony who were also ambassadors of **France** in **Ethiopia**. The two functions were separated by decree January 9, 1899, which gave the colony its administrative autonomy. In the wake of the 1967 **referendum**, the title was changed to **Haut Commissaire**, although the attributions remained unchanged. The governor was appointed by the Council of Ministers and had to report to the Ministry of the Colonies. He was assisted in his mission by the Consultative Council. Though the first governors were civil servants only, some of them were later involved in politics. Among a governor's responsibilities was appointing members to the **Chamber of Commerce**.

GREEKS. Although a few Greek traders had settled in the region, particularly in Harrar (**Ethiopia**) and **Aden** (**Yemen**), well before the French arrived, the **railroad** project brought a massive influx of Greek workers to the area, resulting in the establishment of a large community. These workers played an important part in constructing the railroad, often working as contractors and serving as intermediaries between the native workers and the other European employees. They had fewer advantages and earned lower wages than the latter, which may explain why they were the first in the region to create **labor unions**. Their role increased notably during World War I, when they replaced the railroad company's French employees. In the late 1930s and early 1940s, they were dismissed from the **Chemin de Fer Franco-Ethiopien** (CFE).

GROUPEMENT COMMANDO DES FRONTIÈRES (GCF). *See* MILITIA.

GROUPEMENT NOMADE AUTONOME. The Groupement Nomade Autonome—an auxiliary force of native soldiers that succeeded the former **militia** under the February 1, 1970, decree—supervised the colony's **borders** and the control of the nomadic population in the border areas. This force was placed under the command of the **Haut Commissaire** of the **Territoire Français des Afars et des Issas** (TFAI) and supervised by a lieutenant of the French army. At times it was also used as an intelligence service. Otherwise, it took an active part in the social development of the colony by working to improve sanitary conditions and water supply facilities. In addition, many of its native officers, also called *goumiers*, made a name for themselves by winning cross-country competitions overseas.

GUDIIS. A **Somali** term used to designate both male and female circumcision. *See also* INFIBULATION.

GUELLEH AHMED, OMAR. Better known under the name of Guelleh Batal, he was one of the **Issa** chiefs who signed the 1917 agreement placing the Issa territories under French supervision. In the early 1900s he was appointed **ukal** of the Mamassan, an Issa subclan. Until his death in the early 1920s, Guelleh Ahmed remained the most influential Issa *ukal*. As such, he received the highest salary ever paid to any Issa *ukal*.

GUELLEH BATAL. *See* GUELLEH AHMED, OMAR.

GUELLEH, ISMAEL OMAR (1947–). Born in the town of Dire Dawa, **Ethiopia**, Ismael Omar Guelleh moved to Djibouti in the years before **independence**. He soon joined the **Ligue Populaire Africaine pour l'Indépendance** (LPAI), in which he played a predominant role. When the country achieved independence, Ismael Omar was appointed **Hassan Gouled**'s principal private secretary and controlled the security services. He held this position until he was elected **president** of the Republic of **Djibouti** in May 1999.

– H –

HABBASH. This is the name the local population uses for **Ethiopia**, mainly when referring to the Christian state. The people are referred to as the Habbasha, although the word *habashi* is sometimes used in a derogatory way.

HADAL MAHISS. Considered to be the founder of sultanic authority, Hadal Mahiss is, according to legend, the mythical founder of the **Adaïl** dynasty that is at the head of the **sultanates** in the **Afar** territories. He is said to have appeared for the first time in the village of Adaïlou, located on the banks of the **Waima** River about 50 kilometers from **Tadjourah**. As the legend goes, the daughter of **Ali Abliss**, the village chief, had gone to fetch some water when she saw in the water the reflection of a man perched on a tree. She ran to tell the story to the villagers, who came to the spot where she had seen the apparition. The man was asked to get down from the tree but he demanded that the villagers place two steerhides, one brown and the other white, on the ground. When that was done, he got down from the tree and, almost at the same time, fantastic things happened: rivers started flowing, birds started singing, and grass started growing. Hadal Mahiss was then given Ali Abliss' daughter for his wife. Eventually, they had a son who became the first of the dynasty still holding power in the **sultanate**. The two steer-hides, which are still part of the ritual of enthronement, represent the **Asay Mara** and the **Adoy Mara**.

HADJ DIDEH. Although he was one of the city of **Djibouti**'s founders, very little is known of this man whose name was given to a neighborhood, and to the school and the mosque established there.

HAGBAD. This is a type of savings association in which each subscriber deposits a fixed amount of money into a common fund on regular dates. The capital is then given to one of the subscribers as a sort of loan without interest. All of the subscribers benefit from the loan in turn. The money is generally used to carry out individual or collective projects.

HAMAD LAADE (1940–1981). A poet and song-composer, Hamad Laade was one of the most prolific contributors to the **Afar** literary heritage. He was an active participant in the country's cultural life, and was involved in *Egla Ma'o,* an association that was formed by **Mohamed Talha**. Hamad Laade is the author of one of the first **dramas** in the Afar language.

HAMOUDI AHMED (?–1930). He was a rich merchant from **Yemen** and was involved in the **arms** and slaves (*see also* SLAVERY) **trade**. Hamoudi was also an important real-estate owner and contributed to the urbanization of the cosmopolitan city of **Djibouti**, of which he was one of the first notables in the early 1900s. He is better remembered today for his philanthropic deeds, which include the construction of the capital city's first mosque and the establishment of the first Muslim cemetery at **Ambouli**. Before he died, Hamoudi bequeathed all his estate to the **Sharia**.

HANDICRAFTS. The traditionally nomadic way of life of both the **Afar** and the **Issa**, together with the scarcity of natural resources, has limited the development of handicrafts to what is strictly necessary. The materials used by the craftsmen basically consist of hides, used to make containers such as milk pots; vegetal fibers for wickerwork; wood; and scrap metal for weapons.

HANFARE HASSAN (?–1993). Hanfare Hassan, who was from the region of **Dikhil** in southwest **Djibouti**, was, in the 1940s, one of the founding members of the Club Somali et Dankali (*see also* CLUBS), which counted among its militants most of the future **Afar** and **Issa** political figures. He was a fervent supporter of unifying the Afar and the Issa to counter the clout of the **Gadaboursi** and Arab politicians and to establish a more proportional participation in the social and political institutions. He was imprisoned in 1949, because he had become too virulent against the colonizers, and violent demonstrations were organized to free him. In the 1950s, Hanfare became closer to **Hassan Gouled**, with whom he created a party called Défense des Intérêts Economiques et Sociaux du Territoire. He achieved one of his political goals when he became one of the signers of the 1963 **Accords D'Arta**. Two years later, he went into exile in **Ethiopia** and joined the **Mouvement de Libération de Djibouti** (MLD).

HANLE. This vast plain in western **Djibouti** is characterized by its considerable wealth in underground water reserves. These reserves are supplied by the **Awash** River. Hanle is a potential agricultural zone suitable for the establishment of small-scale agro-pastoral farming. However, due to overgrazing, the region has been affected by the phenomenon of desertification.

Traditionally claimed by the **sultan** of **Awsa**, this region has been the site of various clashes either between the **Debne** and the **Assay Mara** or between the Assay Mara and the **méharistes** who were entrusted with the control of the border. One of the largest such clashes occurred in 1934, one year before the **Moraito** incident, and ended with the defeat of the nomad-warriors of the sultan of Awsa. During World War II, the region remained in turmoil because the frontier between the French colony and Italian-occupied **Ethiopia** was not clearly marked. As a result, the Italians settled in Hanle—sometimes beyond the French defense lines—creating a confusing situation. The frontier was finally delimited in 1954.

HANOLATO. *See* PAN-SOMALISM.

HARBI, MAHAMOUD FARAH (1924–1960). A native of **Ali Sabieh**, Harbi had been a workman before becoming involved in politics as a representative to the Union Française. In 1946, he was a member of the Club Somali and Dankali (*see also* CLUBS). On January 2, 1956, he became the first native to be elected to **Parliament** and went to Paris as a representative of **Djibouti** in the French National Assembly. In July 1957, following the implementation of the **Loi Cadre**, he was elected the first vice president of the colony's **Conseil du Gouvernement**.

The surprise he created at the 1958 **referendum** by calling for a pro-independence vote brought about his disgrace. However, in spite of his defeat in the vote, he maintained public support and, on October 2, 1958, he was reelected vice president of the Conseil du Gouvernement. In reaction to his electoral success, the **Assemblée Territoriale** was dissolved October 21, 1958, and new elections were organized on November 29, 1958. These were won by his main rival, **Hassan Gouled Aptidon**.

Soon after, Harbi exiled himself to **Somalia**, where he became the president of the Mouvement National Pan-Somali (*see also* PAN-SOMALISM). The dissension that grew between him and the Somalian government during the congress that gathered all pan-Somali organizations, in December 1959, led him to move to Cairo. There, he gained an increased audience for his movement by effectively using the Egyptian media.

Harbi died in 1960, when the plane that was taking him from Geneva to Rome crashed. Many believe that Harbi, who was trying to establish links with communist countries such as China, was eliminated by the French secret services. *See also* DEUXIEME BUREAU.

HASSAN GOULED APTIDON. Hassan Gouled, president of the Republic of **Djibouti** from 1977 to 1998, was born in the early 1910s in the town of Garissa, in northern **Somalia**. He received a formal education at the **Catholic Mission** of Djibouti, and worked successively as a **port** employee and a primary school teacher. His political commitment dates back to 1946, when he became a member of the Club de la Jeunesse Somali et Dankali, an organization created by **Mahamoud Harbi**. Six years later, he was appointed Conseiller de la République, mainly because he was in favor of keeping the colony within the French Republic. It was thus at the head of the Défense des Intérêts Economiques et Sociaux du Territoire (DIEST) that he ran against Mahamoud Harbi in the 1957 **Assemblée Territoriale** elections.

A fervent partisan of the colony's progressive evolution toward emancipation, Gouled called for a vote against **independence** in 1958. He founded the **Union Démocratique Issa** (UDI) in 1959 and was appointed minister of education two years later. He kept this position until January 1, 1967, when, together with three other ministers, he resigned to join the **Parti Mouvement Populaire** (PMP), a party he had always criticized until then. He eventually became this party's political secretary and campaigned against maintaining the colony within the French Union during the March 19, 1967, **referendum**.

In 1971, the Union Populaire Africaine he had created merged with the Ligue pour l'Avenir et l'Ordre, led by **Ahmed Dini** and **Sheikho**, to give birth to the **Ligue Populaire Africaine** (LPA). The creation of this national party marked a major stage in Gouled's political career. In 1975, the LPA merged with the Action pour la Justice et le Progrès (led by Moumin Bahdon and Idriss Farah Abaneh), giving birth to the **Ligue Populaire Africaine pour l'Indépendance** (LPAI). Soon after the creation of the LPAI, Ahmed Dini and Hassan Gouled went to Mogadiscio to sign an agreement, titled Accord Cadre de Gouvernement, with the **Front de Libération de la Côte Somalie** (FLCS).

By the end of 1975, Gouled was at the head of the main local opposition party fighting for independence. On the eve of independence, the party was in the foreground of the political stage and appeared as the exclusive interlocutor of the colonial power. The demonstrations and violent outbreaks in 1976 gave way to a parliamentary crisis, which led to the resignation of **Ali Aref** from the presidency of the **Conseil du Gouvernement**. Consequently, Gouled and his party remained alone to prepare the independence process. This was partly done during the **roundtable** that was held in Paris on February 28, 1977, to fix the calendar and the terms of the consultations, to determine the administrative and political organization of the future state, and to agree on the nature of future relations with **France**.

At the May 8, 1977, referendum, Gouled was elected a member of the future state's first **parliament**, which in turn elected him president of the Republic of Djibouti on June 27, 1977. From then on, the new president devoted all his efforts to creating a strong presidential regime along the lines of the Gaullist tradition. This orientation was, among other things, at the origin of Gouled's first dissension with his principal ally, Ahmed Dini, who resigned from his post as prime minister five months after the country's first government was formed (*see also* CRIMINAL ATTACKS). As a part of this presidential power consolidation scheme, Gouled founded, on March 4, 1979, the **Rassemblement Populaire pour le Progrès** (RPP), which remained, until 1992, the sole legal political party. The single-party state was given a legal foundation with the enactment of the **Loi de Mobilisation Nationale** of October 1981, four years after Gouled's reelection as president for a six-year term.

Considered to be France's closest ally in Africa, Gouled was urged by the latter to put an end to the one-party system within the framework of the democratization process that was given a boost during the 1990 summit of La Baule. The electoral calendar fixed on that occasion resulted in the renewal of the parliament, the adoption of a **constitution**, and the institution of quadripartism. The short-lived years of political effervescence—aroused by the emergence of a legal political opposition built around a handful of political figures—did not outlast the death of some of them and the lack of substance of the others. Weakened by health problems, Hassan Gouled decided not to run for the 1998 presidential elections. His former principal private secretary, **Ismael Omar Guelleh**, won the elections.

HASSAN HERSI, OGAZ (?–1994). This traditional chief of the **Issa** clan, who resided in **Ethiopia** and reigned from 1930 to August 1994, was the 18th Issa **ogaz**. His reign, the longest ever, coincided with an era of considerable social and political changes within the Issa community, including the settling of this basically nomadic population. One of the factors of this settling process was the construction of the **railroad** linking **Djibouti** to Addis Ababa.

Despite the troubled nature of the period in which he reigned, Ogaz Hassan Hersi constantly played his role as a moral arbitrator and contributed to the unification of the Issa beyond the political rivalries, particularly in Djibouti. His death was followed by a succession crisis that remains unsolved to this day.

HAUT COMMISSAIRE (High Commissioner). This title is given to the man at the head of the colony, and who locally represents the French government. Since June 28, 1967, this title has been used in lieu of governor (**gouverneur**).

HAYOU (Hayu). *See* OBOCK.

HEEDHO. A traditional container made of woven palm-tree fibers and used to preserve the **muqmad** (*see also* FOOD). The *heedho*, which is part of a young **Somali** girl's trousseau, is generally woven by the bride's mother. However, it can also be presented to the newly married couple by friends. In that case, the container has to be returned to its owner with a gift in it.

Although the tradition is slowly dying, the *heedho* is generally opened on the occasion of a ceremony called *dhiqho,* gathering all of the couple's male and female friends. During that ceremony, the *heedho* is dressed in a way that makes it look like a bride and tied with a string. The master of ceremony, usually a young girl, chooses a young man among the guests to untie the knots. Failure to do so gives way to a quiz session on Somali culture.

HEELO. A poetic genre derived from the **belwo**. The name *heelo* was chosen to mark the difference between these two genres because, in its early days, the *belwo* was solidly opposed by religious leaders. Thus, avoiding taboo themes, *heelo* composers gave special attention to the literary quality of their lyrics. As a consequence, the *heelo* became the way to express political messages through the 1950s and beyond.

HEER. The **Somali** use this form of sociopolitical oral contract to settle their legal and political disputes. Among the **Issa**, this form of contract appeared toward the end of the 16th century, following the defeat of the **Adal** kingdom by the Christian kingdom of **Ethiopia** and the former's subsequent breakup.

The *heer* is the foundation stone of the Issa tribal confederation and regulates all aspects of the **nomads'** life. Its objectives are essentially concerned with gathering and protecting the Issa. The *heer* is also a political constitution and, as such, establishes the conditions of the choice and the enthronement of the **ogaz**, as well as his attributions.

HIRAD. *See* ALI FARAH AHMED.

HOFFMANN, BERNARDIN, Monseigneur (1909–1979). Born in Sieviller, **France**, Mgr. Hoffmann was ordained in April 1935 and later sent as a missionary to Madagascar, where he spent seven years. He then served as an almoner in Vietnam during World War II. In September 1945, Pope Pius XII appointed him apostolic prefect of **Djibouti**, where he served until his death. A prolific writer, he attached a printing press to his diocese, from which he launched several publications (*Carrefour Africain, Le Semeur de Somalie*) and published a **Somali** grammar book. Mgr. Hoffman was also involved in the first attempts to create a press in Somali language.

HOLIDAYS. Public holidays are of two kinds, civil and religious. The latter consist of Muslim as well as Christian celebrations: Christmas, Id al Fitr, Id al Kabir, **Mawlid al Nabi,** and the Islamic New Year. Civil holidays include New Year (January 1), Labor Day (May 1), and Independence

Day (June 27). Muslim holidays are established using the Islamic lunar calendar.

HOUMED LOITA AHMED (1820–1902). As the paramount chief of the **Debne,** Houmed Loita played an important role in the various attempts made by French and other European expeditions to reach the Ethiopian highlands through the arid plains of the **Afar Depression.** Thus, in 1841, he served as a guide to French explorer and diplomat Rochet d'Héricourt. In 1875, he agreed to help the **Munzinger expedition** travel through the **Afar** desert in exchange for **arms,** but he abandoned them in the Lake **Abhe** region, where they were crushed by the troops of the **sultan** of **Awsa** near Lake Udumi. On August 9, 1884, he and **Léonce Lagarde** signed a treaty of **trade** and friendship that gave away to **France** the coastal strip extending from **Sagallou** to **Goubet-el-Kharab.**

HOUSSEIN ROBLEH FARAH, Ogaz (?–1942). Also called **ogaz** of the French or *ogaz* of the rail, Houssein Robleh Farah was appointed by the French in 1913 in an attempt to weaken the customary **Issa** institutions and control Issa resistance, mostly insofar as the construction of the **railroad** was concerned. Houssein Robleh, who reigned at the same time as Hassan Hersi, the legitimate *ogaz,* died in 1942.

– I –

IFTINE. *See* ABDILLAHI DOUALEH WAISS.

ILLALTA. *See* MOHAMED HANFARE.

INDEPENDENCE. Djibouti was the last French colony on the African continent to become independent, on June 27, 1977. This event took place at a time when the French colonial power, concerned with preserving its interests in the region on a long-term basis, had decided to set the country on the rails of a sort of programmed independence. This was done during the **roundtable** in Paris that regrouped most of the main actors of the local **political life.**

INDUSTRY. The scarcity of natural resources makes it difficult to set up any significant industry whereas the high cost of **electric power** discourages potential investors in this sector. The attempts at setting up state-owned, small-scale concerns, such as a mineral-water bottling factory and a dairy plant, have failed because of mismanagement. At the moment, industry is limited to a government printing press, a power plant, and a Coca-Cola factory owned by **Said Ali Coubèche**. *See also* ECONOMY.

INFIBULATION. This sexual mutilation, which consists of sewing up the vaginal opening, is a common practice among the **Afar** and the **Somali**. A series of debates have been held on the trauma caused by this practice, and its medical consequences, and it seems that fewer and fewer families are imposing it on their female children. Moreover, the conjugated efforts of the World Health Organization and the Union Nationale des Femmes Djiboutiennes resulted, in 1995, in the enactment of Law No. 333, condemning all forms of sexual mutilations.

INSTITUT SUPÉRIEUR D'ETUDE ET DE RECHERCHE SCIENTI- FIQUES ET TECHNOLOGIQUES (ISERST). Established in 1978, to replace the Centre d'Etudes Géologiques de Djibouti (CEGED), the Institut Supérieur d'Etudes et de Recherches Scientifiques et Techno- logiques is a government research institution that covers several fields. The institute, supervised by a general director, has four departments: human sciences, earth sciences, biology, and energy. It is more concerned with fundamental rather than applied research. A considerable share of its funds has been invested in the search for new sources of energy, no- tably **geothermal energy**, but no tangible result has been seen to this day. The institute also runs, in collaboration with the Institut de Physique du Globe of Paris, a geophysics observatory located at **Arta**, 40 kilometers from the capital city.

INTER-GOVERNMENTAL AUTHORITY ON DROUGHT AND DE- VELOPMENT (IGADD). The agency was set up in **Djibouti** in 1986. Its goal was to establish cooperation between the countries in eastern and northeastern Africa in the fight against recurrent droughts. The found- ing member countries (recently joined by **Eritrea**) are Djibouti, **Ethio- pia**, Kenya, Uganda, **Somalia**, and Sudan. In 1996, on the occasion of its 10th anniversary, the organization changed its acronym into IGAD (Inter-Governmental Authority for Development). This coincided with a change in its goals, which are now also concerned with settling regional conflicts and establishing political stability.

ISLAM. Because of the vicinity of the Arabian Peninsula and the **trade** links among the people on both shores of the Red Sea, Islam was introduced to **Djibouti** very early (around the eighth century) and in a peaceful way. It gradually spread through the ancient cities of **Zeila** and **Tadjourah** to the hinterland, leading to the conversion of the **Somali** and the **Afar nomads**. The conversion trend amplified from the 14th century on, in the aftermath of the confrontation between the Christian empire of **Ethiopia** and the Islamic sultanates of **Adal**.

Today, more than 90 percent of the population consists of Sunnite Shafiite Muslims and all the acts of civil life (weddings, births, burials, and so on) are infused with Islamic precepts. The number of Koranic schools, mostly for children, is a witness to the presence of this religion in the daily life of the population. *See also* Sharia.

ISLAMIC ORDERS. Two pieces of history led to the regrouping of people who advocated a return to a stricter interpretation of the Koran: the decline of the **Ottoman empire** (especially in 1822 with the nomination of Mehemet Ali as viceroy of **Egypt**, representing the Ottoman **sultan** in the territories situated on the shores of the Red Sea) and the emergence of revivalist religious leaders opposing the decline of morality among the Ottoman-influenced ruling elite in the urban centers. The groups formed into brotherhoods, such as the **Qadiriya**, the **Ahmediya**, and the **Salihiya**, which in turn were usually organized around a **sheik** and favored the strengthening of links based on a common faith rather than on ethnic kinship. Although they professed the same **religion**, the brotherhoods were in active rivalry with one another, especially as far as the recruitment of new members was concerned.

ISLANDS. The territorial waters of the Republic of **Djibouti** are dotted with small, uninhabited islands, including the Sept-Frères archipelago in the north and Moucha and **Maskali** at the entrance of the Gulf of **Tadjourah**, whose beauty and wealth of sea life represents a potential for tourist activities. Throughout history, the role played by these islands in organizing maritime traffic in the Gulf of **Aden** and Tadjourah has been considerable. These have often been used as storing caches for goods illegally transported, especially by the **boutres**. They were also used as an advanced post in the system of maritime and coastal security watch.

During the **blockade** imposed on Djibouti from 1940 to 1942, these islands represented a real stake for the British and French protagonists as well as for the *dhows,* vessels that carried food products from **Yemen** and tried to clandestinely supply Djibouti's starving population.

ISMAEL OMAR GUELLEH. *See* GUELLEH, ISMAEL OMAR.

ISSA. The Issa, who belong to the Deer group, are the northernmost of the six **Somali** clans. The territory on which they live, straddling **Ethiopia**, **Somalia**, and Djibouti, is located in a strategically important area, especially as it is crossed by the **railroad**. Consequently, they are in contact with other ethnic groups, such as the **Afar** and the Oromo. Historically, the Issa are listed as the signers of the main colonial **treaties** with **France**, in March 1865 and August 1917, respectively.

ISSAK. One of the **Somali** clan families predominantly living in northwestern **Somalia**, the Issak group represents a large portion of the capital city's population. Many of them originally came to **Djibouti** in the 1920s, at a time when the booming colonial economy was in need of labor. This period also witnessed a transformation of the pastoral and rural economies, which was at the origin of a migratory movement of the Issak community toward the region's ports, such as **Aden** in **Yemen**.

In Djibouti, the colonial administration recruited many of them in the local **militia**, particularly during the two world wars. And yet, the colonial policy held the Issak, who were labeled *allogènes* (nonnatives) as opposed to the autochtons, apart from the rest of the population in conformity with its ethnic quota-based representation scheme. They were consequently deprived of civil rights and could easily be expelled from the colony. Since the country's **independence**, the Issak have been regarded as one of the elements in the national fabric.

– J –

JEWS. Among the first nonnative communities to settle in the nascent town of **Djibouti** was a small group of Jewish traders originating from neighboring **Yemen**. This community, which had established itself in what is now the town's center, largely contributed to the city's construction. Some of the buildings they constructed at the beginning of the century still stand witness to that.

Soon after the state of Israel's birth, in 1948, the nation organized a repatriation operation that was named Flying Carpet. Most of the Jews of Djibouti seized this opportunity to settle in the Promised Land, often leaving their properties behind.

JUDICIAL SYSTEM. The organization of the judicial machinery in **Djibouti** is characterized by the coexistence of three systems: customary courts, the **Sharia**, and the modern judicial system. The Supreme Court supervises all three, but each has its own field of competence. The customary courts, which have been reorganized by the modern state, are competent as far as minor litigation cases concerning housing are concerned. These courts sit in the premises of the **arrondissement**. The *Sharia,* which is the Islamic judicial system, is competent in social matters, particularly litigation arising from divorces and successions. The judges are the **caadis** at the head of the various subsidiaries or arrondissements (in the case of the capital city). The modern judicial system consists of a first instance court and a court of appeal. Both courts comprise three divisions: civilian and commercial, correctional, and social. Penal affairs fall within the competence of the Criminal Court, whereas the Administrative Litigation Council essentially deals with administrative conflicts concerning civil servants.

– K –

KABOBA REVOLT (1943–1945). Kaboba is the name of a confederation of **Afar** clans settled in the **Goda** mountains, in northern Djibouti. The clans making up this confederation are the Namad Ali, Balawta, Gadido, and Able. In 1943, a revolt broke out after French soldiers violated pastures belonging to the Kaboba in the town of Birseha. The subsequent death of a French soldier provoked a series of reprisals. When the revolt finally ended, in 1945, the region had come under the control of the **méharistes**.

KALO. *See* AWSA.

KHAMSIN. The *khamsin,* a hot sand-wind that blows from the northwest, is so named because it is supposed to last 50 days. It usually starts blowing after the passage of the intertropical front at the end of June.

KHAT (Qat). Khat, or *catha edulis,* is a plant grown in most countries of the Horn of Africa as well as in **Yemen**. Although many people in the area use it, the plant is particularly appreciated in **Djibouti**, where more than eight tons are imported and consumed daily. This represents a considerable source of income for the Ethiopian government and to a lesser extent for the farmers in Harrar, from which this narcotic plant is imported. On the Djiboutian side, the import and distribution of khat is in the hands of a private company called Société Générale d'Importation du Khat (SOGIK).

Men, and sometimes women, usually gather in a **mabraz**, after lunch, to chew this plant, which creates a sort of euphoria. Surveys have shown the nefarious consequences of khat chewing on health, family life, and the economy. However, apart from a timid attempt on the part of the government at prohibiting it in 1979, there has been no real effort to eradicate this social plague.

– L –

LABOR UNIONS. The development of a colonial economy with the successive constructions of the **port** and the **railroad** provoked a rush of labor originating from various social and geographical horizons. Contact among the workers, especially rail workers, gave birth to a union movement that expanded to the neighboring countries as early as the 1920s. **Greek**, Armenian, and Italian workers who were involved in railroad construction constituted a large portion of the original union members. But in the same period, another movement developed among the port workers, most of whom were **Yemenites**.

The massive involvement of the native workers in unions began in 1947, the year of the great railroad strike. This event also marks native workers' first entry into **political life**. Most of the leading political figures of the 1950s had made their debuts in unions. This period of mass unionism ended with the 1956 strike, which was met with fierce repression.

The establishment of the Union Générale des Travailleurs Djiboutiens (UGTD) coincided with the birth of the **Rassemblement Populaire pour le Progrès** (RPP). However, a split within the UGTD soon resulted in the creation of the Union Démocratique du Travail. Although workers are free to join the union of their choice, fewer than 20 percent actually do so. Labor unions are almost never associated in the decisions made by the government.

LAGARDE, LÉONCE (1860–1936). Lagarde, a civil servant in the navy, arrived in **Obock** in late 1883. He took an active part in the life of the colony and was among the signers of the **treaty** by which the **Issa** chiefs transferred their territory to **France**. A few years later, in 1887, he was appointed governor (**gouverneur**) of the Obock et Dépendences colony and eventually decided to transfer the French settlement from the northern shores of the Gulf of **Tadjourah** to the present site of the capital city. There, in 1890, he had a palace built that was later to become the president's palace. When the colony changed its name to **Côte Française des Somalis** in May 1896, Lagarde, who had also been appointed France's ambassador to **Ethiopia**, remained governor. Two years later, in March 1897, he headed the mission that negotiated border conventions with that country (see also BORDERS). Lagarde left Djibouti in 1899, after having laid the foundations of the colony's **administrative organization**.

LAMBERT, HENRI (1828–1859). Lambert was from a family of wealthy plantation owners who lived in Mauritius, a British colony. He arrived in **Aden** in September 1855 to organize the migration of labor from the East African coast to Mauritius. **Slavery** having been abolished in **France** as well as in all of the French colonial possessions, Lambert was looking for a disguised way to supply plantation owners with labor. When he arrived in the region, he went to **Tadjourah**, where he established good contacts with local authorities and more particularly with **Aboubaker Pasha**, one of the wealthiest local merchants. On his second trip, from March 1855 to April 1856, he explored the coastline and was subsequently appointed France's consular agent in Aden in 1857.

In July 1858, Lambert convinced the Navy Ministry to remit to Aboubaker Pasha the sum of 4,000 thalers on behalf of the French government and later transmitted Aboubaker's proposal to give France a territory on the northern shore of the Gulf of Tadjourah, between Ras Ali and **Goubet-el-Kharab**. Lambert was assassinated on June 4, 1859, on board a *dhow* taking him to Tadjourah to bid farewell to Aboubaker before returning to France. He had already convinced the French government of the importance of establishing a colony opposite the British stronghold of Aden. The inquiry into his death by French authorities revealed that the assassination had been organized by **Ali Charmarke** and led to the creation of the colony in 1862.

LEGENTILHOMME, PAUL, General. It was in a context of the Italian expansionist threat to the colony that General Legentilhomme—the first high-ranking military officer to be appointed in the colony—arrived on January 12, 1939. His arrival coincided with an intensive militarization of the colony with the permanent settlement of 8,000 soldiers and the erection of a defense system consisting of bunkers and fortifications to protect the **port**, the airport, and the **railroad**. However, when, despite all his efforts, the colony fell under the control of the **Vichy** government forces, General Legentilhomme fled to **Somalia** to fight on the side of the British.

LIGUE POPULAIRE AFRICAINE (LPA). *See* LIGUE POPULAIRE AFRICAINE POUR L'INDEPENDANCE (LPAI).

LIGUE POPULAIRE AFRICAINE POUR L'INDÉPENDANCE (LPAI). The Ligue Populaire Africaine (LPA) was a political organization that arose in 1972 from the merger of the Union Populaire Africaine created by **Hassan Gouled** in the wake of the 1967 events (*see also* REFERENDUM) and the Ligue pour l'Avenir et l'Ordre of **Ahmed Dini**. When the LPA failed to have its representatives elected at the 1973 local elections, it decided to boycott all elections; it then began to structure local opposition and to organize the population by creating political branches with their own militias in all neighborhoods.

In 1974, the LPA changed its name to Ligue Populaire Africaine pour l'Indépendance and gained the support of most French left-wing parties. It started stating clearly its pro-independence aims in November 1974 and became the main opponent to the government of **Ali Aref**. However, seeing that the French colonial administration refused to recognize the league, the LPAI leaders decided to bring the case of **Djibouti** to international organizations such as the **Organization of African Unity** (OAU) and the Arab League. On May 25, 1976, the organization was officially recognized by Paris and demanded the resignation of Ali Aref.

From July 29, 1976, to May 11, 1977, the LPAI participated in the transitional government of **Abdallah Mohamed Kamil** and changed its name to **Rassemblement Populaire pour l'Indépendance** (RPI) in preparation for the May 1977 elections. The RPI was in fact a sort of umbrella coalition, including Abdallah Mohamed Kamil supporters, **Front de Libération de la Côte Somalie** (FLCS) members, members of the parliamentary opposition led by **Barkat Gourad Hamadou**, and LPAI members.

LIPPMAN, ALPHONSE. Lippman, kin to Governor **Chapon-Baissac**, arrived in the colony in 1921 and was appointed chief administrator of the region of **Dikhil** in 1928. At the time, the administrative post of Dikhil had just been established to control the route to **Awsa**. Thus, Lippmann, who was entrusted with the mission of promoting French penetration into Awsa, met opposition from **Sultan** Mohamed Yayou. However, with the support of the **Debne** and the **Issa**, he succeeded in developing the Dikhil district. His contact with the local populations was made easier because he had converted to **Islam** and also could speak the local languages. The interest he had in local customs led him to write an ethnological study. In 1934, Lippmann, who had also served as an intelligence agent, was replaced by **Albert Bernard.** A few years later, he got involved in the colony's **political life** and took part in the elections of the **Conseil Représentatif** of April 26, 1946, but was defeated by the coalition of **Said Ali Coubèche** and **Jean Martine**.

LITERATURE. With the recent emergence of a new generation of Djiboutian writers expressing themselves in French, it can be said that Djiboutian written literature is still in the making. On the other hand, oral literature, whether in **Somali** language or in **Afar**, is quite developed and includes such varied genres as **poetry**, **drama**, storytelling, and proverbs.

LOI CADRE. The Loi Cadre of June 23, 1956, was elaborated by Gaston Deferre, who was then **France**'s minister of the interior. This law concerned all of France's colonies in Africa and was devised to enable them to become autonomous as far as local affairs were concerned. Defense and finance, though, remained under the control of the colonial administration.

In **Djibouti**, this resulted in the creation of ministerial departments, such as Health, Education, Public Works, and Interior, as early as 1957, and the establishment of the **Assemblée Territoriale** in June 1957. The period corresponds to one of initiation to party politics for local figures and the emergence of new political personalities, most of whom were previously engaged in **labor unions** or other associations.

LOI DE MOBILISATION NATIONALE. Enacted on October 24, 1981, the Loi de Mobilisation Nationale, which stated that political divergence could be expressed only from within the **Rassemblement Populaire**

pour le Progrès (RPP), officially established the single-party system. As a result, all political parties other then the RPP were banned.

LOYADA. A small coastal town at the intersection of the border of the Republic of **Djibouti** and the **Republic of Somalia**. Most of the trade exchanges between the two countries are made via Loyada, which is the frontier zone nearest the capital city. Given the collapse of the state in Somalia and the upsurge of a rebel order in the self-proclaimed Republic of Somaliland, Loyada plays a crucial role in terms of security.

– M –

MABRAZ. A word of Arabic origin used to designate a room that is specially prepared for chewing **khat**, usually in a group. As khat consumption has increased within all social and ethnic groups, so has the number of *mabraz*, which often reflect the social and ethnic origin of their members. The most outstanding character of the *mabraz* is its function as a place where public opinion is formed.

MAGENDIE, Colonel. This French army officer arrived in British Somaliland in August 1941 to prepare the liberation of **Djibouti** from the **Vichy** government. The **Somali** detachment of the Forces Françaises Libres that he was heading gathered at Ourso, in southeastern **Ethiopia**, in April 1942 and succeeded in liberating the colony in December 1942. Eventually, Magendie got involved in politics as the head of the Gaullist movement in Djibouti and was elected to **Parliament** in 1951. He was the last French MP to represent Djibouti in the French National Assembly. He was later replaced by **Mahamoud Harbi**, whom he had introduced to **political life**.

MAJLISS. *See* SULTAN.

MAKABANTU, Makaban (plur.). An **Afar** term that means decision maker and that corresponds to the title given to an elder who is chosen to be a member of a traditional assembly (*see also* MARO). In fact, the *makabantu*, whose function is hereditary, is a mediator and has no power to impose his decisions, although he may be obeyed out of respect and his individual personality.

MANDAYTOU, Sheik. Mandaytou was a legendary Arab missionary who traveled in the region to propagate **Islam**. As the legend goes, Sheik Mandaytou and his disciples were in the area of **Dikhil** one day, and were without drinking water. As his desperate companions prepared to die from thirst, he advised them to pray and to be optimistic. Soon after he had spoken to them, his horse started to neigh and kick out; then it started to dig the soil with its hooves, and water sprang from the ground, to the surprise of the **sheik** and his disciples. They soothed their thirst and ate some dates. The pits they negligently dropped on the floor later gave birth to the now famous palm grove that is at the entrance of the town of Dikhil. Sheik Mandaytou was buried in Harissa, **Ethiopia**, where he had gone in search of the tomb of his father, Sheik Sabir. Both men are revered during the annual pilgrimage that draws Muslims from the whole region.

MARO. An **Afar** term meaning circle and designating the general assembly, which meets in case of litigation in the traditional **judicial system**. The assembly is composed of the makaban (*see also* MAKABANTU), the disputants, and the public. Although the *makaban* play a predominant role, all participants may express their views freely. The decision ultimately made by the *maro* is usually based on the propositions made by the participants in a spirit of compromise.

MARTINE, JEAN. Jean Martine, a member of the local branch of the French Communist Party, was the colony's representative at the French National Assembly from 1946 to 1950. Originally employed at the **Chemin de Fer Franco-Ethiopien** (CFE), Martine was involved in the **railroad labor union** that he represented within the **Conseil Représentatif**.

MASKALI. One of the small, uninhabited **islands** at the entrance of the Gulf of **Tadjourah**, about 10 kilometers from the **port**. This island once hosted the colony's lazaret before being given as a concession to **Henri de Monfreid** for the culture of pearls.

MAWLID (Maoulid). A ritual celebration organized yearly by most Muslim families or individuals to commemorate the death of a relative, ancestor, or saint. This celebration opens with the ritual sacrifice of a sheep, ox, or camel that is consumed during a collective meal to which relatives, neighbors, and poor people living in the area are invited. The meal is followed by a prayer session that can last a whole night. This practice, condemned by the partisans of a stricter interpretation of **Islam**, is a remnant of pre-Islamic beliefs.

MAWLID AL NABI (Maoulid al Nabi). Celebrated on the 12th day of the third month of the Muslim calendar, Mawlid al Nabi is a religious holiday commemorating the birth of the Prophet Mohammed. Activities include distributing food to the poor, sacrificing sheep or camels, and overnight praying sessions. *See also* HOLIDAYS.

MEDICINE. *See* PUBLIC HEALTH.

MEHARISTES. A corps of **militia** on camelback created in 1930 with the task of controlling the southwestern **borders**. This corps, operating in a nomadic environment, also served as an intelligence unit for the colonial army. Its name was changed to **Groupement Nomade Autonome** in 1970.

MICHEL-CÔTE, CHARLES (1872–1959). Michel-Côte, who was from the town of Lyon, **France**, was an agricultural engineer who had also studied political science. From 1896 to 1898, he accompanied the Beauchamp mission that had left from **Djibouti** and was heading to Fashoda via **Ethiopia** to rescue Colonel J. B. Marchand, who had been routed by the British at Fashoda. In Ethiopia, Michel-Côte became a close friend of Emperor Haile Selassie and later organized Ethiopian resistance to Italian occupation. From the 1920s until his death on February 24, 1959, Michel-Côte was the general manager and one of the main stockholders of the **Chemin de Fer Franco-Ethiopien** (CFE), which he helped to modernize. As a witness of his time, Michel-Côte published two books relating the Fashoda incident: *A la Rencontre de la Mission Marchand* and *Vers Fashoda à Travers l'Ethiopie.*

MILITIA. This was a corps of armed native soldiers whose initial role consisted in protecting the **railroad** construction sites and that gradually evolved to become a border patrol force. When the June 2, 1910, decree established it officially, the militia had already existed for 13 years. A few years later, when World War I broke out, many of the men enrolled in the colonial army to fight the German troops. Militia members also captured Ethiopian Emperor Lej Iyasu on November 28, 1916, who was hiding in the region of **Afambo** after being defeated by Haile Selassie's troops. Lej Yasu was then given to Haile Selassie.

The militia took part in the 1934 battle at Tewaho in the **Hanle** plain to protect the Ado Rassoul **nomads** from the **Asay Mara** and, one year later, in the **Moraito** clash where many of them died. In 1968, the corps, which was essentially made up of **Somali** former nomads, was reformed and saw its role strictly limited to border control. In 1970, the militia was renamed **Groupement Nomade Autonome**. The name was changed again to Groupement Commando des Frontières after **independence**.

MODAHTOU. *See* MORAITO.

MOHAMED AHMED ISSA (1940–1997). Better known under the name of "Sheikho," Mohamed Ahmed Issa was a major figure of **Djibouti**'s political opposition. An influential member of the **Union Démocratique Afar** (UDA) in the 1960s, he became its leader in July 1966 and imposed his pro-**independence** views. He was at the origin of its rapprochement with the main opposition party of the time, the **Parti Mouvement Populaire** (PMP), with which the UDA organized the pro-independence demonstrations that shook the city in August 1966, during French President Charles de Gaulle's visit to Djibouti. As a consequence, Sheikho was arrested and his party was dissolved in April 1967, in the aftermath of the March 1967 **referendum**. In continuous opposition to **Ali Aref**, whom he regarded as a supporter of colonialism, he created the Ligue Africaine pour l'Ordre with **Ahmed Dini** to continue his struggle for liberation.

After independence, Sheikho was first appointed minister of education and then minister of public health and social affairs—a position he held from February 5 to September 30, 1978, and again from October 2, 1980, to July 1981. Following the enactment of the **Loi de Mobilisation Nationale** in October 1981, Sheikho and other politicians, including Ahmed Dini and **Moussa Ahmed Idriss**, founded the short-lived **Parti Populaire Djiboutien** (PPD) in August 1981. Later, he joined the **Rassemblement Populaire pour le Progrès** (RPP) and started fighting from the inside, calling for more democracy within the party. Sheikho resigned from **Parliament** following the 1991 **Arhiba** bloodshed and participated in the creation of the Front Uni de l'Opposition Djiboutienne. His death on November 26, 1997, along with that of **Djamah Elabe**, resulted in a leadership vacuum.

MOHAMED HANFARE, Sultan. Better known under his nickname "Illalta," which means the gatherer, Mohamed Hanfare was at the head of the most powerful **Afar sultanate**, the sultanate of **Awsa**, from 1858 to 1902. This period corresponded to the penetration and settlement of European colonizers in the region. Because his territory was strategically located at the crossroads of the various caravan routes linking the coast to the Ethiopian highlands, Mohamed Hanfare's goal was to unify all the Afar sultanates against this penetration. Concerned with preserving the independence of his sultanate, he refused to take sides in the conflict between Emperor Yohannes IV and Menelik, then king of Shoa. In the same way, he refused to participate in the Egyptian scheme to create a greater Muslim confederation in northeastern Africa. Ultimately, he defeated the expedition led by **Werner Munzinger** at Lake Uddumma, to the north of lake **Abhe**. The succession of conflicts that followed Mohamed Hanfare's death brought about the annexation of what remained of his sultanate by the Ethiopian empire.

MOHAMED KAMIL MOHAMED. Mohamed Kamil, also known as Hadj Kamil, is a native of the coastal town of **Obock**, and is one of the pioneers of the colony's **political life**. He was territorial representative in 1946; representative of the Union Française from 1953 to 1958; senator from 1959 to 1965; and vice president of the **Conseil du Gouvernement** from 1966 to 1967. Although he was in favor of gradual **independence**, he finally voted to uphold French rule in the 1967 **referendum**. Eventually, despite his antagonism with **Ali Aref**, he was appointed minister several times in Aref's government. Moreover, Mohamed Kamil, who stood as one of **Hassan Gouled**'s most faithful political allies, was one of the founding members of the Défense des Intérêts Economiques et Sociaux du Territoire, whose political strategy was to seek more internal autonomy for the colony in order to head gradually toward independence.

MOHAMEDALLY, GOLAN M. Golan M. Mohamedally was one of the wealthiest traders in the region in the late 19th and early 20th centuries. He was an Indian native and had established his company in Bombay in 1888. Very quickly, he opened branches in Sidhpur, **Aden**, Dire Dawa, Addis Ababa, and **Djibouti**. Most of the products he imported to the region were destined for the Ethiopian market, including Indian cotton fabrics, **arms** and ammunition, furniture, hardware, spices, and silk. To India he exported coffee, civet, wax, hides and skins, ivory, and gold. He also worked as a money changer.

MONFREID, HENRI DE (1879–1974). This French adventurer, trafficker, and writer left his country at age 32 to begin a smuggling operation on the coasts of the Red Sea. Monfreid landed on the **Côte Française des Somalis** in 1912 and went to work as a clerk in a commercial firm in Dire Dawa, **Ethiopia**. Unsatisfied with his Ethiopian experience, notably because of the problems he had with the Ethiopian courts, he returned to **Djibouti** in 1914 and became involved in oyster culture. However, when the concession he had been granted on the island of **Maskali** was found to be an **arms** cache, he was arrested and sentenced to three weeks imprisonment. He then settled in **Obock**, where he devoted all his energies to trafficking in both arms and slaves (*see also* SLAVERY). His skills as a seaman and his capacity to mingle with the native population contributed to making him a legendary figure on the Red Sea.

Monfreid, who supported the colonization of Ethiopia by the Italians under cover of a civilizing mission, served as a guide to the writer Joseph Kessel. Under Kessel's influence, Monfreid wrote a number of books telling the story of his sea adventures. The most famous among these, *The Secrets of the Red Sea,* has been turned into a television series.

MORAITO (Modahtou). This site is located in southwestern Djibouti, near **Lake Abhe**, along the Ethiopian border. On January 17, 1935, a clash between the colonial **militia**, led by the French administration officer **Albert Bernard**, and **nomads** belonging to the **Afar** tribe of the Galeela ended in the death of all the militiamen. Prior to this confrontation, the French officer **Alphonse Lippman** had been kidnapped by the men of the **sultan** of **Awsa** and was later released, following the signing of a peace agreement between the French authorities and the sultan. The clash that occurred at **Moraito** resulted from the violation of the peace agreement by the French. Until the end of the colonial era, the Moraito incident was regularly commemorated. Two memorials were erected, one on the site of the battle and the other in **Dikhil**, at the center of a square bearing the French officer's name.

MOUCHA (Musha). *See* ISLANDS.

MOUSSA AHMED IDRISS (c. 1933–). This historic leader of the **Parti du Mouvement Populaire** (PMP) appeared on the political stage in 1957, when he was elected councilor to the **Assemblée Territoriale** on **Mahamoud Harbi**'s roll. Then, in 1962, to the surprise of the local administration, he was elected to Parliament representing **Djibouti** in the French National Assembly. In 1963, he was elected to the Assemblée Territoriale as a candidate of the PMP, of which he became the president in 1965.

An active pro-**independence** militant, Moussa Ahmed was among the organizers of the August 1966 demonstrations during French President Charles de Gaulle's visit to Djibouti. After campaigning for independence in the March 1967 **referendum**, Moussa Ahmed disappeared from the political scene until August 1981, when he became president of the **Parti Populaire Djiboutien** (PPD). He was almost immediately arrested and was imprisoned from September 1981 to January 1982. After some time spent in the wilderness, he was elected to **Parliament** in the 1992 legislative **elections**. In the midst of the 1998 campaign for presidential elections, Moussa Ahmed Idriss resigned from Parliament and decided to run against the coalition list presented by the **Rassemblement Populaire pour le Progrès** (RPP) and the **Front pour la Restauration de l'Unité et de la Démocratie** (FRUD).

MOUSSA ALI, Mount. Moussa Ali, located in northern Djibouti, along the border with **Ethiopia** and **Eritrea**, is a volcano and the highest peak in the country (2,100 meters). With the signing of the November 1954 treaty with Ethiopia, part of Mount Moussa Ali was transferred to Ethiopia.

MOUVEMENT DE LIBÉRATION DE LA CÔTE SOMALIE (MLCS). It is following **Mahamoud Harbi**'s death, in 1960, that the Mouvement de Libération de la Côte Somalie was established under the direction of Abdourahman Djama Andole and **Ahmed Goumaneh Robleh**. The new organization immediately gained the support of the Arab League.

MOUVEMENT DE LIBÉRATION DE DJIBOUTI (MLD). The Mouvement de Libération de Djibouti, which was established in Dire Dawa, **Ethiopia**, in 1964, was an instrument of the Ethiopian government aimed at counterbalancing the **Front de Libération de la Côte Somalie** (MLCS). Its major figure and founder was **Ahmed Bourhan Omar**, alias Minister Arab, who had been a member of the **Conseil du Gouvernement** from December 1958 to June 1960.

MOUVEMENT POPULAIRE DE LIBÉRATION (MPL). This political organization appeared on the political stage in the capital city in

December 1975. The MPL, which was made up of **Afar** youth, was regarded as radical to the extent that it demanded immediate and total **independence** and opposed the presence of the French army after independence. Moreover, it refused to take part in the political process initiated on January 22, 1976, and that was to lead to independence. When a bomb exploded at the **Palmier en Zinc** on December 15, 1977, the MPL was immediately suspected and the party was dissolved two days later. This brought about a political crisis within the government and Premier **Ahmed Dini** resigned. Most of the militants of the MPL went into exile in **Ethiopia**, where they re-formed the movement. In 1979, the MPL merged with the **Union Nationale pour l'Indépendance** (UNI) to give birth to the **Front de Libération de Djibouti** (FDLD).

MOUVEMENT D'UNION RÉPUBLICAINE (MUR). This organization, founded by **Mahamoud Harbi**, was formed to get the population as a whole involved in the colony's **political life**. Although MUR had the support of the colonial administration in its early days, the administration's attitude changed when, during the 1958 **referendum** campaign, Harbi called for a pro-**independence** vote. He was immediately dismissed from his position as vice president of the **Assemblée Territoriale**.

MUNZINGER, WERNER (1832–1875). Werner Munzinger was a Swiss businessman who settled in **Eritrea** in 1855 and worked successively for the British and the Egyptians. In September 1872, the Egyptians entrusted him to organize an expedition that was to start from **Tadjourah**. The expedition's goal was to reach and colonize the region of **Awsa**. Most of the 365 men who made up the expedition, including Munzinger, were killed in the region of Lake **Abhe** on November 14, 1875. *See also* MUNZINGER EXPEDITION.

MUNZINGER EXPEDITION. After the defeat of its troops at Gura in 1874, the Khedive of Egypt attempted to colonize the region of **Awsa** in order to take Emperor Yohannes of Ethiopia from the rear. On September 24, 1872, **Werner Munzinger** was entrusted with organizing the expedition. He arrived in **Tadjourah** on October 5, 1875, to establish the camp of the Egyptian expeditionary corps of 365 men, most of whom were mercenaries recruited among U.S. Confederate soldiers.

The expedition left Tadjourah on October 27, 1875, on board a steamer. The men landed on the shores of the **Goubet-el-Kharab** and started walking in the direction of the **Hanle** plain. They reached the region of **Lake Abhe** on November 7 and tried to negotiate their passage on the **Afar** territory of Awsa. But on November 14, the three Egyptian companies were almost utterly destroyed. Of the 365 men, only 150 survived and managed to reach Tadjourah on November 21, 1875. This was the second most severe Egyptian defeat in the Horn of Africa (after the defeat of Gundet on October 16, 1875) and the end of the Egyptian hegemonic aspirations in that region.

MUQADDAM. *See* SARANDJ.

MUQMAD. Cured camel meat that is often soaked with *ghee* and sometimes accompanied with dates. This preparation, which is part of the **Somali** food tradition, is usually set in a **heedho** and given as a present to newly married couples. The *muqmad* is normally prepared for periods of drought, when food is scarce.

MUSIC. The limited range of traditional instruments, which essentially consist of flutes and percussions, is probably a sign that music as such was not important in both **Afar** and **Somali** traditional societies in **Djibouti**. It was adjunct either to labor or religious rituals. However, traditional chants were quite developed and adapted to the circumstances of rural life. Work songs, war chants, and love songs constitute an important part of Djibouti's cultural heritage today. The establishment of a **radio** broadcasting station in 1955 and the subsequent introduction of modern instruments definitely marked the opening of a new era in the development of music. Bands, which were originally created to accompany theater companies, gradually became an integral part of the show and finally started organizing exclusively musical performances. The lack of adequate infrastructure, the absence of musical education in schools, and also the disregard with which the artists in general are treated may be part of the reason why Djiboutian music is still at an early stage.

– N –

NAGAD. The name of one of three hills, located about 10 kilometers from the capital city, that were part of the defense system set up by General **Paul Legentilhomme** during World War II in order to protect the **rail-**

road and the port of Djibouti. The two other hills are Fara Had and Douda. Between 1967 and 1977, Nagad hosted a Foreign Legion camp that controlled the entrance to the capital city. It is at this camp that a police academy bearing the name of the late Idriss Farah Abaneh (once the country's minister of the interior) was established in 1981. Today, the premises are used officially as a transit center for illegal immigrants before they are repatriated. In reality, Nagad is a center of provisional detention for opponents of all kinds.

NAJAH AL ISLAMIYA, MADRASA. An educational institution, also known as Ecole Franco-Islamique, that was established in 1931 to dispense formal education, in both Arabic and French, essentially to the children of the **Yemenite** community. The school was subsidized by the Yemenite traders, who viewed it as a way to preserve their culture and to escape the grip of colonial education. Most of the members of the country's first generation of religious elite were trained in it. In the 1940s, with the foundation of the Arab League, the institution was used as a center to propagate Pan-Arabian ideas, at times collecting funds for the Palestinian movement. The 1950s were marked by the development of academic links with **Egypt**. A number of students of the Najah Al Islamiya were granted scholarships to pursue their higher studies at Egyptian universities.

NAKHUDA. An Arabic term used to designate the helmsman of a **boutre**. The *nakhuda* is one of the main characters in the history of navigation in the Red Sea and the Indian Ocean. The *nakhudas* were also instrumental in bringing **Yemenite** and **Somali** immigrations to the Gulf states, and in the development of the **arms** and slave **trade** (*see also* SLAVERY). In 19th-century literature, the *nakhuda* is often equated to a pirate or an adventurer, as can be testified by **Henri de Monfreid**'s works.

NATION DE DJIBOUTI, LA. *La Nation de Djibouti* is a government weekly newspaper in the French language that was created in 1981, to replace *Le Réveil de Djibouti* and to help create a national entity. It is supervised by the Secrétariat Général à l'Information, which also controls the **radio** and **television** broadcasting services, the national printing press, and the Centre National de Documentation.

NATIONALITY. From the early days of the colony, the question of nationality has been at the heart of the social and **political life**. When the country was first colonized, the natives were regarded as **France**'s "protégés" in conformity with the statute provided for in the various **treaties** signed between the end of the 19th century and the beginning of the 20th century. Then, with the official establishment of the **Côte Française des Somalis** in 1897, the administration started to make a distinction between the colony's inhabitants, who were classified either as French subjects or *allogènes* (nonnatives). All members of communities who had signed the treaties that established the colony were considered French subjects, whereas the members of the other communities, who had usually settled in the urban center, were considered *allogènes*.

The members of the former group, or the *autochtons* (as they were also called), could be granted French citizenship under the guarantee of their administratively recognized **ukal**. The members of the latter group could be granted French nationality only as a privilege for services rendered to the nation. Naturally, the members of communities who were regarded as enemies of France would in no way be granted French nationality.

The importance of this notion of *autochton* and *allogène* is illustrated by its use by courts of justice when sentencing offenders. For the same offense, the sanction befalling an *autochton* was usually imprisonment, whereas the *allogènes* could be banished.

Electoral policies and political representation were based on these notions, which are at the root of the ethnic quota system. The system is still so much at the root of the government's political and administrative organization that any serious crisis that has occurred since **independence** has usually been directly related to the respect or nonrespect of the balance of ethnic quotas.

NOMADS. The ancestral way of life of the population living on the present territory of **Djibouti** was based on nomadization. This was mainly because the environment is so arid that the nomads, trying to preserve it, had to keep their herds moving in order to maintain a balance between the size of the herds and the available pastures.

Although both the **Issa** and **Afar** populations living in the hinterland remain deeply rooted in it, this way of life is nonetheless slowly disappearing, because of repeated droughts and wars. Today, the nomadic population is estimated at 20 percent of the total population.

NOUAILHETAS, PIERRE. The governor (**gouverneur**) of the **Côte Française des Somalis** from September 1940 to September 1942. His two years at the head of the colony, at the time of **Vichy** rule, were characterized by the terror he imposed on the population, notably by issuing a letter (circular letter No. 457 of May 7, 1941) commanding all administrative officers to shoot by firing squad any native caught carrying a message from the Gaullist troops into the colony. As a consequence, a number of illiterate people were killed without even understanding their crimes. When the colony was liberated from Vichy rule, Nouailhetas escaped to Portugal. He was tried and sentenced to death in absentia, and was eventually pardoned by General Charles de Gaulle in 1953.

NOUR ROBLEH, OGAZ. The **Gadaboursi** traditional chief who signed a treaty ceding the Gadaboursi territory to **France** in October 1885. However, the quick establishment of a frontier between British Somaliland and the French colony voided the treaty. This started the policy of appointing Gadaboursi notables to office, even outside the French-controlled territory, thus becoming part of the extension of a French zone of influence.

– O –

OBOCK. Situated in northeastern Djibouti, at the entrance of the Gulf of **Tadjourah**, this small town lives off trade and to some extent fishing, and is a meeting point between the **nomads** of the hinterland and the seamen from **Yemen**. On their arrival at Obock in 1862, the French signed a treaty with the local chiefs. Almost immediately, French traders settled there with a view to exploring the area and penetrating the Ethiopian market.

When **Léonce Lagarde** was appointed governor **(gouverneur)** of the Territoire d'Obock et Dépendances on September 5, 1887, the town had about 2,000 inhabitants. However, moved by the desire to establish a well-sheltered deep-water harbor, and worried by the problems related to the difficulty of supplying the place with drinking water, Lagarde decided to move the capital to **Djibouti**. This decision was motivated by the need for an easier and safer access to the Ethiopian hinterland, among other concerns.

Ever since, Obock—which was once called Hayou—has remained an isolated spot, the growth of which has been further slowed by the three-year **armed conflict**, during which its center was devastated.

OGADEN WAR. The region of Ogaden in southeastern **Ethiopia**, at the border with **Somalia**, has long been claimed by the Republic of Somalia as one of its lost provinces. The Somali state's dream of a greater Somalia consisted of bringing together the three Somali-inhabited territories, namely the Northern Frontier District of Kenya, the territory of **Djibouti**, and the region of Ogaden. These territorial claims were at the origin of two wars between Ethiopia and Somalia.

The first conflict broke out in 1964 and ended soon after with a cease-fire supervised by the **Organization of African Unity** (OAU). The second began in July 1977, immediately after Djibouti's **independence**, and ended in late 1978 with the intervention of Warsaw Pact troops on the side of the Ethiopian state. The economic and social impacts of this war on the young Republic of Djibouti were considerable. An unprecedented flock of **refugees** fleeing the war zones inundated the country and brought about a modification of the social fabric, particularly in the capital city. Moreover, the partial destruction of the **railroad** interrupted the traffic, generating a shortage of fruits and vegetables.

OGAZ (Ugas, Ugaz). Among the **Somali**, the *ogaz* is the man at the head of the clan. Despite his position at the apex of the hierarchical organization, he actually has little power and only plays the role of an arbitrator. However, all members of the clan must pay him respect. Within the **Issa** clan, the *ogaz*, who must belong to the tribe of the Wardiq, is chosen by an assembly of 44 elders from the various Issa tribes. The symbolic abduction that precedes his enthronement and the ceremony itself are conducted according to carefully codified rituals. Once enthroned, the *ogaz* is regarded as a man with no tribe but the king of all. Failure to fulfill his role as an arbitrator or adviser may result in his dismissal, a decision that can be made only by the **Gande**, the council of elders.

OKKAR. The name by which the natives of **Dikhil** and (by extension) its region are known. The name is actually derived from the basaltic massifs standing to the southeastern part of town.

OMAR FARAH ILTIREH (c. 1933–). Omar Farah Iltireh is a politician who started as a primary school teacher and later worked as a journalist before becoming the first president of the **Union Démocratique Issa** (UDI) in 1963. He held this position until November 1968 when he became a member of **Parliament** in the newly established **Chambre des**

Députés. In 1972, Omar Farah was elected to Parliament to represent Djibouti in the French National Assembly. Two years later, he decided to join the parliamentary opposition that put an end to **Ali Aref**'s reign and initiated the move toward **independence**. In the postindependence era, Omar Farah was appointed Djiboutian ambassador to **Ethiopia** and later elected to Parliament to represent the district of **Ali Sabieh**. He was reelected again in 1992 and still holds his seat.

OMAR KAMIL WARSAMA (1920–1986). After fighting on the French side in the Compagnie Somalie during World War II, Omar Kamil enrolled in the merchant navy and traveled around the world. He was already in his forties when he became involved in politics. He was elected councilor to the **Assemblée Territoriale** in 1958 and kept the seat until he was elected to **Parliament** on **Hassan Gouled**'s roll in 1968. However, when Gouled was defeated in the 1973 elections, Omar Kamil lost his seat and helped Hassan Gouled create the **Ligue Populaire Africaine** (LPA), of which he became the vice president. The first difference between the two men occurred during the **roundtable** that was held in Paris to prepare for independence. Nonetheless, Omar Kamil was, from the early days, a member of the politburo of the **Rassemblement Populaire pour le Progrès** (RPP) and later became its vice president. He was minister of public works from July 15, 1977, to June 12, 1981, and minister of justice and Islamic affairs from May 1982 until his death.

OMAR OSMAN RABEH (c. 1946–). Rabeh is a political activist and nationalist intellectual who, as a teenager, was an active member of the **Parti Mouvement Populaire** (PMP). He dropped out of school to take part in the demonstrations organized during French President Charles de Gaulle's visit in 1966. He was arrested a few months later and imprisoned for two weeks. In May 1968, he was accused of trying to assassinate **Ali Aref** and sentenced to death. However, after being pardoned by de Gaulle, who commuted his sentence to life imprisonment, he was transferred to the French prison of La Santé and shortly after to Le Muret in Toulouse. He spent his years in prison working toward a doctorate in philosophy.

In March 1975, a **Front de Libération de la Côte Somalie** (FLCS) commando kidnapped the French ambassador to Somalia, and demanded Omar Osman Rabeh's liberation. He was sent to **Aden**, where the exchange took place. Immediately after, he became the FLCS public relations chief. As a member of the radical FLCS Pan-Somali wing, he was in sharp disagreement with **Aden Robleh**, the organization's secretary general.

In 1979, Omar Osman Rabeh started teaching at the capital city's only high school but remained under close watch by the government. Nonetheless, he was a founding member of the **Parti Populaire Djiboutien** (PMD), which was created in August 1981. Soon after, he was jailed once more and released in January 1982. Aware that he could not live freely in Djibouti, he went into exile. When, in November 1984, the Djiboutian government withdrew his citizenship, he started working with the Republic of **Somalia** and, in 1986, founded the bilingual *Somali Studies Review* in Paris. In addition to the numerous articles he has contributed to the government newspaper, *La Nation*, Omar Osman Rabeh has published several books, including his autobiography, *Le Cercle et la Spirale*.

ORBISSO GADITO (c. 1930–). Born in the **Goda** mountains, Orbisso Gadito joined the Pan-Afarist movement soon after he had completed his secondary studies. He started working as a primary school teacher in government schools but was harassed by the administration because of his political commitment. When the **Union Démocratique Afar** (UDA) was established in 1961, Orbisso became its first president, a position he kept even after the crisis that occurred within the organization in 1965. Although he was a fervent partisan of **independence**, he left the UDA in 1967 to join the sort of sacred union that was formed by the **Afar** to counter the Somali pro-independence movement. The latter was perceived by the Afar as a Pan-Somali menace (*see also* PAN-SOMALISM). As a reward for his joining the sacred union, Orbisso was elected to **Parliament** on **Ali Aref**'s roll in 1968. He retired from politics soon after independence.

ORGANIZATION OF AFRICAN UNITY (OAU). The Organization of African Unity was established in Addis Ababa, **Ethiopia**, in 1963, with all independent African states as members. Its most important activity at that time was decolonization, for which it formed a Decolonization Committee. This committee had set up an inquiry commission entrusted with the mission of studying the Horn of Africa as early as September 1964. But it was only in the aftermath of the violent political events that occurred in **Djibouti** in 1966 that, under the pressure of a few African countries such as **Somalia**, the case of the French colony was finally presented. In October 1966, a resolution of the OAU Decolonization Committee exhorted **France** to engage in the decolonization process as far as Djibouti was concerned. Then, in November 1966, the Council of Ministers of the OAU adopted a resolution condemning violence, urging France to use more restraint, and recommending it organize the **referendum** that was to take place before July 1967 in a free, democratic, and impartial way. In April 1976, an OAU delegation was authorized to visit Djibouti. Eventually, the OAU's observers played an active part in the supervision of the May 8, 1977, referendum on self-determination that resulted in the colony's accession to **independence**. The Republic of Djibouti became the OAU's 49th member state in 1977.

OTTOMAN EMPIRE. In 1557, the Turks who were already in control of the whole Abyssinian Peninsula settled at the port of Massouah, in **Eritrea**. Their objective was to monopolize the trade with Christian **Abyssinia** and prevent Portugal from penetrating the Red Sea basin, considered by the Ottoman empire as the Islamic Sea. After imposing its domination on the coasts and main ports of Arabia, the Ottoman empire extended its authority to the African shores along the Red Sea and the Gulf of **Aden**. Thus, ancient ports such as **Zeila**, Berbera, and Bulhar remained under its rule until the early 19th century. Titles such as **pasha**, **wali**, and **bey** bear witness to the age-old Turkish influence on the populations of these Horn of Africa ports.

OUED (Wadi). An Arabic term designating a seasonal river that flows in the rainy season, or its bed. *Oueds,* which form the essential part of the country's hydrographic network, are used by the **nomads** as communication axes to bypass the mountainous region. Nomadic camps are usually set up on their banks. As a result, among the **Afar**, several clans derive their name from that of the neighboring *oued.*

– P –

PALMIER EN ZINC. The name of a bar and restaurant initially owned by a Frenchman named Armand Savouré and located in the capital city's center. The choice of the name (zinc palm tree) reveals the state of mind of the first European settlers, who tended to propagate the idea that nothing could be grown in **Djibouti**. The bar later became famous following two bomb attacks that almost destroyed it, killing several Europeans (*see also* CRIMINAL ATTACKS). The first one happened January 24, 1970, in the midst of the struggle for **independence**. The second one took place December 15, 1977, a few months after the country achieved independence. Mythified by the logs of the various travelers, the name Palmier en Zinc itself has become a cliché and a visit to the café a must.

PAN-SOMALISM. The end of World War II in the region was marked by the development of a nationalistic trend that aimed at freeing all the **Somali**-inhabited territories from colonial domination and regrouping them within a single state. These included, along with Italian Somalia and British Somaliland, Kenya's Northern Frontier District, **Ethiopia**'s Ogaden region, and **Djibouti**. This political movement, which emerged in 1943, was formally established in 1947 under the name Somali Youth League, although it was often referred to as *Hanolato,* the slogan that its adherents used and that meant "long live" in Somali. It developed quickly and reached the region of Ogaden *(see also* OGADEN WAR) in Ethiopia, where it opened a branch in 1948. In Djibouti, the French intelligence service pointed out the existence of this movement in 1951 and suspected **Mahamoud Harbi** of having connections with it. From then on, the control of the Pan-Somali movement became one of the major preoccupations of the colonial administration, which feared the possible repercussions on the colony's political evolution. *See also* SOMALIA, REPUBLIC OF.

PARLIAMENT. *See* ASSEMBLÉE NATIONALE; ASSEMBLÉE TERRITORIALE; CHAMBRE DES DÉPUTÉS.

PARTI MOUVEMENT POPULAIRE (PMP). Supporters of **Mahamoud Harbi** established this political party following the 1958 **referendum**. The PMP, which had existed informally, became legal in November 1960 and started campaigning for the territory's emancipation from colonial supervision. In January 1961, during a visit by the French minister of the colonies, it organized demonstrations in the whole country, demanding autonomy. In July 1962, a joint delegation with the **Union Démocratique Afar** (UDA) went to Paris to plead the cause for **Djibouti**. Despite the animosity of the colonial administration, the PMP succeeded in having its candidate, **Moussa Ahmed Idriss**, elected to the French National Assembly in the November 1962 legislative **elections**.

Following this event, the party faced increased hostility on the part of the colonial administration. In May 1963 its president, Obsieh Bouh Abdallah, was sentenced to nine months imprisonment for publishing "false news." In February 1965, he was sentenced to 15 months under the same charges. The repeated imprisonment of its president provoked some disarray within the PMP, which confined itself to limited activity. It rose up again to take an active part in the demonstrations that were organized in August 1966 during French President Charles de Gaulle's visit. On the same momentum, it campaigned for **independence** in the March 1967 referendum but was dissolved almost immediately after, on July 13, 1967.

PARTI NATIONAL DÉMOCRATIQUE (PND). One of the three offi-cially authorized opposition parties that were formed in the middle of the three-year **armed conflict** that shook Djibouti. Despite its name, the PND, which was founded in 1993 by, and around, **Aden Robleh Awaleh**, is exclusively anchored to the district of **Ali Sabieh** and, to a lesser ex-tent, to the capital city. Most of the party's militants were recruited among former members of the **Front de Libération de la Côte Somalie** (FLCS).

PARTI POPULAIRE DJIBOUTIEN (PPD). The creation of this short-lived party, in August 1981, was an attempt by a group of politicians, who were dissatisfied with the postindependence era, to take advantage of the absence of laws forbidding the creation of **political parties**. Its founding members—**Sheikho, Ahmed Dini, Moussa Ahmed Idriss**, and **Omar Osman Rabeh**—were former party leaders in the colonial era. This initiative took place at a time when the **Rassemblement Populaire pour le Progrès** (RPP) was strengthening its grip on the country's **po-litical life**. As a response the **Loi de Mobilisation Nationale**, which for-mally established the one-party system, was enacted on October 24, 1981. The leaders of the PPD were imprisoned; Omar Osman Rabeh lost his citizenship and went into exile.

PARTI DU RENOUVEAU DÉMOCRATIQUE (PRD). Mohamed Djama Elabe formed this political party soon after his resignation as minister of health. This party, which emerged in the context of the **armed conflict** between the government and the **Front pour la Restauration de l'Unité et de la Démocratie** (FRUD), was made legal during the pro-cess of democratization initiated by the government.

In its early days, the PRD appeared as a serious rival to the **Rassemblement Populaire pour le Progrès** (RPP), organizing mass meetings and publishing a weekly leaflet, *Le Renouveau*. However, it lost much of its credit when it chose to take part in the May 1993 presidential **elections**, which the other opposition parties had decided to boycott. The internal conflicts that arose following Elabe's death in 1996 led to a split that weakened the party.

PASHA. This term of Turkish origin was initially the honorary title given to the representative of the **Ottoman empire** in the territories it colonized. The term gradually came to designate dynasties of ruling families. The fact that the title was placed right after the first name is probably why some of its bearers, such as **Aboubaker Pasha**, adopted it almost as a family name.

PINO, ELOI (1845–1905). The man who founded the company now known as Marill was originally a seaman. He opened the first trade route to Shoa from the newly created **port** of **Djibouti** and set up, between 1887 and 1891, a commercial network consisting of small factory units in Djibouti, Harar, and Ankober.

POETRY. The major form of oral **literature** among the **Afar** and **Somali** is poetry. Somali poetry consists of two dominant genres: the **gabbay**, a form of poetry now in decline, and the *burambur*. Whereas the first one deals with political issues, the second one, exclusively reserved for women, is more concerned with household matters. Other genres such as **belwo**, which was invented by Abdi **Sinimo**, and **heelo** are specially composed to be sung.

In Afar culture, *gad* often consists of poems that are sung or danced to either in evening gatherings or in religious or traditional ceremonies. *See also* DANCE; MUSIC.

POLITICAL LIFE. Intercommunity relations have been at the core of political life from the early days of the colony. It was impossible to create real **political parties** because of the colonial administration's monopoly on political issues. Thus, the political life of the country can be divided into three main periods.

In the period between 1887 (the creation of **Djibouti**) and 1945, the population as well as its leading figures were essentially concerned with social issues—particularly the living conditions—and community representation. The debate was therefore rather limited. At this time, the colonial administration, assisted by the **Chamber of Commerce**, which was represented in the colony's board, stood as the absolute master.

After the end of World War II, with the establishment of a **Conseil Représentatif** in 1945, the colonial administration gradually broadened the representation. This was particularly emphasized from 1956 onward, following the enactment of the **Loi Cadre**, which gave natives access to political institutions. This decision was an attempt to channel any possible opposition. Therefore, political parties were authorized as long as they recognized the sovereignty of French rule. The main issues concerned representation and the future status of the colony.

The period from 1977 onward was marked by the power consolidation of the notables leading the country's political activities. The most significant event in the immediate postindependence period is probably the creation of the **Rassemblement Populaire pour le Progrès** (RPP) and the subsequent banning of all other parties. This situation of single-party rule was strengthened with the enactment of the **Loi de Mobilisation Nationale** on October 24, 1981. The **armed conflict** that was started 10 years later was partly a refusal of this political monopoly at a time when most African states were engaged in a forced democratization process.

To calm things down, a **constitution**—Djibouti's first—was adopted in September 1992. A certain form of multipartism was consequently installed, with the legalization of four parties. All this was done as the country prepared for the succession to the aging president. Following the signing of a peace agreement with the **Front pour la Restauration de l'Unité et de la Démocratie** (FRUD) and the subsequent alliance between FRUD and RPP, the political debate shifted from democratization to structural adjustment.

POLITICAL PARTIES. Until the enactment of the 1992 **Constitution**, which opened the era of quadripartism, all legal political groupings had to conform with the French law, Loi 1901, which regulated the creation of non–profit-making organizations. Therefore, there were no local political parties recognized as such, although the existing organizations (such as the **Parti Mouvement Populaire** [PMP] and **Union Démocratique Afar** [UDA]) were in fact political parties playing their role fully. They presented candidates to the local elections, and had militias and official headquarters. They also developed alliances with one another. However, to be authorized by the colonial administration, these parties had to avoid declaring any pro-independence claims.

Shortly after **independence**, the **Loi de Mobilisation Nationale** made all political parties illegal, whatever their official status. All the provisions in the Loi 1901 that banned associations from being involved in political activities were strictly enforced from then on. The **Rassemblement Populaire pour le Progrès** (RPP) became the sole legal party.

In the early 1990s, following the Conference of Franco-African Heads of State at La Baule in France and the democratization process recommended by the French government, the first constitution in the history of the Republic of Djibouti was adopted; it allowed the creation of new parties but limited the number to four. These are today the RPP (the state party); **Parti du Renouveau Démocratique** (PRD), created by **Mohamed Djama Elabe; Parti National Démocratique** (PND), led by **Aden Robleh Awaleh;** and **Front pour la Restauration de l'Unité et de la Démocratie** (FRUD), which was originally an armed group created by **Afar** opponents. After a four-year **armed conflict** (1991–1994) against the ruling government and its subsequent defeat, a FRUD wing agreed to sign a peace treaty on December 26, 1994, and to participate in a sort of "cohabitation" government that was set up on June 8, 1995.

PONCHARDIER, DOMINIQUE (1917–). Appointed to head the colony on February 6, 1969, replacing **Haut Commissaire** Louis Saget, Dominique Ponchardier arrived in **Djibouti** on March 8, 1969. He had previously served as head of department at the Direction Générale des Etudes et Recherches (DGER), the French intelligence service (*see also* DEUXIEME BUREAU), from 1940 to 1945. On April 7, 1971, Mr. Delmotte, the French chief administrator of the town of **Tadjourah**, and his wife were kidnapped by two escaped prisoners who used them as a shield to drive across the frontier to Somaliland. The two prisoners, Ali Guelleh Dirir and Abdi Hassan Liban, were members of the **Front de Libération de la Côte Somalie** (FLCS) who had been sentenced to life with hard labor and to 20 years of hard labor, respectively, following the failed bomb attack against **Ali Aref** on May 6,1968. They succeeded in reaching the border and released their hostages. After this eventful episode, Ponchardier, who had tried to serve as a mediator, published a novel, titled *La Dame de Tadjourah*. He had already started his career as a writer in 1948 and had written more than 40 thrillers under the pseudonym of Antoine Dominique. After leaving the colony, he devoted himself entirely to his literary career.

PORT. France's search for a convenient site on the Red Sea, where it could establish a naval base, led to the birth of the colony of **Djibouti**. Originally conceived of as a coaling station, the port of **Obock** was used from 1862 to 1887. However, when it became obvious that a larger port was needed, Obock was gradually abandoned to the profit of Djibouti. The March 9, 1894, concession—by which Emperor Menelik of **Ethiopia** authorized the construction of the **railroad** and designated Djibouti as the outlet of Ethiopia's trade—played a crucial role in developing the future modern port of Djibouti. With the boom experienced by the railroad throughout the 1920s and into the early 1930s, the port developed considerably and upgraded its infrastructure. Among other things, a new jetty was constructed in 1934 over the wreck of the *Fontainebleau*, and the first fuel-storing unit was built in 1937. Activities came to a relative standstill during the war years, particularly during the **blockade**.

Then, from 1948 to 1957, the construction of additional quays, sheds, and fuel-storing units induced the establishement of major oil companies. The port started to be used as a fueling station on the Asian route. The late 1950s, however, were lean years, marked by the decline of the major colonial shipping lines. In addition, the forming of the Ethiopia-**Eritrea** federation in 1952, and the subsequent development of the port of Assab in Eritrea, had serious impacts on the traffic. This situation was further aggravated by the Suez crisis. The closing of the **Suez Canal** from 1967 to 1973 followed by the outbreak of the **Ogaden War** resulted in a sharp decrease in the port's activities.

After a period of lethargy, the installation of a container terminal in February 1985 opened new perspectives for the port, which, despite periodic ups and downs, has always played the role of an economic lung to Ethiopian trade. This role was further increased with the 1998 outbreak of a conflict between Eritrea and Ethiopia

POSTAL SERVICES. The installation and development of the European trading and administrative activities called for the creation of postal services. The first Colonial Post Office was opened in **Obock** on September 1, 1884. The **Messageries Maritimes** liners sailing from Marseille to **Aden** via Obock transported the mail. In 1888, a new system sent mail from Obock to **Djibouti** by boat and, four years later, the first stamps bearing the name of Obock were printed.

The development of postal services in Djibouti influenced the introduction of modern postal services in **Ethiopia**, which became the first African state to join the International Postal Union in 1894. In the same period, Emperor Menelik II granted a concession for the construction of a **railroad** that would connect Djibouti to Addis Ababa. The railroad's construction was accompanied by the installation of the telegraph.

The Obock post office was transferred to the city of Djibouti in September 1899 and served the whole territory until 1952, when branches were opened in the country's four regions: **Ali Sabieh** in March, **Tadjourah** in May, **Dikhil** in September, and Obock, which reopened in November. The postal services have continued to develop. After **independence**, they were transformed into a real showcase of the government's will to make Djibouti a communications crossroads. The Office des Postes et Télécommunications, as it is now called, is an autonomous establishment ranking among the best-organized postal services in Africa.

POUDRIERE, LA. This destitute neighborhood is located on the site of what was once the French colonial army's arsenal. Soon after the transfer of the arsenal to the newly established camp of **Nagad**, the premises were used as a detention center, more particularly during the March 1967 riots (*see also* REFERENDUM). Thousands of people were detained for a few days at the center, which was commanded by General Vatinelle, and then deported to Somaliland. However, when Somaliland decided to close its frontiers, the colonial authorities started to abandon the deportees on the border without food or water.

POUNT, LE. The **Société d'Etudes d'Afrique Orientale** (SEAO) published a quarterly journal, *Le Pount,* from 1964 to 1987. Despite its irregular publication in the final years, *Le Pount* was and still remains a great source of information for anyone interested in Djibouti and its region. Its contributors formed a sort of intellectual elite that included officers of the colonial administration as well as Catholic missionaries (*see* CATHOLIC MISSION) and native politicians. The journal's name was derived from the ancient **land of Punt**.

PRATT, HUGO (1927–1995). Pratt, whose father had worked in the region as an administrative agent for the Italian administration in Eastern Africa, was born in Venice and came to live in the Horn of Africa from 1937 to 1943. In 1941, he and his family were imprisoned by the Allied forces in a concentration camp in Dire Dawa **(Ethiopia)** and then deported to Berbera **(Somalia)** in 1943.

A talented artist, Pratt used his experience in the region as a source of inspiration for the series of successful comic strips he created. He returned to the region, first to Ethiopia in 1971, and later to Djibouti, from 1981 to 1982.

PRESIDENT. Despite the existence of an appointed prime minister, the president is the cornerstone of the political system of the Republic of **Djibouti.** He is elected by universal suffrage for a six-year term and can be reelected only once. The president is the political head of the government, the head of state, the supreme head of the armed forces, and the head of the public administration. The president appoints all the ministers, on the advice of his prime minister. The ministers answer to the president and have only a consulting role.

The political and administrative system as a whole is based on a certain form of ethnic balance: The president has always been an **Issa** and the prime minister, an **Afar.**

PRESS, THE. The history of the **Djibouti** press starts in 1899 with the creation of *Le Djibouti,* a newspaper published by the company that built the **railroad**: the **Entreprise Générale des Travaux Publics.** During World War II, the pro-**Vichy** colonial administration published a propaganda bulletin called *Djibouti Française,* whereas the Free French Forces published *Djibouti Libre.*

In 1943, at the end of the war, the official paper, *Le Réveil de Djibouti,* appeared. Three years later, another medium was started: a monthly magazine, *Le Semeur en Terre Somalie,* which changed its name to *Carrefour Africain* in 1952. The magazine was published by the Catholic apostolic prefecture and included articles in the **Somali** language. Thus, from the 1940s to the 1970s, the local press was limited to the publication of the administration-controlled *Le Réveil de Djibouti* and the **Catholic Mission**'s journal.

The intensification of the struggle for **independence** in the 1970s was reflected by the number of publications attempting to overcome the government's monopoly on information. These leaflets were usually the organs of political parties, such as the **Ligue Populaire Africaine** (LPA), which published *Fraternité, Egalité, Unité,* and the **Mouvement Populaire de Libération** (MPL), which published *L'Avant Garde.* Sometimes the publications were the initiative of individuals such as **Abdillahi Doualeh Waiss,** who launched *Iftine* in 1974. After the country achieved independence, the number of publications gradually faded, leaving the ground to *Le Réveil de Djibouti* until 1981, and to *La Nation* thereafter.

After more than a decade of lethargy, the appearance of a number of publications—following the 1992 enactment of a law on freedom of information and communication, authorizing the creation of nongovernmental media—marked the country's political evolution from a single-party system to a multiparty one.

PROGRAMME D'AJUSTEMENT STRUCTUREL (PAS). In the early 1990s, the decrease in the country's economic activities and, more particularly, the slowdown in **port** and airport activities, brought about a budgetary deficit aggravated by the constant increase of the public expenditure and the rise of imports. Added to the freezing of international aid prompted by the war the government was waging in northern **Djibouti**, this economic crisis brought the Republic of Djibouti to the brink of collapse. It was under the pressure of both the International Monetary Fund and the French government that the Structural Adjustment Program (SAP) was signed on April 15, 1996.

The declared objectives of the SAP consisted of reducing the government's budget by cutting payroll, which represented 20 billion Djibouti francs. This meant, among other things, that the government had to demobilize more than 12,000 soldiers who had been enlisted during the **armed conflict** of 1991 to 1994.

PUBLIC HEALTH. The first hospital in the country was built in **Obock** between 1884 and 1886 in order to treat the patients evacuated from Indochina and Madagascar by the French navy. In 1898, following the transfer of the capital city of **Djibouti** to its present site, another hospital was inaugurated by the **railroad** company on December 26. In 1901, the colonial administration decided to buy this hospital and extend its services to the whole population. The staff then consisted of Catholic nuns belonging to the Franciscaines de Calais order.

To satisfy the local population's increasing needs for health care, a series of dispensaries were built at regular intervals between 1907 and 1951. A Ministry of Health was established in 1956 as a result of the enactment of the **Loi Cadre**. The ministry's policy was to give the population access to partially free health care, later to be financed by contributions from employers and taxes paid by workers. It remained efficient for some time but became unable to cope with the changes caused by the numbers of displaced people fleeing war zones (*see also* REFUGEES). Combined with the lack of qualified staff, this gradually brought about the decline in the quality of health care provided by the public system. The public health system is now in a dire state, accentuated by the country's economic difficulties and the staff's dissatisfaction.

PUNT (the land of). Punt, which means "land of the gods," was the mythical name given by the ancient Egyptians to the Horn of Africa. The Egyptians believed that their deities originated from this land. This belief was reinforced by the fact that the two sacred products used in mummy-making—incense and myrrh—as well as many spices were imported from there. An engraving in the bas-reliefs of the Deir Al Bahari temple near Thebes in **Egypt** represents an expedition organized by Queen Hatshepsut.

– Q –

QADIRIYA. The great Muslim saint Abdoulkader Jilani created this **Islamic order** in the 12th century. **Somali** Islamic awareness of this brotherhood spirit dates back to 1820. By the 1880s Sayyid Abdoulkader Jilani's Qadiriya order was the established Sufism in the Somali territories. The practice of *tawassel,* the mediation of saints for intercession with Allah, was one of the cornerstones of the Qadiriya order in the region.

QAT. *See* KHAT.

QUARTIERS. A French word commonly used in **Djibouti** in reference to the various working-class neighborhoods. The use of the label *quartier,* followed by the number (1 through 6) assigned to each precise neighborhood, was part of the colonial administration's attempt to control urban development. The *quartier* numbers matched the chronological order in which the neighborhoods were created during the time that saw waves of rural exodus and conflicts. On the part of the natives, the *quartiers* reflected their need for a communitarian area. The *quartiers* constitute today the essential part of the old city. All buildings within the neighborhoods were made of wood, as stone houses were not allowed. After **independence**, the government offered to rehabilitate the *quartiers* and set up an urban development project. Among other things, some improvements were made to the wastewater collection system, although a lot still remains to be done.

– R –

RADIO. The radio broadcasting in Djibouti started in November 1955 with the creation of Radio Djibouti. From the early days, the three local languages—**Afar**, Arabic, and **Somali**—were used, along with French, to broadcast the news. The radio stimulated the emergence and consolidation of urban culture. The first musical bands, singers, songwriters, and playwrights (*see also* DRAMA) emerged in those days. In April 1967, a **television** station was inaugurated and shared the newly built premises with the radio station. The radio and television stations that were supervised by the Office de la Radio et de la Télévision Française, the French national broadcasting corporation, became Radio et Télévision de Djibouti (RTD) soon after **independence**. The facilities and equipment were fully modernized in 1992 within the framework of Djibouti-Japanese cooperation. This was part of a series of projects funded by the Japanese government.

RAHAITA (Rahaito). This small town, located along the border of **Eritrea** and the Republic of **Djibouti**, hosts the headquarters of the eponymous **Afar sultanate** extending from **Obock** to Assab in Eritrea. Rahaita represents a landmark in the expansion of **Islam** in the Horn of Africa. Its main activities consist of **trade** exchanges with **Yemen**, across the Red Sea.

RAILROAD. Railroad construction began in 1894 when Emperor Menelik II of **Ethiopia** granted a private concession to his Swiss adviser, Alfred Ilg, who, with **Léon Chefneux**, set up a private company chiefly financed by British capital. It was the first such project in the Horn of Africa. In 1896, the **Compagnie Impériale d'Ethiopie** (CIE) was established and work started in July 1897 on the Djiboutian side. By 1902, the line reached the Ethiopian town of Addis Harar, which was later to become Dire Dawa.

The project, which was seen as a way to control the economy of northeast Africa, initially intended to connect **Djibouti** to the ancient city of Harar and the Nile basin via Ankober. However, it was reviewed and modified for a number of reasons, political as well as financial. Work was first interrupted in 1902 for lack of funds. From 1902 to 1908, the Bank of Egypt, controlled by the British, pumped new capital into the project and started to supervise it. In 1908, the French government bought the private shares from the British and granted a subsidy to a new company, the **Chemin de Fer Franco-Ethiopien** (CFE). The second section was built in 1915 and the line opened in June 1917. Covering a total distance of 780 kilometers, from Djibouti to Addis Ababa, the railroad had a strong impact on the region's economy and more particularly on the development of the **port** of Djibouti, which quickly became Ethiopia's official outlet.

From the invasion of Ethiopia by Italy in 1934, to its liberation in 1941, the railroad remained under the control of the Italian Army. The British military administration took over from 1941 until 1945, when the Franco-Ethiopian Protocol gave control back to the initial company, the CFE. In November 1956, the second Franco-Ethiopian Protocol gave Ethiopia the majority of the shares.

The CFE disappeared, without officially going into liquidation, in 1977, when Djibouti became independent. In March 1981, following the end of the **Ogaden War**, which had caused an interruption of railroad traffic, a new company, the Chemin de Fer Djibouto-Ethiopien (CDE) was created.

Today, although traffic has considerably decreased, the railroad remains the symbol of cooperation between Ethiopia and Djibouti. It is clear that the railroad has greatly contributed not only to the economic development of the region but also to the emergence of a new urban culture. It has especially transformed the way of life of the **Issa nomads** who live in the areas it crosses.

RASSEMBLEMENT DÉMOCRATIQUE AFAR (RDA). Daballe Ahmed Kassim established this political organization in 1966. Its creation resulted from the split within the **Union Démocratique Afar** **(UDA)** following the election of **Ahmed Dini Ahmed** and **Mohamed Kamil Mohamed** as members of the UDA's bureau. The RDA regrouped the partisans of **Ali Aref Bourhan**.

RASSEMBLEMENT POPULAIRE POUR LE PROGRÈS (RPP). Established in the town of **Dikhil** on March 4, 1979, two years after **Djibouti** gained **independence**, the Rassemblement Populaire pour le Progrès (RPP) was, until 1992, the sole legal party in the Republic of Djibouti. Although this political party was effective from its very early days, the one-party regime was not officially established until October 24, 1981, in the wake of the first presidential elections held June 12, 1981. **Hassan Gouled Aptidon**, the sole candidate, won that election with 84 percent of the votes. The **Loi de Mobilisation Nationale**, which gave all powers to the government, stated that the "democratic" debate between the various tendencies had to be conducted within the RPP. All political parties were therefore dissolved and banned. The following year, a number of measures modifying the party's organization were taken to reinforce the president's authority.

RASSEMBLEMENT POUR L'INDÉPENDANCE. *See* LIGUE POP-ULAIRE AFRICAINE POUR L'INDÉPENDANCE.

REEDO, JAMALEDDIN ABDULKADER. Reedo, a founding member of a political organization called Ugugumo (**Afar** for "revolution"), was at the head of the Afar militia in **Ethiopia** under the Derg military regime, which ruled the country from 1974 to 1991. However, his name, together with that of **Dimis**, is usually associated with the transcription method of Afar language both men devised.

REFERENDUM. Almost every decade since the late 1950s has had its referendum in **Djibouti**. This is the legacy of the Gaullist institutional model that was at times qualified as "constitutional Caesarism." Three out of the four referenda were organized at the time of French domination. What all these referenda have in common is that they generally mark a turning point in Djibouti's political history.

The campaign for the first referendum, which was to take place September 28, 1958, started on August 7, 1958, with a surprising declaration by **Mahamoud Harbi**, then vice president of the **Côte Française des Somalis** (CFS), and its representative to the French National Assembly. In a statement published in the French daily newspaper *Le Monde,* Harbi called for a negative vote regarding CFS remaining within the French colonial empire. Despite the overwhelming victory of those who wanted to keep Djibouti as a French colony, the "nays" represented 25 percent of the ballots. This referendum, which was simultaneously organized in all French colonies, marked the failure of Djibouti's first pro-independence aspirations.

The second referendum was organized March 19, 1967, in the wake of the violent riots that shook the capital city on August 26, 1966. Once again, an overwhelming majority of voters favored French rule. However, the announcement of the vote's outcome generated violent uprisings. A few months later, on June 14, 1967, the French National Assembly adopted a law that defined the new status of the colony and that changed its name to **Territoire Français des Afars et des Issas** (TFAI).

The May 8, 1977, referendum, which was a vote on self-determination, resulted in the emancipation of the colony from French rule.

The referendum organized in 1992 dealt essentially with changing the political system and resulted in the adoption of the country's first **Constitution** in a context of democratization advocated by **France**.

REFUGEES. The existence of a number of politically unstable zones in the Horn of Africa led to waves of refugees entering the Republic of Djibouti before and after **independence**. The first substantial group of refugees arrived in 1966, with the outbreak of the first conflict between **Ethiopia** and **Somalia**. The group consisted of the **Issa** population of the town of Aichaa, which moved en masse into Djibouti. In 1974, the followers of Sultan Ali Mirah fled the region of **Awsa** to escape the possible consequences of the military coup that had overthrown Emperor Haile Selassie. In 1978, 70,000 Issa refugees fleeing the **Ogaden War** settled in the small towns of the hinterland. Given the importance of the issue, the U.N. High Commissioner for Refugees (UNHCR) opened an office in the capital city of **Djibouti**.

In 1982, a program of voluntary repatriation was initiated by Djibouti and Ethiopia. The last refugee camp for Ethiopians was closed in 1994 and the repatriation program ended in November 1995. However, the collapse of the Somali state in 1991 resulted in the massive arrival of some 40,000 refugees who settled in camps near the villages of Assamo, Ali Adde, and Holl Holl, in southern Djibouti. In the meantime, the **armed conflict** that pitted the **Front pour la Restauration de l'Unité et de la Démocratie** against the Djiboutian governmental troops provoked the exodus of the rural population of northern Djibouti to Ethiopia. This was the first time in the country's history that civilians had to seek asylum in another country.

These massive population movements have not only had unfortunate consequences in the economy of the country, but they have also wrought changes in the country's demographic constitution and the way of life for city dwellers.

RELIGION. Before the introduction of **Islam** in about the eighth century, the various nomadic tribes that controlled what is now the Republic of Djibouti held animistic beliefs. Today, although Islam is, without any doubt, the dominant religion, most of today's major religions have established places of worship in the capital city of **Djibouti**. In terms of number, the largest religious communities after Islam are the Orthodox and the Catholics. Despite the numerous attempts made by the early missionaries to convert the natives, the number of Catholic natives is not significant. Today's Catholic community consists essentially of the French expatriates. This community has established several places of worship, the largest one being the Cathédrale Notre Dame du Bon Sauveur.

Among the first active Christian churches that were established in Djibouti is the Greek Orthodox Church. Its activities have been considerably reduced with the decline in the number of Greek traders (*see also* GREEKS). In addition, members of the Ethiopian Coptic Church, who once shared the place of worship with Greek Orthodox members, have now built their own church.

In terms of social involvement, the Protestant church, which was established in colonial times, remains quite active. Its focus is mainly with the mass of Ethiopian **refugees** who have settled in the capital city of Djibouti.

As for the Jewish community, only the ruins of an ancient synagogue and the mural sculptures ornamenting the halls of former Jewish-owned buildings remind the informed observer of its once significant presence. *See also* JEWS.

REVEIL DE DJIBOUTI, LE. This weekly French-language newspaper was launched in 1943, after the colony's liberation from **Vichy** government rule. The name of the newspaper, which can be translated as "The Awakening of Djibouti," was chosen to mark the end of Djibouti's long period of lethargy during the pro-Vichy period. Published by the government's information department, *Le Réveil* remained the only regular newspaper for 38 years. Four years after **independence**, its name was changed to *La Nation*. *See also* PRESS.

RIMBAUD, ARTHUR (1854–1891). A French poet who gave up writing and started living as an adventurer, Rimbaud landed at the port of **Aden** in **Yemen** in June 1880 and was hired by a trader named **Alfred Bardey**, who decided to send him as his representative to Harar, **Ethiopia**. During his stay in Harar, Rimbaud, who was the first Frenchman to live in that city, organized caravans from the ports of **Zeila** and **Tadjourah** to Harar. Although he got involved in the lucrative slave (*see also* SLAVERY) and **arms** trade, he never fulfilled his dream of getting rich and left the region to die in Marseille.

ROUNDTABLE. The roundtable that was held in Paris in March 1977 was organized to prepare the French colony for a smooth passage to

independence when it had become obvious that its colonial status could not be maintained in a peaceful way. A year earlier, a series of meetings had been held in **Djibouti** with Olivier Stirn, the French state secretary for the overseas territories. The three legally recognized political organizations—**Union Nationale pour l'Indépendance** (UNI), **Ligue Populaire Africaine pour l'Indépendance** (LPAI), and the parliamentary opposition—had refused to sit at the same table and so separately, on June 8, 1976, signed the agreements concerning the amendment of the legislation on French citizenship.

When **Ali Aref**, who felt that he had been betrayed, resigned from his position as chairman of the **Conseil du Gouvernement**, the UNI, LPAI, and parliamentary opposition finally made an alliance and took part in the roundtable, where the foundations of the future independent state were laid.

– S –

SAGALLOU. This small coastal village is located on the Gulf of **Tadjourah** and at the foot of the northern massifs of **Goda**. The relative abundance in water and the palm-tree gardens lining its coast helped to make it a crucial halt for both **nomads** and sailors. Thus, between 1864 and 1874, Sagallou was an important port of call for the Egyptian navy. In 1884, European traders tried to organize caravan trade to **Ethiopia** from Sagallou in order to avoid the traditional caravan routes, which were controlled by the local traders. *See also* SAGALLOU INCIDENT; SOLEILLET, PAUL.

SAGALLOU INCIDENT. Toward the end of the 19th century, Russian Czar Alexander III planned to create a base in the Red Sea that would give his navy a place to stop on the route to the Middle East and Asia via the **Suez Canal**. To that end, he encouraged the creation of a Russian colony either in **Ethiopia** or on the shores of the Red Sea. The Russian expedition gathered at the port of Odessa on the Black Sea and set sail on December 22, 1888. It consisted of 120 crew members led by a Cossack officer named **Atchinoff**. Among them were four women and four priests. On January 16, 1889, they entered the Gulf of **Tadjourah**, eluding the French navy, and landed on the coast to raise the Russian flag. The French navy ordered them to leave but they refused. On January

24, 1889, the Russian ambassador to Paris was called for an interview. To minimize the incident, the Russian government said the attempted settlement was a private initiative. On January 28, 1889, the Russian crew took position at the ancient fort of **Sagallou**, built by the Egyptians, and prepared to resist. On February 8, 1889, French battleships were sent to dislodge them; the battle took place on February 16 and resulted in the defeat of the Cossacks, who were eventually transferred to Suez and sent back to Odessa.

SALIHIYA. This **Islamic order** was the military branch of the **Ahmediya**. It derived its name from its leader, Mohamed Saleh (1835–1917).

SALINES. Now the name of a developing neighborhood, Salines used to designate the marshes on the eastern and western coasts of the capital city, where **salt** was extracted to be exported all over the world. *See also* COMPAGNIE DES SALINES DU MIDI ET DE DJIBOUTI.

SALT. Industrially tapped from 1899 to 1956 by various firms (*see also* COMPAGNIE DES SALINES DU MIDI ET DE DJIBOUTI) that had dug out salt marshes on the coastal plains of the capital city, salt constitutes one of the country's scarce resources. Until the late 1950s, it was part of the trilogy, along with the **port** and the **railroad**, that made up the colony's **economy**. The **trade** in industrial salt was at its peak from the late 1920s to the early 1930s, when it was exported as far as India and Japan. In addition, salt is found in large quantities on the banks of the lakes located in the **Afar Depression**, from which it is extracted by the Afar **nomads** and carried on camel back to the Ethiopian highlands along age-old caravan tracks (*see also* AMOLLE). Paradoxically, the local consumption of salt depends on **imports** from countries such as the Netherlands.

With the outbreak of the conflict between **Ethiopia** and **Eritrea** in May 1998, Ethiopia found itself cut off from the maritime outlet of Assab port and also from the Eritrean salt supplies. Djiboutian businessmen seized this opportunity to develop the exploitation of the **Lake Assal** salt on a large scale.

SARANDJ. The hiring of labor from **Yemen** to meet the needs of the **port** of **Djibouti** was part of an organization that consisted of avoiding all sorts of relationships or direct contact between employers and employees. The *sarandj,* or *muqaddam,* was therefore a middleman in charge of hiring workers, paying them, and organizing work as a whole. Employers were totally dependent on his services and acknowledged his role by paying him well. *See also* YEMENITES.

SCHEFER. Schefer was Napoleon III's secretary and interpreter. Following the March 11, 1862, treaty signed in Paris, he came to the region to take over the territory conceded to **France** by the **sultans** of **Tadjourah** and **Rahaita**.

SHARIA. An Arabic term referring to a body of codified Islamic laws. In **Djibouti**, it designates a court that was officially set up in 1933 to deal with all social matters concerning the Muslim community. The *Sharia* is thus in charge of settling matrimonial and patrimonial disputes. The head of the *Sharia,* the **caadi**, is a leading figure in the community's public life. *See also* JUDICIAL SYSTEM.

SHEIK. Among the Cushitic populations of northeast Africa, and particularly the **Afar**, the **Somali**, and the Oromo, the term can have three meanings: a saint, a teacher of Islamic precepts, or a traditional leader. Pilgrimages to the places where famous sheiks are buried are common, even though the practice is condemned by most **Islamic orders**, and especially the **Salihiya**. Five sanctuaries define the old city of **Djibouti** itself: Sheik Siradj to the north, Sheik Osman and Sheik Mohamed to the south, Sheik **Gabode** to the east, and Sheik Rufahi to the west.

SHEIKHO. *See* MOHAMED AHMED ISSA.

SHERSHARI. Women traders who started traveling on the **railroad** linking **Djibouti** with Addis Ababa in the mid-1940s, to import and export petty goods, were called *shershari.* With the development of road **transport**, these women traders expanded their activities to **Somalia**. In the years that followed the country's attainment of **independence**, this form of woman entrepreneurship triggered a boom in the informal sector. These women, who now use air transport, import most of the luxury goods from Asia and the Gulf states that are available on the local market.

SINIMO, ABDI. *See* ABDI DEEQSI.

SITTI. Hassan Gaditshe drafted the **heer**, the sociopolitical contract binding the **Issa**, at the foot of this mountain, near the town of Hadagalla, in

Ethiopia. It is following the adoption of the *heer* that the name of Hassan Gaditshe's mother, Sitti, was given to the site.

SLAVERY. Enslaving the vanquished has been part of the history of this part of the world for centuries. However, this practice developed considerably with the massive introduction of firearms (*see also* ARMS) in the 18th century and the outbreak of feudal wars. It is in this context that slaves were brought to the Arab countries via the Djiboutian coasts, and more particularly through the port of **Tadjourah** and the anchorage of Ambabo. The slaves were used as a bartering tool between the Ethiopian princes and the **Afar** traders on the coast. In October 1889, **France** and the sultan of Tadjourah signed an agreement to abolish and prohibit slavery. More than 40 years later, in 1930, French author Joseph Kessel, in a novel titled *Fortune Carrée,* and adventurer **Henri de Monfreid** criticized the practice of this infamous activity.

SOCIÉTÉ D'ETUDES D'AFRIQUE ORIENTALE (SEAO). Founded in 1964, the Société d'Etudes d'Afrique Orientale was a circle of French and, to a lesser extent, native intellectuals who were concerned with the study of the **Djibouti** region in various fields, such as **geology, archaeology**, anthropology, and history. Most of the early studies conducted in these fields can be attributed to this association. The quarterly journal *Le Pount*, which the group published until it disbanded in 1987, remains a useful tool for people interested in or conducting research on the country.

SOCIÉTÉ DES MESSAGERIES MARITIMES. A French shipping line that opened its first regular link from **Suez** to Indochina via **Obock** in 1888, after acquiring a concession on the Plateau des Gazelles to establish a coal storage and workshops for its ships. The company left the port of Obock to settle in **Djibouti** in July 1894. It played an important role in creating the **postal services** in the colony and took an active part in developing the port. As a matter of fact, one of the quays was built on the wreck of the *Fontainebleau*, a ship belonging to that company. The Messageries Maritimes long remained the colony's main job provider but they were also at the forefront of the first ethnic clashes in September 1935.

SOCIÉTÉ INDUSTRIELLE DE DJIBOUTI (SID). Established in 1919, the Société Industrielle de Djibouti was a private company that was responsible for the supply of water of the capital city. Its early operations were complicated by the fact that the nearest water sources were saturated with **salt**. As a consequence, in 1935, the company started exploiting the groundwater of **Ambouli**, which remains Djibouti's main reservoir.

SOLEILLET, PAUL (1842–1886). A French explorer who arrived at **Obock** in November 1881 to be the manager of the Société Française d'Obock, Soleillet quickly established relations with the **Afar sultans** and bought several concessions. He also bought the port of **Sagallou** on the Gulf of **Tadjourah**. In 1883, he traveled to **Ethiopia**, from which he received a concession to construct a **railroad** to connect Obock to Ankober.

SOLET. An **Afar** term used to designate both female circumcision and **infibulation**.

SOMALI. A group of some 10 million individuals who live in a territory that spreads over four of the Horn of Africa countries: the Republic of **Somalia**, **Ethiopia**, Kenya, and the Republic of **Djibouti**. The Somalis, who are almost all Sunnite Muslims, are a linguistically homogeneous group. Their traditional social organization consists of six clan families: the Hawiye, who settled in the central parts of southern Somalia and in northeastern Kenya; the Darod, in the eastern provinces of Somalia, in Kenya, and in southeastern Ethiopia; the **Issak** and the **Gadaboursi**, in northwestern Somali and in southeastern Ethiopia; the **Issa**, in Djibouti, southeastern Ethiopia, and to a lesser extent in northwestern Somalia; and the Rahanweyn, in southern Somalia, on a territory bordered by the Wabe Shaballe River to the east and the Juba River to the west.

Despite the linguistic and confessional homogeneity, a somewhat rare characteristic in Africa, clan and genealogical controversies and conflicts are common. The collapse of the Somali state, following the civil war that raged from 1981 to 1991, has brought about a backlash of clan sectarianism.

SOMALIA, REPUBLIC OF. The Republic of Somalia was born in 1960 from the unification of two former colonies: British Somaliland and Italian Somalia. It was one of the few countries that, following the creation of the **Organization for African Unity** (OAU) in 1963, refused to recognize the intangibility of frontiers inherited from colonization. As a matter of fact, it wanted to unify five territories inhabited by Somalis, including **Ethiopia**'s Ogaden province, Kenya's Northern Frontier District, and **Djibouti**. The project was symbolized by the five-branched star ornamenting the Somali flag. It was with this goal in mind that the Somali government supported pro-independence movements such as the **Front de Libération de la Côte Somalie** (FLCS).

In 1967, the Republic of Somalia opened a consular representation in **Djibouti**, despite **France**'s strong feelings against the move. The French animosity was calmed by discussions between French President Charles de Gaulle and Premier Mohamed Ibrahim Igal, now president of the self-proclaimed Republic of Somaliland. With the onset of the socialist military regime of Siyad Mohammed Barre in 1969, which advocated nationalism and **Pan-Somalism**, Somali became extremely active within the OAU and the Arab League concerning the decolonization of Djibouti

In 1975, Jean Gueury, the French ambassador to Somalia, was kidnapped by members of the FLCS, and a year later a school bus transporting French children was hijacked to Somalia. These two actions contributed greatly to the acceleration of the decolonization process in Djibouti. It was not surprising then that the Republic of Somalia became the first country to officially recognize the République de Djibouti (RDD).

From the birth of the RDD to the fall of the Barre regime in January 1991, relations between the two countries were based on mutual esteem and solidarity. With the exacerbation of the civil war in the Somali republic, however, relations gradually deteriorated from 1986 on. In May 1991, the Somali republic split into two separate states corresponding to the territories of the former British and Italian colonies.

SPORTS. The introduction of a sports culture in the Republic of **Djibouti** is quite recent and much indebted to the educational system. Although sports do not receive much support in the school curriculum, it cannot be denied that school is the only place where young people can become familiar with activities otherwise inaccessible to them. The main obstacle to the development of sports is the lack of infrastructures, which in turn results from the absence of real interest on the part of the political decision makers. Yet, sports has become a real factor for the development of new types of relations between the communities and goes hand in hand with the formation of associations.

As in many Third World countries, football (soccer) holds a predominant position because of the number of people who practice it. But athletics, and more particularly running, has now become the national sport, highlighted by the victories of **Ahmed Salah** and the emergence of a generation of first-rate runners, most of whom were originally **nomads** scouted by the sports department of the national **army** for their endurance.

STRUCTURAL ADJUSTMENT PROGRAM (SAP). *See* PROGRAMME D'AJUSTEMENT STRUCTUREL (PAS).

SUEZ CANAL. The opening of the Suez Canal in 1869 inaugurated a new era in the race between the European powers to settle the banks of the Gulf of **Aden** and the Indian Ocean and to create ports for their respective navies. This was why **France** started showing new interest in the colony it had possessed in **Obock** since 1864. The division of the coastal area and sea territory into zones of influence was initiated then. As a consequence, the Red Sea basin became a zone dominated by Great Britain, and France decided to create the **port** of **Djibouti** to counter British domination. Generally speaking, the opening of the Suez Canal induced the creation of several colonial ports.

Very quickly, the canal became vital for the activities of Djibouti's port, so much so that these activities decreased dramatically when the canal was closed from 1967 to 1975.

SUUGAN. The **Somali** word for oral **literature**. *Suugan* can be divided into two categories: *tih,* or verses, and *tiraab,* or prose.

SULTAN. Also called *dar-dar* (particularly until 1557), the sultan is the head of the traditional sociopolitical structure among the **Afar**. He holds a hereditary function and is always a member of the **Adaïl** clan. The sultan is a sort of arbitrator, and the dean of the *makaban* (*see* MAKABANTU). They meet in the traditional assembly—the *majliss*— to settle all matters concerning the Afar community. With the advent of colonization, however, the sultans' real power was gradually reduced. Thus, in 1928, the French deported the reigning sultan from **Tadjourah** to Madagascar, and then named a sultan to replace him. The role of the sultan today is limited to managing customary affairs.

SULTANATES. The geographical area in which the **Afar** live is divided into four sultanates: **Tadjourah**, Baylul, **Rahaita**, and **Awsa**. This form of organization, which is thought to have started in Tadjourah in the 12th century, reflects among other things, the divisions existing within the Afar nation—Tadjourah, Rahaita, and Baylul being the sultanates of the **Adoy Mara**, and Awsa that of the **Assay Mara**.

SYAD, WILLIAM (1930–1993). This pioneer of written **literature**, in a society with a predominant oral tradition, started his career as a journalist for the local **radio** and **television** broadcasting services in 1956. A passionate advocate of **Pan-Somalism**, he left the country in 1960 and sought exile in **Somalia**, where he worked as an adviser to the Ministry of Tourism and Culture until 1964. He was eventually hired by the Tanzanian Ministry of Culture and worked in Dar es Salaam from 1964 to 1967, before becoming a civil servant in UNESCO in Paris, where he lived from 1968 to 1988. William Syad wrote **poetry** in both English and French.

– T –

TADJOURAH (Tajura, Tagori). This small port town on the shores of the Gulf of Tadjourah, in northern Djibouti, is one of the oldest sites in the region and hosts the headquarters of the oldest **sultanate**. Tadjourah is a town with ancient marine traditions that, as early as the 13th century, was described by Ibn Batuta as a place with a strong Islamic culture. As a port, it handled most of the **trade** of the regions of Shoa and **Awsa** in **Ethiopia**. Slaves, ivory, grains, wheat, **salt**, and **durra** were the major products exported to the Arabian peninsula or India via Tadjourah, whereas tobacco, clothes, knives, dates, and rice were imported from these regions. This sea trade reached its height in the second half of the 19th century.

TALHA, MOHAMED ALI (c. 1933–). Talha, one of the most talented and popular **Afar** songwriters and singers, left **Obock** to settle in **Djibouti** in 1950 and started working as a cook. In 1956, when the new **radio** broadcasting services were inaugurated, he started composing songs for singers such as Djilani, Ali Oudoum, and Sheik Ahmed. Eventually, he was joined by the famous poet **Hamad Laade**, with whom he founded a band called *Date Ma'o*. He left the band in the 1960s to create *Egla Ma'o,* a cultural association whose main goal was to fight illiteracy. Talha ended his artistic career in the 1980s. Before that, however, he had composed more than 250 songs. Following a palsy attack, Talha lost the power of speech.

TELEVISION. The television broadcasting services were inaugurated April 14, 1967, in one of the most dramatic periods of the country's history. The new department was part of the Office de la Radiodiffusion et de la Télévision Française (ORTF), which controlled the **radio** broadcasting services as well. Djiboutian television broadcasts its programs in four languages: **Afar**, Arabic, French, and **Somali**. However, despite the growing Arabization, most of the programs are still in French.

TERRITOIRE FRANÇAIS DES AFARS ET DES ISSAS (TFAI). On June 14, 1967, as a consequence of the March 1967 **referendum**, a new law changing the status of the colony was enacted. This law (No. 67-521 of July 3, 1967) among other things, changed the name of **Côte Française des Somalis** (CFS) to Territoire Français des Afars et des Issas. Instead of a governor (**gouverneur**), the colony was supervised by a **haut commissaire** representing the French government and in charge of the state's public affairs. Concomitantly, the **Assemblée Territoriale** was transformed into the **Chambre des Députés**. The change in name of the colony corresponded to **Ali Aref**'s effort to cut short the pan-Somali (*see also* PAN-SOMALISM) propaganda by mentioning for the first time the presence of the second local community—the **Afar**. Organizations such as the **Front de Libération de la Côte Somalie** (FLCS) contested this change in name, which could be interpreted as an attempt at isolating the **Issa** from the rest of the **Somali**.

TRADE. From 1555 to 1820, the Red Sea could be considered as an **Ottoman** sea, closed to all other maritime powers. During that period, trade was controlled by merchants from the Arabian Peninsula and from the Red Sea coastline. They bartered products such as gold, amber, and musk as well as slaves (*see also* SLAVERY). Indian merchants too were actively involved. The major event back then was the great fair of Berbera, to which merchants from places as remote as the Indian province of Gujrat came to buy and sell various products.

The opening of the **Suez Canal** in 1869 upset this type of trade. European merchants settled on the coast and created new trade poles, thereby causing the decline of the caravan trade. In the 1880s, several European trading houses opened in **Obock**, and later transferred their offices to **Djibouti**. Among them were the Société Française d'Obock, run by **Paul Soleillet**, and the Maison **Pino**.

The construction of the **railroad**, at the beginning of the 20th century, gave the final blow to the age-old trading habits through caravan tracks and *dhows* (*see also* BOUTRES). The **port** of Djibouti became the official outlet of the Ethiopian trade. Several import-export companies established themselves in the capital city and contributed to the development of service-providing infrastructures that are still at the base of the Djiboutian economy.

Traditionally, the import-export business had been in the hands of Yemenite-Jews (*see also* JEWS; YEMENITES) and Indian (*see also* BANYANS) traders, such as **Mohamedally**, who controlled almost all of the trade of the Ethiopian empire and, consequently, that of Djibouti. However, with the population's growing urbanization and the repatriation of the Jewish community, which took place after the State of Israel was established in 1948, more and more natives started to get involved in trade and to compete with the foreign traders. Starting in the 1980s, with the development of air links with the countries of the Arabian Gulf, a large portion of the import business began to shift into the hands of the native traders (*see also* SHERSHARI).

In the absence of local industries and significant **agriculture**, most consumer goods available on the market are imported from Asia and Europe, and, to a lesser extent, from other African countries. Strange as it may seem, even **salt**, which is one of the scarce natural resources of the Republic of **Djibouti**, is imported. All in all, in 1996, imports represented an estimated total of $200.5 million (US).

Most of the products imported from Asia consist of textiles, electronics, and automobile spare parts. Building materials are imported from Europe, whereas food products are essentially imported from **Ethiopia**.

TRANSPORT. The creation of the colony was a direct consequence of the transportation revolution that was taking place in Europe. In fact, **France**'s decision to establish itself in the region was principally motivated by the need to have a coaling station for its steamers on route to Asia and the Indian Ocean. The opening of the **Suez Canal** in 1869 convinced France, whose settlement in **Obock** had provoked a rush of French traders wishing to conquer the Ethiopian market, of the strategic importance of such a project. This in turn triggered the second transportation revolution, which materialized with the opening of the **Djibouti**-Addis

Ababa **railroad** in 1917. Its success gave the final blow to the traditional transport chain constituted by the *dhows* (*see also* BOUTRES) and the caravans. At the same time, the boost given to sea traffic induced the need to modernize and develop Djibouti's **port**.

The advent of air transport was stimulated by the outbreak of the Italo-Ethiopian war in November 1934. However, because of the isolation caused by the three-year **blockade**, the civil aerodrome was not established until 1949. Ever since, air transport has been in constant development, with only a few periodic ups and downs.

One of the conditions of the railroad stipulated that no roads were to be built between Djibouti and **Ethiopia**, in order to protect the monopoly held by the railroad company. Because of this, the first asphalt road connecting Djibouti to Ethiopia via **Galafi** was not built until 1975. Today, the development of road transport, especially as far as freight is concerned, is the order of the day. Air, rail, road, and sea transport, combined with modern telecommunication infrastructures and a free banking system, are the foundations of Djibouti's **economy** that relies on service activities.

TREATIES, ISSA. Following the signing of the March 11, 1862, treaty with the **Afar sultanates** of **Rahaïta** and **Tadjourah**, **France**, which had been granted a territorial concession on the littoral extending from Ras **Doumeira**, in the north, to **Goubet-el-Kharab**, in the south, started exploring the southern coast of the Gulf of Tadjourah. It was during this exploration period that the colonial authorities came into contact with the **Issa** populations and signed two historic treaties, one in March 1885 and the other in August 1917. These treaties, signed with the main Issa notables, helped France to consolidate its hold on a colony that had been in gestation since the mid-19th century. *See also* AMBADO.

TURKEY. *See* OTTOMAN EMPIRE.

– U –

UKAL. A word derived from the Arabic *aqil* and now meaning tribal chief. The colonial administration used the chiefs skillfully to consolidate both its hold on the local populations and its influence on the territories controlled by the *ukal* beyond the frontiers, and to maintain law and order. Thus, during the construction of the **railroad**, the colonial administration nominated *ukals* all along the track to ensure that security was guaranteed in territories crossed by the train. Today, *ukals* are still used by the government and remain useful auxiliaries to the administration, notably in terms of conflict management.

ULAMMA. An Arabic term designating a highly learned man of **religion**. The *ulammas* generally travel from country to country and share their knowledge at large Islamic centers.

UNION DÉMOCRATIQUE AFAR (UDA). The Union Démocratique Afar was a political organization created in 1961 by a group of **Afar** notables and civil servants, following the enactment of the **Loi Cadre**. Concerning the question of **independence**, which was the main issue in those days, the UDA evolved from an attitude of conciliation with the colonial administration to a radical commitment for independence. This evolution was a reflection of both the internal rivalries and the clanic divisions of the Afar political elite that constituted the organization.

Until late 1963, there was a form of entente between the two groups composing the movement and respectively led by **Ali Aref**, a native of **Tadjourah**, and **Mohamed Kamil**, a native of **Obock**. The contested election of **Orbisso Gadito** to the head of the organization, in December 1963, brought to light the internecine feuds. The succession crisis lasted until February 1965, when the two groups agreed to form an arbitration committee, with **Abdallah Mohamed Kamil** at its head, to organize other elections. These took place in April 1965 and confirmed the victory of Orbisso Gadito over Daballe Ahmed Kassim, the man representing Ali Aref. From then on, the UDA began to adopt radical policies and was joined by a number of politicians opposed to Ali Aref, then vice president of the colony.

During French President Charles de Gaulle's visit to the country in August 1966, the UDA, led by **Ahmed Dini**, together with the dominantly Somali **Parti Mouvement Populaire** (PMP), was among the main organizers of the pro-independence demonstrations that were violently repressed. *See also* SHEIKO.

UNION DÉMOCRATIQUE ISSA (UDI). This predominantly **Issa** political organization represented the region of **Ali Sabieh** and was established in the early 1960s. The UDI was characterized by its collaboration with the colonial administration and its anti-independence stances.

UNION NATIONALE POUR L'INDÉPENDANCE. Faced with growing opposition from within his own party, the Union Démocratique

Républicaine, **Ali Aref** started, in 1975, to acknowledge that **independence** was inevitable. He consequently changed the name of his party to Union Nationale pour l'Indépendance in an attempt to remain on the political stage.

UNION NATIONALE DES ETUDIANTS DE LA CÔTE AFAR ET SOMALIE (UNECAS). This national union of students from French Somaliland was established in early 1975 under the wing of a West Berlin-based student organization called the Student Union of the Somali Coast (SUSOC) and included SUSOC itself, the Association des Etudiants Afars en France, and the Organisation des Etudiants Somalis en France. The goal of UNECAS was to transcend the tribal divisions in order to prepare for the country's **independence**. But internal conflicts and personal ambitions quickly led to its disintegration.

– V –

VICHY. When the German forces occupied **France** during World War II, a political regime presided over by Marshall Philippe Pétain was established in the town of Vichy. This regime, which collaborated with the Nazis, fought the Forces Françaises Libres (Free French) over control of the colonies. In **Djibouti**, after long debates and a vote, the colony's board decided in June 1940 to join the Vichyists. This decision was followed by a number of drastic measures imposed by **Pierre Nouailhetas**, then governor (**gouverneur**) of the colony. Pressure exerted by British troops, notably by means of a **blockade**, and the defeat of Vichy's Italian allies in **Ethiopia**, brought an end to Vichy domination in November 1943.

– W –

WAIMA (Weima). A valley hosting an eponymous river and located on the **Djibouti** and **Eritrea border**. The site, which is populated by a number of **Afar** clans, constitutes an important jurisdiction.

WALASMA (Oualashma). This royal family reigned over the kingdom of Ifat, in the eastern part of the province of Shoa (in **Ethiopia**) from the 13th century to the 17th century. The founder of this dynasty, Omar Walasme, arrived from the region of Hedjaz, in present-day Saudi Arabia, to settle in the city of Ifat in the early 13th century. Very quickly, the man's family was noticed for its piety and integrity. One of his descendants, Omar Ben Dounyahouz, was appointed governor of the city, thus inaugurating a long dynastic reign that was marked by never-ending wars against the Christian state of **Abyssinia**. These wars brought instability to the Walasma kingdom, whose capital was displaced on many occasions. Thus, in 1435, the capital was moved to the region of Harar and the name of the kingdom was changed to **Adal**. In 1569, it moved again, this time to the region of what is now **Awsa**.

WALI. A term of Arabic origin that is used to describe the person at the head of an administrative region called *wilayat*. During the colonial period, natives used this word to refer to the governor (**gouverneur**), and the governor's palace was called *beit el wali*.

WEDDAD. This Arabic term designates a preacher belonging to a brotherhood (*see also* ISLAMIC ORDERS). In traditional **Somali** society, there is a social distinction between the *weddad* (the men of prayer) and the *warranley* (the warriors).

WOMEN. In the traditional society, whether it is among the **Afar** or the **Issa**, the most difficult chores have always been reserved for women. Gathering wood, carrying water, or setting up the *toukouls* or *daboitas* (the traditional huts) are some of their responsibilities. However, despite their crucial role in the rural economy, women are rarely consulted when important decisions are made concerning either society as a whole or families.

Over the years, however, urbanization has profoundly affected the status of women. This transformation was accelerated, to a large extent, by the broadening of access to education for girls, despite the unwillingness of many parents to allow their daughters to receive an education. Thus, women have been able to gain access to office jobs, mostly as secretaries. Although more and more female employees can be found in positions of high responsibility, the number of women taking part in decision making remains low. The first female deputy minister was appointed in 1999.

Yet, political leaders have never underestimated the power of women when it comes to mobilizing voters, promoting candidates during electoral campaigns, or implementing official decisions affecting social aspects. It is to that end that the Union Nationale des Femmes Djiboutiennes (UNFD) was established in 1980, chaired by President **Hassan Gouled**'s wife, Aicha Bogoreh. Even though its main function is political recruitment, this organization also plays a significant role in the struggles against **infibulation** and illiteracy.

Trade is probably the sector in which the role of women is most visible. Whether they work as **shershari**, traveling as far as Thailand, or simply as **khat** vendors at the corner of a street, women have become important breadwinners. With the increasing number of female graduates trained in foreign universities entering the job market, the place of women in Djibouti's society is bound to change in the coming decades

– Y –

YEMEN. Throughout its history, Yemen, once known as Arabia Felix, has developed close links with the countries in the Horn of Africa. The country's strategic location on the eastern shore of the Red Sea, at the crossroads of the trade routes among Africa, Asia, and Europe, undoubtedly played a part in the relations it established with its neighbors across the Red Sea and, to a certain extent, with **Djibouti**. The creation of the port of Djibouti in 1887 was followed by a significant immigration of Yemenite (*see also* YEMENITES) skilled workers. These were particularly needed in the construction industry. Ever since, the Yemenite community has been part of the ethnic mosaic of the city of Djibouti.

The relations between the independent Republic of Djibouti and Yemen, both before and after the merger between the two Yemenite states, have always been stable.

YEMENITES. The Yemenites, a part of the colony as a community since its foundation, were used by the colonial administration as a relay group in its relations with the native populations. The migratory movement of this community was encouraged by the creation of the **port** and the subsequent maritime traffic between **Aden** and **Djibouti**. The early immigrants worked either in the construction industry, where their skills were highly demanded, or as merchants. A significant portion of this community was also employed by the **Messageries Maritimes**. The preference granted by this company to Yemenite laborers was the basis of a number of conflicts with the other **dockers**.

The growth of this community and the emergence of wealthy families, such as the Doranis, the Coubèches (*see also* COUBECHE, SAID ALI), and the Banabilas, resulted in more involvement in the colony's **political life**. The Club Arabe was thus created in 1937. However, following the hostility they encountered, particularly in the 1950s, the community as a whole chose to refrain from any participation in political events and to devote itself entirely to **trade**. Until the colony gained **independence** in 1977, the Yemenite community held the monopoly on trade in the formal sector.

Today the Yemenites hold seats in the **Parliament** as a form of balance in the representation of ethnic communities. They represents about 6 percent of the population and almost all of them live in the capital city, where they work in the fields of trade, fishing, or in small-scale **agriculture**, and to a lesser extent in the public sector. They have a considerable impact on the country's **economy**, especially in regard to **port** activities.

– Z –

ZEILA (Zeyla). The past cultural wealth of this port, located in northern **Somalia**, greatly influenced the communities living in the region. Zeila, which was the capital of the **Adal** kingdom throughout the kingdom's existence, from the 13th century to the second half of the 16th century, was an important outlet to sea for **Ethiopia** in the Middle Ages. As a port, it played the role **Djibouti** plays today and was characterized by the cultural diversity of its population. With the defeat of Ahmed Gragne's troops in 1547, Zeila ceased to be the capital.

In the early 18th century, the **Ottoman** Turks took control of the city and installed a **pasha**, whose main roles included raising taxes. From 1882 to 1885, the town remained under Egyptian control. When the British settled there and created British Somaliland, most of the city dwellers moved to Djibouti. The creation of the **port** of Djibouti in 1887 accelerated the Zeila's decline.

ZEILA'I. *See* DJAMA ALI MOUSSA.

ZERIBA. This word of Turkish origin was once used to designate a small enclosure that served as a guardhouse. Today, Zeriba is the name of the central market of the capital city of **Djibouti**.

Appendix 1
Rulers of the Colony, 1887–1977

Until 1967, the rulers of the colony bore the title of "gouverneur"; since June 28, 1967, they were called "haut commissaire."

1887–1899	Léonce LAGARDE
March 1899–April 1900	Alfred MARTINEAU
August 5, 1904–April 1913	Pierre PASCAL
1913–1916	A. BONHOURE
October 8, 1916–August 31, 1917	FILLON
1917–1924	LAURET
1924–1934	CHAPON-BAISSAC
May 7, 1934–July 18, 1935	Jules Marcel DE COPPET
July 18, 1935–November 10, 1935	Achille SILVESTRE
November 10, 1935–May 1, 1937	Armand ANNET
May 1, 1937–March 19, 1938	Marie-Pierre ALYPE
May 1938–July 1940	Hubert DESCHAMPS
July 1940–September 1940	General GERMAIN
September 2, 1940– September 1942	Pierre NOUAILHETAS
September 1942–November 1942	General TRUFFERT
November 28, 1942–December 4, 1942	General POUVREAU
December 4, 1942–December 28, 1942	General DUPONT
December 30, 1942–June 1943	General BAYARDELLE
June 22, 1943–January 7, 1944	Raphaël SALLER
May 1, 1944–May 1945	Jean CHALVET
May 14, 1945–December 1945	Jean BEYRIES
April 30, 1946–February 1950	Paul-Henri SIRIEX
March 1, 1950–1954	Numa SADOUL
April 6, 1954–August 1954	Roland PRÉ
August 13, 1954–August 7, 1957	René PETITBON
August 7, 1957–December 1958	Maurice MECKER
December 1958–November 1962	Jacques COMPAIN
November 1962–September 9, 1966	René TIRANT

September 11, 1966–February 6, 1969	Louis SAGET
March 8, 1969–August 1971	Dominique PONCHARDIER
September 16, 1971–July 1974	Georges THIERCY
July 1974–February 1976	Christian DABLANC
February 1976–June 1977	Camille D'ORNANO

Appendix 2
Members of Government since Independence

Prime Ministers

July to December 1977	Ahmed Dini Ahmed
February to September 1978	Abdallah Mohamed Kamil
September 1978 to present day	Barkat Gourad Hamadou

Ministers of Education

July 1977 to September 1978	Hassan Houssein Banabila
October 1978 to November 1987	Mohamed Djama Elabe
November 1987 to December 1991	Souleiman Farah Lodone (resigned)
January 1992 to February 1993	Omar Chirdon Abass
February 1993 to April 1999	Ahmed Guirreh Waberi
Since May 1999	Abdi Ibrahim Absieh

Ministers of Health

July 1977 to December 1977	Ahmed Youssouf Ahmed (resigned)
February 1978 to July 1981	Mohamed Ahmed Issa
July 1981 to May 1982	Ahmed Hassan Liban
May 1982 to October 1986	Mohamed Adabo Kako
January 1987 to 1989	Ougoureh Hassan Ibrahim
1989 to December 1991	Mohamed Djama Elabe (resigned)
January 1992 to February 1993	Idriss Harbi Farah
February 1993 to December 1997	Mohamed Saïd Saleh
December 1997 to April 1999	Ali Mohamed Daoud
Since May 1999	Mohamed Dini Farah

Ministers of Defense

July 1977 to September 1978	Ahmed Hassan Ahmed
October 1978 to July 1985	Habib Mohamed Loïta

1985 to 1989	Ali Barkat Siradj (dismissed)
1989 to 1993	Ismaël Ali Youssouf
February 1993 to March 1996	Ahmed Boullaleh Barreh (dismissed)
March 1996 to April 1999	Abdallah Chirwa Djibril
Since May 1999	Ougoureh Kifle Ahmed

Ministers of the Interior

July 1977 to September 1978	Moumin Bahdon Farah
October 1978 to July 1982	Idriss Farah Abaneh (died in office)
October 1982 to 1986	Youssouf Ali Chirdon (died in office)
May 1986 to February 1991	Khaireh Allaleh Hared (dismissed)
May 1991 to February 1993	Ahmed Boulalah Bareh
February 1993 to March 1997	Idriss Harbi Farah
March 1997 to April 1999	Elmi Obsieh Waïss
Since May 1999	Abdallah Abdillahi Miguil

Ministers of Foreign Affairs

July 1977 to September 1978	Abdallah Mohamed Kamil (also prime minister)
October 1978 to February 1993	Moumin Bahdon Farah
February 1993 to December 1997	Abdou Bolock Abdou
December 1997 to May 1999	Mohamed Moussa Chehem
Since May 1999	Ali Abdi Farah

Bibliography

LIST OF ABBREVIATIONS

ACCT	Agence de Coopération Culturelle et Technique
ADEN	Association Djibouti Espace Nomade
BCAF	*Bulletin du Comité de l'Afrique Française*
BCEOM	Bureau Central d'Etudes pour les Equipements d'Outre-Mer
BRGM	Bureau de Recherches Géologiques et Minières
BSA	*Bulletin de la Société d'Anthropologie*
BSG	*Bulletin de la Société de Géologie*
BSGCB	*Bulletin de la Société de Géographie Coloniale de Bordeaux*
BSGCH	*Bulletin de la Société de Géographie Commerciale du Havre*
BSGE	*Bulletin de la Société de Géographie de l'Est*
BSGM	*Bulletin de la Société de Géographie de Marseille*
BSKG	*Bulletin de la Société Khédivale de Géographie*
BSNG	*Bulletin de la Société Normande de Géographie*
CEA	*Cahier d'Etudes Africaines*
CEAN	Centre d'Etude sur l'Afrique Noire
CEGD	Centre d'Etudes Géologiques et de Développement
CHEAM	Centre des Hautes Etudes sur l'Afrique et l'Asie Moderne
CNRS	Centre National de la Recherche Scientifique
CQRI	Centre Québécois de Relations Internationales
CRAS	*Comptes Rendus de l'Académie des Sciences*
DEA	Diplôme d'Etudes Approfondies
DESS	Diplôme d'Etudes Supérieures Spécialisées
EHESS	Ecole des Hautes Etudes en Sciences Sociales
ENFOM	Ecole Nationale de la France d'Outre-Mer
FAO	Food and Agriculture Organization
ICES	International Conference on Ethiopian Studies
IEMVT	Institut d'Etudes de Médecine Vétérinaire Tropicale
IEP	Institut d'Etudes Politiques
IES	Institute of Ethiopian Studies
IHPOM	Institut d'Histoire des Pays d'Outre-Mer

IJAHS	International Journal of African Historical Studies
INALCO	Institut National des Langues et Civilisations Orientales
ISERST	Institut Supérieur d'Etudes et de Recherches Scientifiques et Techniques
JAH	Journal of African History
JAS	Journal of African Studies
JATBA	Journal d'Agriculture Tropicale et de Botanique Appliquée
JES	Journal of Ethiopian Studies
JGEG	Jahresbericht der Geographisch Ethnographischen Gesellschaft in Zürich
JORD	Journal Officiel de la République de Djibouti
JORF	Journal Officiel de la République Française
JRGS	Journal of the Royal Geographic Society
JSA	Journal de la Société des Africanistes
JSPS	Journal of Social and Political Studies
MTPUL	Ministère des Travaux Publics de l'Urbanisme et du Logement
ONTA	Office National du Tourisme et de l'Artisanat
RC	Revue Coloniale
RFEPA	Revue Française d'Etudes Politiques Africaines
RFHOM	Revue Française d'Histoire d'Outre-Mer
RGPGD	Revue de Géographie Physique et de Géographie Dynamique
RGSJ	Royal Geographical Society Journal
RHA	Revue Historique des Armées
RHCF	Revue de l'Histoire des Colonies Françaises
RIS	Revue Internationale de Sociologie
RSGB	Revue de la Société de Géographie de Bordeaux
RSGCP	Revue de la Société de Géographie Commerciale de Paris
SCET	Société Centrale pour l'Equipement des Territoires
SGAC	Société Générale de l'Aviation Civile
SHAA	Services Historiques de l'Armée de l'Air

INTRODUCTION

One of the first difficulties encountered in writing this work was the scantiness of available documentation related to the subject. The imbalance existing among the various categories in the bibliography reflects this difficulty. This lack of documentation is due to the way in which various historical periods were handled by the few researchers who became interested in Djibouti's history. Thus, aspects relating to the French colonial period are rather well documented because of the existence of colonial archives. In that regard, the numerous international, regional, or local crises have given researchers the opportunity to proceed to an inventory of the existing literature and produce better documented historical studies on that period.

The imbalance affecting the documentary sources also reflects the one that exists between 100 years of colonialism and the two decades of existence as an independent state. Unsurprisingly, the overwhelming portion of the primary and secondary literature is in French, with also a smattering in Italian, due to Italy's colonial interests. Works in these and other European languages are included in the bibliography, but not works in Arabic.

Articles in journals, magazines, and newspapers, rather than larger monographs and books, provided much of the information on the period of independence. Where appropriate, doctoral dissertations and master's theses at various universities, especially those in France, are included. However, many more can certainly be found; of particular interest are those by Djiboutian students studying in France and other countries.

A useful introduction to the precolonial history is certainly Jean Doresse's *Histoire Sommaire de la Corne Orientale de l'Afrique* (Paris: Paul Geuthner, 1971). This comprehensive study of the Horn of Africa presents a detailed picture of the region from antiquity to the eve of World War II. Philippe Oberlé and Pierre Hugot's *Histoire de Djibouti: des Origines à la République* (Paris: Présence Africaine, 1985) is a valuable account of the colonial period with, in its latest edition, a short study on the first decade after independence. Based on a thorough scrutiny of the colonial archives, Colette Dubois's *Djibouti, 1887–1967. Héritage Ou Frustration ?* (Paris: L'Harmattan, 1997) provides researchers with a well-documented chronicle on the colony's gradual development and interesting leads yet to be explored. Virginia Thompson and Richard Adloff's *Djibouti and the Horn of Africa* (Stanford, Calif.: Stanford University Press, 1968) is among the scarce comprehensive studies on the region written in English. More recently published, Ali Coubba's *Le Mal Djiboutien* (Paris: L'Harmattan, 1996) is rich with information on the decades after independence.

For a detailed study on the native populations of the Republic of Djibouti, Adou Abdallah's *The Afar: A Nation on Trial* (Stockholm: Abdallah A. Adou, 1993) and I. M. Lewis's *Peoples of the Horn of Africa: Somali, Afar and Saho* (London: International African Institute, 1955) are among the most useful works.

ARCHIVES

For those interested in conducting in-depth historical studies on the Republic of Djibouti, the archives held by the following institutions may be a valuable starting point:

- Le Centre National de Documentation (CND). This Djiboutian institution archives the copies of the former *Le Réveil de Djibouti* and the current weekly government paper, *La Nation*.
- The archives of the Chambre Internationale de Commerce et d'Industrie de Djibouti consist essentially of correspondence between some of the economic and, sometimes, political actors in the former colony's early days. (Chambre Internationale de Commerce et d'Industrie de Djibouti, P.O. Box 84 Djibouti, Republic of Djibouti. Web site: www.intnet.dj/public/cicid).
- The archives of the British Public Records Office located in Kew, Richmond, Surrey TW94DU, United Kingdom, are particularly well stocked.
- The main institution in France is the Centre d'Accueil et de Recherche des Archives Nationales (60, rue des Francs-Bourgeois, 75141 Paris Cedex 03). However, most of the documents concerning French former colonies are stocked in the Centre des Archives d'Outre-Mer (29, Chemin du Moulin de Testa, 13090, Aix-en-Provence).

Other interesting archive institutions are the Archives du Ministère des Affaires Etrangères (Quai d'Orsay, Paris) and the Service Historique de la Marine and the Service Historique de l'Armée de Terre (SHAT), both located in Paris, Château de Vincennes.

In this age of electronic communication, this bibliographical tool would not be complete if we forgot to mention Web sites that provide users with instant information on the country. The following are among the most useful sites:

- The site of the Intergovernmental Authority on Development (www.igad.org) publishes regular press releases on the member countries.
- The site of the Agence de Coopération Culturelle et Technique (www.francophonie.org/pays/djibouti.htm) has a directory for Djibouti.
- The Djibouti page hosted by the University of Pennsylvania site (www.sas.upenn.edu/African_Studies/country_specific/Djibouti) is interesting for the various links it provides.

- Information on the country's diplomatic relations can be found on the official site of the Embassy of Djibouti in France (www.amb-djibouti.org).

GENERAL

Bibliographies

Clarke, Sheldon, W. *A Current Bibliography on African Affairs,* vol. 10, no. 1 (1977–1978): 3–31.

———. "A Developmental Bibliography for the Republic of Djibouti." Typescript document, Djibouti, 1979.

Darch, Colin. *A Soviet View of Africa: An Annotated Bibliography on Ethiopia, Somalia and Djibouti.* Boston: G.K. Hall, 1980.

Janvier, Roger, and Christian Dupont. *Bibliographie. Côte des Somalis et Dépendances.* Paris: Bibliothèque de la Documentation Française, 1933.

Marcus, Harold G. *The Modern History of Ethiopia and the Horn of Africa: A Select and Annotated Bibliography.* Palo Alto, Calif.: Hoover Institution Press, 1972.

Ministère Français de la Coopération. *Bibliographie de la République de Djibouti.* Djibouti: Imprimerie Nationale, 1980.

Pankhurst, R. *Register of Current Research on Ethiopia and the Horn of Africa.* Addis Ababa: IES, 1969.

Schraeder, Peter J. *Djibouti.* Santa Barbara, Calif.: ABC-CLIO, World Bibliographical Series, vol. 118, 1991.

Biographies

Borer, Alain. *Rimbaud en Abyssinie.* Paris: Seuil, 1984.

Comte, J. M. *A. Bernard. Vie et Mort d'un Savoyard Tombé pour l'Afrique.* Paris: Fontaine de Siloé, 1944.

Farrère, Claude, and Alfred Sexer. "Monfreid en Côte des Somalis." *Livres de France* (1955).

Grandclément, Daniel. *L'Incroyable Henri de Monfreid.* Paris: Grasset, 1990.

Gros, J. *Paul Soleillet en Afrique.* Paris: Alcide Picard et Kahn, 1988.

Keller, Conrad. *Alfred Ilg, sein Leben und sein Wirken.* Frauenfeld: Huber, 1918.

Petitfils, P. *Rimbaud.* Paris: Julliard, 1982.

Poinsot, Jean-Paul. "Hommage à Léonce Lagarde. Un Diplomate et un Bâtisseur." *Le Réveil de Djibouti* (February 1966).
Starkie, Enid. *Arthur Rimbaud in Abyssinia*. Oxford: Clarendon Press, 1937.
———. *Rimbaud*. Paris: Flammarion, 1982.
Tubiana, Joseph. "Alfred Bardey à Zeila en 1880." *Le Pount*, no. 11 (1973).

Exploration and Travels

Alvarez, Ernest-Eugène. *Obock et Abyssinie*. Paris: L. Baudoin, 1894.
Aubry, Marie-Christine. *Djibouti l'Ignorée*. Paris: L'Harmattan, 1988.
Bardey, Alfred. *Barr-Adjam, Souvenirs d'Afrique Orientale. 1880–1887*. Paris: CNRS, 1981.
Brazza, Savorgnan de. "La Côte Orientale d'Afrique et son Avenir Commercial." *BSGCB*, no. 3 (February 1880).
Burton, Richard, Sir. *First Footsteps in East Africa, or an Exploration of Harar*. 2 vols. London: Longmans, 1856.
Castro, Lincoln de. "De Zeila au Harar." *BSKG* 5 (1898): 133–161.
Charmetant, Félix. "Un Voyage à Djibouti." In *Bulletin de la Société de Géographie de Lyon*, vol. 15 (1898): 490–506.
Delabergerie, Guy. *Fleuron de la Mer Rouge. Le Territoire Français des Afars et des Issas*. Boulogne: Delroisse, 1972.
Doody, John. *The Burning Coast*. London: Michael Joseph, 1955.
Ellsberg, E. *Under the Red Sea Sun*. New York: Dodd, Mead, 1946.
Forbes, Rosita. *From Red Sea to Blue Nile*. London: MacAuley Co., 1925; New York, 1935.
Forestier, Patrick. *Le Train du Négus*. Paris: Grasset, 1994.
Galves, Georges. "Randonnées en Pays Afar." *Revue du SGAC*, no. 148 (November 1973).
———. "Djibouti." *Esprit*, no. 430 (December 1973).
———. *Territoire Français des Afars et des Issas*. Djibouti; Boulogne: Delroisse, 1973.
Gil-Artagnan, André. *Expédition Pount: Autour de l'Afrique sur la Route des Phéniciens*. Paris: L'Harmattan, 1994.
Goedorp, Victor. "Chez les Somalis." *A Travers le Monde*, vol. 5 (1899): 369–371.
Guillain, M. *Voyage sur le Côte Orientale d'Afrique. Sur le Pays Galla, Somali, Danakil*. Paris, 1846.
Guyod, Francois. *D'Addis Abeba à Djibouti en Train*. Paris: L'Harmattan, 1996.
Haffiz, Mahmassani R. *Djibouti, Côte Française des Somalis*. Beirut: Dar el Assima, 1965.

Heudebert, Lucien. *Au Pays des Somalis et des Comoriens.* Paris: J. Maisonneuve, 1901.

Hezez, Guillaume. *Odyssée en Mer Rouge.* Grenoble: Glénat, 1996.

Ibn Battuta. *Sur la Côte Orientale de l'Afrique,* vol. 5. Paris: Anthropos, 1968.

James, Frank Linsley. *The Unknown Horn of Africa: An Exploration from Berbera to the Leopold River.* London: G. Philip, 1888.

Kirk, R. "Report on the Route from Tajurra to Ankobar Travelled by the Mission to Showa, under Charge of Captain W. C. Harris, 1841." *JRGS* 12 (1943).

Le Roux, Hugues. *Côte de Somalis; Mission Hugues Leroux.* Paris: Imprimerie Nationale, 1914.

———. "Guerriers et Pillards." *Le Globe-Trotter* (1907).

Lebrun, Keris G. *Djibouti, Terre Nécessaire et Menacée.* Paris: Le Cerf, 1956.

Lobo, Jérôme. *Voyage Historique d'Abissinie du R. P. Jérome Lobo.* Translated from Portuguese by M. Legrand. Paris and La Haye: P. Gosset and J. Neaulme, 1728.

Merch, Charles A. *La Dankalie en CFS.* Brussels: Reflets du Monde, 1965.

Michel, Charles. "Dans les Brousses de l'Ethiopie et du Soudan. Mon Raid de Djibouti à Khartoum." *Lecture pour tous,* no. 15 (March 1921).

Monga, Celestin. *Un Bantou à Djibouti.* Paris: Editions Silex, 1990.

Monmarson, Raoul. *Chez les Clients de la Mer Rouge.* Paris, 1948.

Munzinger, W. "Narrative of a Journey through the Afar Country." *RGSJ,* vol. 39 (1869).

Nesbittt, S. F. "Danakils Transversed from South to North in 1928." *The Geographical Journal* (London Royal Geographical Society), vol. 76, 298–315; 391–414.

Neumann, Oskar. "From the Somali Coast through Southern Ethiopia to the Sudan." *JIGS,* no. 5 (1963).

Nurse, Charles G. "A Journey through Parts of Somali; between Zeila and Bulhar." *RGSJ,* no. 13 (1891).

Pagne, Léon. *Mon Voyage en Abyssinie et Séjour chez les Somalis (Côte Orientale d'Afrique).* Saint-Quentin: Imprimerie C. Pœtte, 1900.

Poncins, Edmond de. "Voyage au Choa, Explorations au Somal et chez les Danakils." *BSG,* no. 19 (1898): 423–488.

Pottier, Louis. "Note de Route d'Aden au Choa." *BSGM,* vol. 2 (1978): 142–146.

Revoil, Georges. "Voyage au Pays des Çomalis." In *BSGM,* no. 20 (1880).

———. "Voyage au Pays Çomali." In *BSGM,* no. 5 (1881).

Rimbaud, Arthur. *Lettres de Jean-Arthur Rimbaud. Egypte, Arabie, Ethiopie.* Paris: Mercure de France, 1899.

————. *Correspondances. 1888–1891.* Paris: Gallimard, 1965.

Rochet d'Héricourt, C. E. X. *Voyage sur la Côte Orientale de la Mer Rouge, dans le Pays d'Adal et le Royaume de Choa.* Paris: A. Bertrand, 1841.

————. *Second Voyage sur les Deux Rives de la Mer Rouge, dans le Pays des Adels et le Royaume de Choa.* Paris: A. Bertrand, 1846.

Russel, S. *Une Mission en Abyssinie et dans la Mer rouge, 23 Octobre 1859–7 Mai 1860.* Paris: Plon, Nourrit et. Co., 1884.

Simonin, L. "Voyages de M. Henry Lambert, Agent Consulaire de France à Aden (1855–1859)." *Le Tour du Monde* vol. 2 (1862).

Soleillet, Paul. "Obock et l'Ethiopie Méridionale." *Bulletin de la Société de Géographie de Lyon* (1882).

————. *Obock, le Choa, le Kaffa; une Exploration Commerciale en Ethiopie.* Paris: M. Dreyfus, 1886.

Stigand, C. H., Captain. *The Land of Zinj: An Account of British East Africa, Its Ancient History and Present Inhabitants.* London: Constable, 1913.

Teilhard De Chardin, P. *Lettres de Voyage 1923–1939.* Paris: Grasset, 1956.

Thesiger, Wilfred. *The Life of My Choice.* London: Collins, 1987.

Treat, Ida. *La Croisière Secrète.* Paris: Gallimard, 1939.

Wheatley, Paul. "The Land of Zanj: Exegetical Notes on Chinese Knowledge of East Africa prior to AD 1500." In *Geographers and the Tropics.* London: Green, 1964.

General Works

Abir, Mordechai. "Ethiopia and the Horn of Africa, 1600–1790." In *The Cambridge History of Africa,* vol. 4. New York: Cambridge University Press, 1977.

Beke, Charles T. *The French and the English in the Red Sea.* London: 1862.

Clark, John Desmond. *The Prehistoric Cultures of the Horn of Africa.* Cambridge: 1954.

Cole, Sonia. *The Prehistory of East Africa.* London: Pelican Books, 1954.

Coupland, Reginald, Sir. *East Africa and Its Invaders.* London: Faber and Faber, 1956.

————. *The Exploitation of East Africa, 1856–1890: The Slave Trade and the Scramble.* London: Faber and Faber, 1939.

Deschamps, Hubert, and Menard Decary. *Côte des Somalis—Réunion—Inde.* Paris: Edition Berger-Levrault, 1948.

Doresse, Jean. *Histoire Sommaire de la Corne Orientale de l'Afrique*. Paris: Paul Geuthner, 1971.

Hachette, René. *Djibouti. Au Seuil de l'Orient*. Paris: A. Redier, 1930.

Marston, T. E. *Britain's Imperial Role in the Red Sea Area, 1800–1878*. Hamden, Conn.: Shoe-String Press, 1961.

Mauham, R. C. F. "Early History of the East African Coast." In *United Empire* 5 (September 1914).

Mohamed Nuh Ali. "History in the Horn of Africa: 1000 BC–1500 AD. Aspects of Social and Economic Changes between the Rift Valley and the Indian Ocean." Ph.D. dissertation, University of California, Los Angeles, 1985.

Oberlé, Philippe. "Afars et Issas. Des Haines Ataviques à la Coexistence." *RFEPA* (January 1973).

Oberlé, Philippe, and Pierre Hugot. *Histoire de Djibouti: Des Origines à la République*. Paris: Présence Africaine, 1985.

Oliver, R., and G. Mathew. *History of East Africa,* vol. 1. 5th ed. London: Oxford University Press, 1976.

Rubenson, S. "Ethiopia and the Horn of Africa, 1790–1870." In *The Cambridge History of Africa*, vol. 5. New York: Cambridge University Press, 1977.

Sommer, John. *A Study Guide of Ethiopia and the Horn of Africa*. Boston: Boston University, 1969.

Tamrat, Taddesse. "Ethiopia, the Red Sea and the Horn, 1050–1600." In *The Cambridge History of Africa*, vol. 3. New York: Cambridge University Press, 1977.

Thompson,Virginia, and Richard Adloff. *Djibouti and the Horn of Africa*. Stanford, Calif.: Stanford University Press, 1968.

Toussaint, Auguste. *Histoire de l'Océan Indien*. Paris: Presses Universitaires de France, 1961.

Wauthier, Claude, and Hervé Bourges. "La Corne de l'Afrique." In *Les 50 Afriques,* vol. 2. Paris: Editions du Seuil, 1979.

HISTORY

Abdourahman Said. "Les Principaux Facteurs d'Islamisation de la Corne de l'Afrique." Master's thesis, Université de Bordeaux, 1987.

Adawa Hassan Ali. "Djibouti: Un Etat en question." DEA thesis in history, Université Paul Valéry, Montpellier, 1992–1993.

Albospeyre, Max. *La Côte Française des Somalis. Problèmes Economiques et Politiques*. Centre d'Etudes Musulmanes, December 1957.

————. "Panorama et Perspectives de la Côte Française des Somalis." *RHA* (1965).

Alvarez, Ernest-Eugène. *Obock et Abyssinie.* Paris: Baudoin, 1894.

Angoulvant, G. *Djibouti, Mer Rouge, Abyssinie.* Paris: J. André, 1902.

Aramis Houmed Soule. "Quelques Données Historiques Relatives à l'Origine des Populations du Royaume Adal du Moyen-Age." In *Proceedings of the 10th ICES.* Paris: *ICES,* 1988.

Aubert de la Rûe, Edgar. "Action Militaire en Côte Française des Somalis. 1939–1945." *RHA,* Documentation Etat-Major des Forces Armées en CFS (1965).

————. *La Somalie Française.* Paris: Gallimard, 1939.

Austen, Ralph A. "The Islamic Red Sea Slave Trade: An Effort at Quantification." In *Proceedings of the 5th ICES.* Chicago: *ICES,* 1979.

Awad Daoud Mohamed. "Les Afars dans la Corne d'Afrique." DEA thesis, Institut des Relations Internationales, Cairo.

Bacquart, André. *Une Colonie de Commerce Française. Etude sur le Protectorat de la Côte Somali.* Paris: Bonvalot-Jouve, 1907.

Banabila. "L'Effort Français à la CFS." Typescript document, Djibouti, 1950.

Beckwith, Carol. *African Ark: People and Ancient Cultures of Ethiopia and the Horn of Africa.* New York: H. N. Abrams, 1990.

Beckwith, Carol, and Angela Fisher. *La Corne de l'Afrique.* Paris: Chêne, 1990.

Berger, Henri. "Le Blocus de Djibouti." *Revue des Deux Mondes* (March–April 1943): 60–71.

Bernard-Dutreil, Maurice. *Djibouti, Création d'une Colonie Française.* Paris: V. Giard et E. Brière, 1900.

Bertin, Francine. "Les Chefs Issa Signataires des Traités avec le Gouvernement Français." *Le Pount,* no. 12 (1973).

Bonnefon, Edmond. "Côte Française des Somalis et Dépendances." In *L'Afrique Politique en 1900,* pp. 439-443. Paris: Charles Lavauzelle, 1901.

Bonnet, P. "Côte Française des Somalis. Son Passé." *Etudes d'Outre-Mer* (January 1954).

Borlée, M. *La Côte Française des Somalis.* Paris: 1947.

Bouet, Colonel. *Historique du Bataillon Somali.* Rochefort-sur-Mer, 1931.

Brockett, A. M. "The British Somaliland Protectorate to 1905." Ph.D. dissertation, Oxford, Lincoln College, 1969.

Brunschwig, Henri. "Une Colonie Inutile: Obock, 1862–1888." *CEA,* vol. 8, no. 8 (1968).

Callières, Nils de. "L'Abolition de l'Esclavage à Tadjourah." *L'Illustration,* no. 2543 (March 1, 1890).

Cassanelli, Lee V. *The Shaping of Somali Society: Reconstructing the History of a Pastoral People, 1600–1900.* Philadelphia: University of Pennsylvania Printing Press, 1982.

Cassim Ahmed Dini. "Contribution à l'Histoire du Peuple Afar." DEA thesis, IEP de Bordeaux, 1986.

Catroux, Général. *Dans la Bataille de Méditerranée, 1943–1944,* chap. 14. Paris: Editions Julliand–Témoignages et Commentaires 1950.

Champion, Paul. "Djibouti et la Question des Voies d'Accès à l'Abyssinie Italienne." Second-year thesis, ENFOM, 1939.

Chedeville, Edouard. "Les Forces Armées de la C.F.S." *Tropiques: Revue des Troupes Coloniales* (May 1955).

Christopher, John Barret. "Ethiopia. The Jibouti Railway and the Powers 1899–1906." Ph.D. dissertation, Harvard University, 1942.

Coats, Peter D. "Factor of Intermediacy in 19th-Century Africa: The Case of the Issa of the Horn." In *Proceedings of the Second International Congress of Somali Studies,* vol. 2, edited by Thomas Labahn, pp. 175-199. University of Hamburg: August 1–6, 1983.

David, A. H. "La Colonie Française d'Obock." *Bulletin de la Société de Géographie de Lille*, vol. 3 (1884): 141–166.

Delahaye, T. "Djibouti et la Côte Française des Somalis." *La Revue Maritime,* no. 191 (1962).

Delvert, Charles. "Djibouti." *Revue des Deux Mondes* (February 15, 1936): 669–682.

Denizet, J. "Du Bal de la Marine à la Côte Française des Somalis." *Neptunia,* no. 16 (1949).

Deschamps (Lieutenant). *Le Commerce des Armes à la Côte Française des Somalis.* Paris: Imprimerie Nationale, 1907.

Deschamps, Hubert. *Le Roi de la Brousse.* Nancy: Edition Berger Levrault, Mémoires d'Autres Mondes. 1975.

———. "La Côte Française des Somalis." In *La Côte Française des Somalis, Réunion, Inde.* Paris: Berger-Levrault, 1948.

Desiré, Captain. *Historique Sommaire de la Milice.* Djibouti: 1967.

———. "Les Troupes Somalies Pendant les Deux Guerres Mondiales." *RHA,* no. 4 (1963).

Desplanches, H. "Les Vichyssitudes de Djibouti; Matériaux pour une Etude Politico-Militaire de la Somalie au Tournant de 1940." DEA thesis, Université d'Aix-en-Provence, 1992.

Djama Omar Idleh. "L'Histoire de la Langue Arabe en République de Djibouti." Master's thesis, Université de Bordeaux III, 1989–1990.

Duarte, Barbosa. *A Description of the Coasts of East Africa and Malabar in the Beginning of the 16th Century,* translated by E. J. Stanley. London: The Hakluyt Society, 1866.

Dubois, Colette. *Djibouti, 1887–1967. Héritage ou Frustration?* Paris: L'Harmattan, 1997.

———. "L'Onde des Indépendances sur l'Evolution Politique de la Côte Française des Somalis (1958–1967)." In *L'Afrique Noire Française: L'Heure des Indépendances,* pp. 629-645. Paris: Editions CNRS, 1993.

———. "Des Résolutions Novatrices au Désenchantement. L'ONU et la Décolonisation de la Corne de l'Afrique (1948–1977)." *Relations Internationales,* no. 77 (1994): 81–98.

Emerit, Marcel. "Le Premier Projet d'Etablissement Français sur la CFS." *RFHOM,* no. 179 (1963): 189–196.

Esme, Jean d'. "Côte Française des Somalis." In *Le Domaine Colonial Français.* Paris: Editions du Cygne, 1930.

Ferry, V. *Des Patates en Zinc: l'Armée de l'Air en Côte Française des Somalis de 1940 à 1944.* Vincennes, Djibouti: SHAA, 1977.

Flory, Maurice. "L'Indépendance de Djibouti." *Annuaire Français du Droit International* 23 (1977): 295–306.

Fontpertuis, F. de. "Les Français sur la Côte Orientale d'Afrique (Obock, le Choa et l'Abyssinie)." *BSGE* (1883): 474–481.

Fontrier, Captain. "Aboubaker Pacha. Commerce et Diplomatie dans le Golfe de Tadjourah." Master's thesis, INALCO, Paris.

Fouquet, G. *Mer Rouge.* Paris: J. Suse, 1946.

Foster, William, Sir. *The Red Sea and Adjacent Countries at the Close of the 17th Century.* London: 1949.

Frantz, Georges-Félix. *Djibouti: Oeuvres Françaises—Avant, Pendant et Après le Conflit Italo-Éthiopien.* Lyon: Editions Lugdunum, 1937.

Gaffarel, Paul. "Obock." *BSNG,* vol. 1 (1897): 123–126.

Gaudillière, Commander. *Ciels d'Empire.* Paris: Edition Jean Renard, Collection Tropiques, 1942.

Geschekter, Charles L. "Anticolonialism and Class Formation in the Eastern Horn of Africa before 1950." *IJAHS,* vol. 18, no. 1 (1985): 1–32.

Gilmour, Thomas Lennox. *Abyssinia, the Ethiopian Railway and the Powers.* London: Alston River, 1906.

Goltdammer, F. *Notice sur Obock, Colonie Française.* Paris: Imprimerie Arnous de Rivière, 1877.

Griaule, Marcel. "Mission Dakar-Djibouti." Rapport Général. *JSA,* vols.1 and 3 (1932).

Guillot, E. *La Mer Rouge et l'Abyssinie.* Lille: Imprimerie de L. Danel, 1890.

Guillain, M. *La Colonisation Française au Pays des Somalis.* Paris: Jouve (n.d.).

Hafiz, Mahmassani. *Djibouti, Côte Française des Somalis.* Beirut: Dar-el-Assima, 1965.

Hallo Aboubaker Houmed. "Djibouti: Evolution Politique (1966–1977)." Master's thesis in history, Université de Bordeaux III, 1981.

Hemous, R. *Le Territoire Français des Afars et des Issas sur la Scène Internationale.* Paris: IEP, 1968.

Hersi Ali. "The Arab Factor in Somali History: The Origins and Development of Arab Enterprise and Cultural Influence in the Somali Peninsula." Ph.D. dissertation, University of California, Los Angeles, 1977.

Hoffmann, Bernardin, Monseigneur. "Historique de la Mission de Djibouti." *Vivante Afrique,* no. 247 (1967).

Imbert-Vier, Simon. "Djibouti et la Politique Française des Années 30 aux Années 50." Master's thesis in history, Université de Nice, 1985.

Ismael Wais. "Djibouti: The Political Stability of a Small State in a Troubled Area." In *Proceedings of the Second International Congress of Somali Studies,* vol. 2, edited by Thomas Labahn. University of Hamburg: August 1–6, 1983.

Joint-Daguenet, Roger. *Aux Origines de l'Implantation Française en Mer Rouge (Vie et Mort d'Henri Lambert, Consul de France à Aden, 1859).* Paris: L'Harmattan, 1992.

———. *Histoire de la Mer Rouge (de Moïse à Bonaparte).* Paris: Perrin, 1995.

———. *Histoire Moderne des Somalis.* Paris: L'Harmattan, 1994.

Jouin, Yves, Lieutenant Colonel. *La Côte Française des Somalis de 1936 à 1940. RHA,* vol. 19, no. 4 (1963).

Jourdain, H., and C. Dupont. *D'Obock à Djibouti.* Paris: Larose, 1933.

Kammerer, Albert. *La Mer Rouge, l'Abyssinie et l'Arabie depuis l'Antiquité.* Paris: Institut Fondamental d'Archéologie Orientale, 1935.

Killion, Tom C. "Railroad Workers and the Ethiopian Imperial State: The Politics of Workers' Organization on the Franco-Ethiopian Railroad, 1919–1959." *IJAHS,* vol. 25, no. 3 (1992).

Kollbrunner, Ulrich. "Die Eisenbahn von Djibouti nach Harar." *JGEG* 4 (1903–1904).

Labrousse, Henri, Admiral. "L'Affaire de Sagallo." *Le Réveil de Djibouti* (December 1961).

———. "Le Blocus de Djibouti." *Histoire pour Tous,* no. 202 (February 1977).

———. "La C.F.S. et son Avenir." *Tropiques* (March 1959).

———. "L'Épopée Portugaise en Mer Rouge (1507–1560)." *Le Pount,* no. 10.

———. "Les Expéditions Maritimes Françaises du XVIIIe Siècle en Mer Rouge et au Yémen." *Le Pount,* no. 6 (1968); also, *Tropiques,* no. 403 (February 1958).

———. "Le Mad Mullah du Somaliland (Vingt ans de Guerre et de Révoltes)." *Le Pount,* no. 7 (1969).

———. "Le Mad Mullah du Somaliland (Suite et Fin)." *Le Pount,* no. 8 (1970)

———. "La Mer Rouge et l'Expédition de Bonaparte en Egypte." *Le Pount,* no. 2 (1967).

———. "Les Négociants Marseillais à Cheikh-Saïd à la Fin du 19e Siècle." *Le Pount,* no. 3 (1967).

———. "L'Occupation Égyptienne de la Côte des Somalis (1874–1884)." Typescript document, Table Ronde d'Histoire de l'Océan Indien, Sénanque, May 1978.

———. "L'Océan Indien sans le Canal de Suez." *Le Pount,* no. 11 (1973).

———. "Renaud de Châtillon, Héros de Légende et la Conquête de la Mer Rouge par les Croisés (1183)." *Le Pount,* no. 9 (1971)

———. "Une Tentative d'Implantation Russe en Côte Française des Somalis en 1889." *Le Pount,* no. 5 (1968).

Lacour, G. "L'Enseignement en Côte Française des Somalis." *Le Réveil de Djibouti* (October–November 1961).

Lagarde, Léonce. *Notice Coloniale sur le Territoire d'Obock.* Melun: Imprimerie Administrative, 1885.

———. "Présentation de la Colonie d'Obock." *Le Tour du Monde* (1885–1886).

Lebrun, G. *Djibouti, Terre Nécessaire et Menacée.* Paris: Le Cerf, 1956.

Le Maresquier, E. *Les Sources de l'Histoire des Pays de l'Océan Indien aux Archives de la Marine.* Paris: 1979.

Lemoine, Robert. "La Côte Française des Somalis." In *La France de l'Océan Indien.* Paris: Editions Géographie Maritime et Coloniale, 1952.

Lepointe, Henri. *La Colonisation Française au Pays des Somalis.* Paris: Librairie Jouve, 1913.

Leroux, Rémi. *Le Réveil de Djibouti, 1968–1977. Simple Outil de Propagande ou Véritable Reflet d'une Société?* Paris: L'Harmattan, 1998.

Lewis, I. M. "The Somali Conquest of the Horn of Africa." *JAH* 1:2 (1960).

———. *Peoples of the Horn of Africa: Somali, Afar and Saho.* London: International African Institute, 1955.

———. *Nationalism and Self-Determination in the Horn of Africa.* Ithaca, N.Y.: Cornell University Press, 1983.

Lewis, David Levering. *The Race to Fashoda*. New York: Weidenfeld and Nicolson, 1988.

Lippmann, Alphonse. *Guerriers et Sorciers en Somalie*. Paris: Hachette, 1953.

Lois, Raphael, A. C. "The Cape to Cairo Dream." Ph.D. dissertation, Columbia University, 1936.

Martin, B. G. "Muslim Politics and Resistance to Colonial Rule: Sheik Uways b. Muhammad al-Barawi and the Qadiriya Brotherhood in East Africa." *JAH* 10:3 (1969).

Martineau, Alfred. "La Côte des Somalis." In *Histoire des Colonies Françaises et de l'Expansion de la France dans le Monde*, vol. 4. Paris: Plon, 1931.

Meggle, Armand. "La Côte Française des Somalis." In *Madagascar et Dépendances*. Paris: Société Française d'Edition, 1931.

———. "Notice Illustrée sur la Côte Française des Somalis." *La Presse Coloniale* (1931).

Michel, Marc. *La Mission Marchand, 1895–1899*. Paris: Mouton, 1972.

Michel-Cote, Charles. *Vers Fachoda*. Paris: Plon, 1900.

———. "La Côte Française des Somalis et les Intérêts et les Droits de la France en Ethiopie." *Bulletin de l'Union des Chambres de Commerce Mixtes et Etrangères* (1936).

———. *La Situation de la CFS et le Chemin de fer Franco-Ethiopien d'Addis Abeba*. Paris: Académie des Sciences Coloniales, 1945.

Minne, Lucien. "Souvenirs sur la Naissance de Djibouti." Typescript document, Paris, 1964.

———. "Lettre sur l'Administration Lagarde." Typescript document, Mont-Saint-Aignan, 1964.

Mohamed Elmi Osman. "La Politique de la Grande Bretagne dans la Corne de l'Afrique, 1897–1914." Master's thesis in history, Paris Sorbonne,1987.

———. "Djibouti et la Seconde Guerre Mondiale." *Revue de l'ISERST,* no. 3 (1988).

———. "Djibouti. Le Commerce et le Transport." *Revue de l'ISERST,* no. 6 (1992).

———. "Note sur l'Etat des Archives Relatives à l'Histoire de Djibouti." *Revue des Etudes Djiboutiennes* (1994).

Montagnon, G. H. *L'Enfer de Djibouti, 1940–1942*. Vincennes: SHAA, 1950.

———. "Blocus à Djibouti." *Historia Magazine* (March 1968): 635–644.

———. "Historique du Bataillon Somali." *RHA* (1973).

Morgan, Edward. "The 1977 Elections in Djibouti: A Tragi-Comic End to French Colonial Rule." *Horn of Africa* 1:3 (1978).

Mugnier-Pollet, J. F., and A. M. Leduff. "Esquisse Historique du TFAI." *Trait d'Union*, no. 1 (1974).

Natsoulas, Théodore. "The Greeks in Ethiopia." Ph.D. dissertation, Syracuse University, 1975.

Naville, Edouard. *Francia Contré Italia in Africa La Questione di Gibouti.* Milan: La Prora, 1939.

O'Mahoney, Kevin. "The Salt Trail." *JES* 8:2 (1970):147–154.

Pankhurst, Richard. "The Franco-Ethiopian Railway." *Ethiopian Observer* 4 (1963): 342–379.

———. "Italian Fascist Claims to the Port of Jibuti, 1935–1941: An Historical Note." *Ethiopian Observer* 14:1 (1971).

———. "The Banyan or Indian Presence at Massawa. The Dahlak Islands and the Horn of Africa." *JES* 7:1 (1974): 185–212.

Picquart, Agnès. "Le Commerce des Armes à Djibouti de 1888 à 1914." *RFHOM,* no. 213 (1971).

Pilatte, L. W. "Obock et ses Dépendances." *BSGM*, vol. 18 (1894): 111–120.

Poinsot, Jean-Paul. *Djibouti et la CFS.* Paris: Hachette, 1964.

———. "Ainsi Naquit Djibouti." *Le Réveil de Djibouti* (October 10,1959–March 12, 1960).

Polydenot, G. *Obock, une Station de Ravitaillement pour la Marine Française.* Paris, 1889.

Prijac Luc. "La Côte Française des Somalis: 1938–1942." Master's thesis in history, Université de Paris VII, June 1992.

Ravier, Théodore. "L'Ethiopie et l'Expansion Européenne en Afrique Orientale." Ph.D. dissertation in law, Faculté de Droit de Lyon, A. Rey, 1910.

Rivoyre, Denis de. *Mer Rouge et Abyssinie.* Paris: Plon, 1880.

———. *Les Français à Obock.* Paris: Picard et Kaan and M. Dreyfous, 1887.

———. *Obock, Mascate, Bouchire, Bassorah.* Paris: 1883.

Riyad, Zahir. "Zaila." *Nahdat Ifriqiyya* 2 (September 1958): 65–72.

Rondot, Pierre. "Quelques Remarques sur le Personnage Historique de Mohammed 'Abdillé Hassan." *Le Pount,* no. 7 (1969).

Rouard, de Card E. "Les Possessions Françaises de la Côte Orientale d'Afrique." *Revue Générale de Droit International Public,* vol. 6 (1899).

Rouaud, Alain. "Pour une Histoire des Arabes de Djibouti, 1896–1977." *CAF* 146, 37-2 (1997): 319–348.

Santelli. "La Côte Française des Somalis." *L'Economie* (January 1952).

Saussus, Roger. "Le Territoire Français des Afars et des Issas." *Vivante Afrique* (1967).

Schneyder, Philippe. "Le Dossier Djibouti." *Communautés et Continents* (October–December 1966).

Simonin, L. "Voyages de M. Henri Lambert Agent Consulaire de France à Aden, 1855–1859." *Le Tour du Monde*, vol. 2 (1862b): 65–80.

Siriex, Paul-Henri. "Djibouti et ses Problèmes." *France-Outre-Mer* (March 1956).

———. *Souvenirs en Vérité, 1930–1980. Oxford, Londres, Afrique, Madagascar, Djibouti, Inde.* Paris: Edition des Ecrivains, 1998.

Trampont, Jacques. *Djibouti Hier, de 1887 à 1939.* Paris: Hâtier, 1990.

———. "Djibouti: Port Colonial Français de 1896 à 1940." Master's thesis in history, Université de Paris VII–Jussieu, 1983.

Trimingham, J. S. *History of Islam in East Africa.* Oxford: Clarendon Press, 1964.

Tubiana, Joseph. "Alfred Bardey à Zeila en 1880." *Le Pount,* no. 11 (1973).

Uzel, B. "La Fondation de Djibouti." *RHCF* 39 (1952): 63–75.

Valran, G. "Contribution à l'Histoire de la Somalie Française." *Revue Indigène* (1928): 234–235.

Van Gelder de Pineda, Rosanna. *Le Chemin de fer de Djibouti à Addis Abeba.* Paris: L'Harmattan, 1995.

Vazeilles, Benoit. "L'Évolution Politique du TFAI depuis 1967." *RFEPA* (1976).

Viator, P. "Obock et les Possessions Françaises du Golfe d'Aden." *BSGCH* (1896): 148–157.

Vigneras, Sylvain. *Notice sur la Côte Française des Somalis.* Paris: Imprimerie Poupont, 1900.

War Office. *Memorandum on Our Relations with French Somaliland.* October 1941.

Youssouf Ibrahim. "Structures Villageoises dans le Nord de la République de Djibouti." Master's thesis in history, Université de Montpellier.

POLITICS

International Relations

Abdi, Said Yusuf. "The Mini-Republic of Djibouti: Problems and Prospects." *Horn of Africa,* vol.1 (April–June 1978): 35–40.

Abir, Mordechai. "The Contentious Horn of Africa." *Conflict Studies* 24 (1972).

———. "Red Sea Politics." *Conflicts in Africa,* no. 94 (1972).

Absieh, Omar Warsama, and Maurice Botbol. *Djibouti: Les Institutions Politiques et Militaires.* Paris: Editions Lettre de l'Océan Indien, 1986.

Adawa Hassan Ali. "Djibouti: Un Etat en Question." DEA thesis in history and civilizations, Université Paul Valéry, Montpellier, 1993.

Aden Robleh Awaleh. *Djibouti, Clef de la Mer Rouge.* Paris: Editions Caractères, 1986.

Adou, Abdallah A. *The Afar: A Nation on Trial.* Stockholm: Abdallah A. Adou, 1993.

———. "Ethnicity and Foreign Relations: The Case of Djibouti." Master's thesis in political science, University of Stockholm, 1989.

Agnofer, Fantu. "Djibouti's Three-Front Struggle for Independence: 1967–1977." Ph.D. dissertation, University of Denver, 1979.

Ali Coubba. *Le Mal Djiboutien.* Paris: L'Harmattan, 1996.

———. *Djibouti, une Nation en Otage.* Paris: L'Harmattan, 1993.

———. *Ahmed Dini et la Politique à Djibouti.* Paris: L'Harmattan, 1999.

Amnesty International. "Djibouti: Prisoners of Conscience—Unfair Trial by Security Tribunal." Press release, December 3, 1992.

———. "Djibouti: Torture et Emprisonnement Politique." Press release, November 6, 1991.

Aramis Houmed Soule. "Ethiopian Afars: Adapting to New Realities." *The Ethiopian Herald,* vol. 49, no. 133 (February19, 1993).

Baa, Frans. Coopération UE-Djibouti. *Le Courrier,* no. 153 (September–October, 1995), 29–31.

Bell, J. Bowyer. *The Horn of Africa.* New York: Crane, Russak Co., 1973.

Bereket Habteselassie. *Conflict and Intervention in the Horn of Africa.* New York: Monthly Review Press, 1980.

Bouden, Majid. "Spécial Djibouti." *Le Monde Arabe* (1979).

Briand, P. "La RDD est Née dans le Calme." *Le Monde* (June 28, 1977).

———. "L'Économie Souffre Gravement des Combats en Ethiopie." *Le Monde* (June 30, 1977).

Brisset, Claire. "Du Soleil, des Pierres et des Idées." *Jeune Afrique,* no. 1197 (December 14, 1983).

———. "Les Réfugiés de la Corne." *Le Monde* (April 26, 1979): 8.

Chabaane, Hamid. "Djibouti, Terre de Volonté." *Jeune Afrique,* no. 1544 (August 7, 1990): 42–72.

Chabalier, H. "Djibouti aux Portes de la Guerre." *Le Matin* (September 6, 1977).

Champion, Paul. "Djibouti et la Question des Voies d'Accès à l'Abyssinie Italienne." Thesis, ENFOM, 1939.

Chapuisat, L. J. "La Côte Française des Somalis." Master's thesis in political science, Paris, 1967.

Cissoko, V. "Un Régime Vulnérable." *Jeune Afrique,* no. 1372 (April 22, 1987).

Comte, Alain. "Djibouti: L'Indépendance sans Liberté." *Le Monde Diplomatique* (December 1979):19.

Couteau Begarie, Hervé. *Géostratégie de l'Océan Indien.* Paris: Economica, 1993.

Crisp, J. "The Politics of Repatriation: Ethiopian Refugees in Djibouti 1977–1983." *Review of African Political Economy* (September 1984).

Darcourt, P. "Djibouti: Présence Française Maintenue." *Le Figaro* (August 27, 1984).

De Backer, Roger. "Djibouti: Payer le Prix de la Paix." *Le Courrier,* no. 153 (September–October 1995): 14–19.

Decraene, Philippe. "Un Nationaliste Combatif et Intransigeant." *Le Monde* (July 14, 1977).

———. "L'Attentat de Djibouti." *Le Monde* (December 18–19, 1977).

———. "Veillée d'Armes aux Portes d'un Empire Défunt." *Le Monde* (February 25–27, 1978).

———. "Djibouti ou la Démocratie en Question." *Le Monde* (September 8, 1982): 16.

Delvert, Charles. "Djibouti." *Revue des Deux Mondes* (February 1936): 681.

Desjardin, T. *Les Rebelles d'Aujourd'hui.* Paris: Presses de la Cité, 1977.

———. *La Poudre et le Pouvoir.* Paris: Nathan, 1977.

Dives, E. "Chez les Afars et les Issas." Thesis No. 3861, CHEAM, Paris, 1963.

Drysdale, John. "The Problems of French Somaliland." *Africa Report,* 11 (November 8, 1966).

Ebo Houmed Alwane. "Djibouti: Tensions Socio-Politiques sur Fond de Succession." *Afrique Politique,* pp. 85–109. Bordeaux: CEAN, 1997.

Economist, The. *The Peaceful Profiteer.* October 3, 1987, p. 45.

Erouart-Siad, Patrick. "Adieu aux Nostalgies Coloniales." *Autrement,* no. 21 (1987): 189–195.

Farer, Tom J. *War Clouds on the Horn of Africa: The Widening Storm.* New York: Carnegie Endowment for International Peace, 1979.

Fidel, Camille. "Djibouti et le Chemin de Fer Franco-Éthiopien." *Revue des Questions Coloniales et Maritimes* (1916).

Fitzgerald, J. "Gunboat Diplomacy and the Horn." *Horn of Africa,* vol.1, no. 3 (1979).
———. "Djibouti: Petrodollar Protectorate?" *Horn of Africa,* vol.1, no. 3 (1978).
Fomekong, Nestor. "La Décolonisation de Djibouti." Thesis, International Relations Institute of Yaounde, 1977.
Francis, Samuel T. "Conflict in the Horn of Africa." *JSPS,* vol. 2 (fall 1977): 155–168.
Gaillard, William J., and Margo Hammond. "The New Republic of Djibouti and Maneuvers in the Red Sea." *New Leader,* vol. 60 (July 4, 1977): 6–8.
Gascon, Alain. "Intégration Économique, Intégration Nationale et Irrédentisme: Le Harar, la Rivalité Somalo-Éthiopienne et l'Emprise de Djibouti." Fifth Conference on the Horn of Africa, April 27–28, 1989, East Lansing, Mich.
Gascon, Alain, and Roland Marchal. *La Corne après les Dictatures.* Paris: EHESS, 1991.
Gaudio, Attilio. "Djibouti, Entre les 'Appétits' Somalien et Éthiopien." *Remarques Africaines,* no. 504 (May 1, 1977).
Gilguy, Christine. *La Question Nationale Djiboutienne.* Bordeaux: IEP, Report 1989–1990.
Goum, Ali. *Djibouti, Création Française et Bastion de l'Empire.* Paris: CAF, 1939.
Guillebaud, Jean-Claude. "Djibouti ou le Temps Suspendu." *Le Monde* (April 2–4, 1974).
———. *Les Confettis de l'Empire.* Paris: Le Seuil, 1976.
Hassan Gouled Aptidon. "La Côte des Somalis, la France et les Autres." *Union Française et Parlement,* no. 85 (July 1957).
———. *Ma Vie Politique pendant Treize Années, 1949–1962.* Typescript document, Djibouti, 1963.
Henze, Paul B. *The United States and the Horn of Africa: History and Current Challenge.* Santa Monica, Calif: Rand, 1990.
Hughes, A. "France: The Reluctant Colonialist?" *Africa Report,* vol. 2, no. 6 (1975).
Idriss Ali Abdallah. "La Coopération Bilatérale entre la République de Djibouti et la République Fédérale Démocratique d'Ethiopie (1977–1996)." Diplomatique Traineeship Report, International Relations Institute of Yaounde, June 1998.
Jarry, I. "Djibouti, Dix Ans d'Indépendance." *Le Figaro* (June 29, 1987).
———. "Oasis de Paix dans une Zone Turbulente." *Le Figaro* (August 15, 1987).

Jeambar, Denis. "Djibouti: Tracer la Voie." *Echanges,* no. 5 (1990): 16–24.

Jeune Afrique. *L'Opposition Décapitée.* Paris: Editions Jeune Afrique, no. 1082, September 30, 1981.

Journal Officiel de la République Française. "Loi Portant Approbation, de la Convention Conclue le 6 Janvier 1902 entre le Protectorat de la CFS et la Compagnie Impériale des Chemins de Fer Ethiopiens, Suivie du Texte de la Convention." February 8, 1902.

Kenfe, Daniel. *The Conflicting Natural Interests of Ethiopia and Somalia on the French Territory of Afar and Issa.* The Hague: The Hague Institute of Social Studies, 1974.

Koburger, J. R., and Captain W. Charles. *Naval Strategy East of Suez: The Role of Djibouti.* New York: Praeger, 1992.

Lamarche, Gabriel. "Djibouti: La Fin des Beaux Jours." *Politique Internationale,* no. 61 (1993).

Laudouze, André. "Djibouti, une République à l'Échelle Humaine." *France-Pays Arabes,* no. 87 (June 1978): 28–30.

———. "La Démocratie à Djibouti." *Le Monde* (September 24, 1982).

———. *Djibouti, Nation Carrefour.* Paris: Karthala, 1982.

Légume, Collin. *Conflict in the Horn of Africa.* New York: Africana Publishing, 1977.

Légume, Collin, and B. Lee. *The Horn of Africa in Continuing Crisis.* New York: Africana Publishing, 1975.

Leymarie, Philippe. "La Ligue Populaire Africaine pour l'Indépendance." *RFEPA* (April 1976).

———. "Naissance de la République de Djibouti." *Marché Tropicaux et Méditerranéens,* no. 1651 (July 1977).

———. "La République de Djibouti entre l'Afrique Noire et le Monde Arabe." *RFEPA* (November 1977).

———. "Début d'Indépendance Difficile à Djibouti." *RFEPA,* no. 154 (October 1978).

Makinda, S. M. *Superpower Diplomacy in the Horn of Africa.* New York: St. Martins, 1987.

Malecot, Georges. "Raisons de la Présence Française à Djibouti." *RFEPA* (1973).

———. "Djibouti, Demain l'Indépendance." *L'Afrique et l'Asie Modernes,* no. 112 (1977).

Mallet, Roger. "Djibouti: Problèmes Ethniques et Politiques." *Revue de Défense Nationale* (December 1966).

Marchal, Roland. "Conflits et Recomposition d'un Ordre Régional dans la Corne de l'Afrique." *Etudes Internationales,* vol. 22, no. 2 (June 1991).

————. "Mitterrand, Djibouti et la Corne de l'Afrique." *Politique Africaine,* no. 58 (June 1995): 65–83.

————. "The Post Civil War Somali Business Class." Typescript document, Paris, European Commission/Somalia Unit Report, September 1996.

Markakis, John. *National and Class Conflicts in the Horn of Africa.* Cambridge: Cambridge University Press, 1987.

Marks, T. A. "Djibouti: Strategic French Toe-hold in Africa." *African Affairs,* vol. 73, no. 290 (1974).

Monde, Le. "L'Accord Relatif au Chemin de Fer Dire Dawa–Addis Abeba." Paris, May 24, 1945.

Nation, La. "Un Attentat à la Bombe Ravage le Café L'Historil." Djibouti, Imprimerie Nationale, March 26, 1987.

Notes Documentaires et Etudes. "Djibouti et le Chemin de Fer Franco-Ethiopien." No.122 (1945).

Omar Osman Rabeh. *Le Cercle et la Spirale.* Paris: Les Lettres Libres, 1984.

————. *République de Djibouti ou Roue de Secours d'Ethiopie?* Paris: Ateliers Silex, 1986.

————. *L'Etat et le Pansomalisme.* Paris: Le Darwish, 1988.

Osman, Sultan Ali. "Djibouti: The Only Stable Country in the Horn of Africa?" *Horn of Africa,* vol. 5, no. 2 (1982): 48–55.

Otayek, René. *La République de Djibouti. Construction Nationale et Contraintes Stratégiques.* Bordeaux: CEAN, 1985.

Pasteau, Michel. "Evolution de la Situation Juridique du Chemin de Fer Djibouti-Addis Abeba." *Proceedings of the 8th ICES.* Addis Abeba: ICES, 1984.

Poidevin, R. "Fabricants d'Armes et Relations Internationales au Début du XXème Siècle." *Relations Internationales* (May 1, 1974): 39–56.

Pomonti, Jean-Claude. "L'Oeil du Cyclone." *Autrement,* no. 21 (1987): 141–147.

Rondot, P. "La Mer Rouge Peut-Elle Devenir un *Lac de Paix Arabe?*" *Revue de la Défense Nationale* (October 1977): 71–84.

Ropp, K. B. V. "The French Territory of Afar and Issa: France's Last Possession on the African Mainland." *Africa,* no. 3: 11–14.

Said Yusuf Abdi. "The Mini-Republic of Djibouti: Problems and Prospects." *Horn of Africa* 1:2 (1978).

Saint-Veran, Robert. *Djibouti: Pawn of the Horn of Africa.* Metuchen, N.J.: Scrarecrow Press, 1981.

Scalabre, Camille. "Deux Années d'Indépendance à Djibouti." *Revue Juridique et Politique* (July–September 1979): 331–336.

Schraeder, Peter J. "La Présence Américaine dans la Corne après la Fin de la Guerre Froide: Ruptures et Permanences." *Politique Africaine,* no. 50 (June 1993): 70–73.

———. "Ethnic Politics in Djibouti." *African Affairs,* no. 367 (April 1993).

Shehim, Kassim, and J. Searing. "Djibouti and the Question of Afar Nationalism." *African Affairs,* vol. 79, no. 315 (April 1980).

Simon Mibrathu. "L'Etat à Djibouti à travers les Rapports Inter-Ethniques." DEA thesis, CEAN, Bordeaux I, 1990.

Skurnik, W. A. E. "Continuing Problems in Africa's Horn." *Current History,* vol. 82 (March 1983).

Soudan, Francois. "La Lutte Armée?" *Jeune Afrique,* no. 967 (July 18, 1979).

Syad, William. "Djibouti, Terre sans Dieu et sans Espoir." Thesis, CHEAM, Paris, 1939.

Tavernier, M. P. "Le Rayonnement de Djibouti." Thesis No. 2919, CHEAM, Paris, 1958.

Terrier, Auguste. "Délimitation de l'Afrique Orientale." *BCAF* 13 (1903).

United Nations. "Assistance to Refugees in Djibouti." Document A/35/409, U.N. Secretary General, New York, 1980.

———. "Assistance to Botswana, Cape Verde, the Comoros, Djibouti, etc." Document A/34/556, New York, U.N. Secretary General, 1979.

———. "Assistance to Djibouti." Document A/34/362, New York, U.N. Secretary General, 1979.

———. "Implementation of the Declaration on the Granting of Independence to Colonial Countries and Peoples; Question of French Somaliland." Document A/32/107, New York, U.N. General Assembly, 1977.

———. "Implementation of the Declaration on the Granting of Independence to Colonial Countries and Peoples; Question of French Somaliland." Document A/32/107/Add. 1, New York, U.N. General Assembly, 1977.

———. "Special Economic and Disaster Relief Assistance: Assistance to Djibouti." Document A/36/281, New York, U.N. Secretary General, 1981.

———. "Assistance to Djibouti." Document A/33/106, New York, U.N. Secretary General, 1978.

Urban, Marion. "Djibouti: Au Carrefour de Toutes les Convoitises." *Le Monde en Développement-Croissance,* no. 348 (1992).

Vali, Ferenc A. *Politics of the Indian Ocean Region: The Balances of Power.* New York: Free Press, 1976.

Yared, Marc. "Le Commencement de la Fin: Djibouti à son Tour." *Jeune Afrique*, no. 1613 (1991): 18–19.

Zelleke, Lij Imru. *The Horn of Africa: A Strategic Survey*. Washington, D.C.: International Security Council, 1989.

Law

Chiroux, René. "Le Nouveau Statut du TFAI." *Recueil Penant, Revue de Droit des Pays d'Afrique*, no. 719 (1968).

———. *Le Problème de la Nationalité en TFAI*. Djibouti, 1974.

———. "La Nationalité en TFAI." *Marchés Tropicaux et Méditerranéens* (June 4, 1976).

———. "Lois Constitutionnelles." *JORD* (June 27, 1977).

Flory, Maurice. "L'Indépendance de Djibouti." *Annuaire Français du Droit International*, 23 (1977): 295–306.

Grignou, G. "Le Droit Coutumier et la Justice chez les Somalis." *RSGCP* (1912).

Hasna Barkat Daoud. "La République de Djibouti et le Droit de la Mer." DEA thesis, Université de Nice-Sophia Antipolis, 1996.

Jacquemin, H. "L'Organisation Judiciaire à Djibouti." *Revue Juridique et Politique*, no. 39 (December 1985): 892–902.

Luchaire, Francois. "Le Conseil Représentatif de la Côte de Somalis." *Recueil Penant de Jurisprudence* (November 1950).

———. "Loi du 3 Juillet 1967 Relative à l'Organisation du TFAI." *JORF* (July 4, 1967): 6643–6647.

Reedo, Jamaleddin Abdulkader. "The Afar Customary Law." Type document, Assab, 1973.

ECONOMY

Agriculture, Industry, Transport

Abdallah Mohamed Kamil. "Les Incidences de la Fiscalité sur la Vie Économique du TFAI." *Le Pount*, no. 4 (1968).

Ali Aref Bourhan. "Le Port de Djibouti Joue à Plein son Rôle de Station-Service." *Communauté France-Eurafrique*, vol. 14 (February 1962).

Amat, J. P., M. Esquerre, and Eddine Silah. *L'Agriculture Maraîchère et Fruitière Traditionnelle en République de Djibouti*. Djibouti: ISERST/ACCT, 1981.

Bernard, G. "Le Franco-Ethiopien." In *La Vie du Rail d'Outre-Mer,* no. 119 (February 1964) and no. 141 (December 1965).

Bovet, Louis. "Les Relations Économiques de Djibouti avec l'Ethiopie." In *Etudes d'Outre-Mer* (January 1954).

———. *Evolution Économique et Sociale de la CFS.* Paris: Imprimerie Nationale, 1954.

Camut, Jean-Georges. *Une Expérience de Réalisation Ferroviaire Africaine: Le Chemin de Fer Franco-Ethiopien de Djibouti à Addis Abeba.* Paris: CAF, 1935.

Chabalian, Pascal. "Air Djibouti." *Revue du SGAC,* no. 148 (November 1973).

Clouet, Alain. "La Pêche à Djibouti." *La Revue Maritime,* no. 275 (April 1970): 477–493.

Coats, Peter. *Djibouti et les Ports de la Mer Rouge 1900–1917.* Aix-en-Provence: IHPOM.

Compain, Jacques. "L'Evolution Economique et Sociale de la CFS." *Revue Française,* no. 168 (May 1961).

Coubèche, Said Ali, and J. Prévot. "Djibouti. Deuxième Port de la Communauté Franco-Africaine." *Revue Française,* no. 128 (May 1961).

Dabanian. "Djibouti. Le Port." *Etudes d'Outre-Mer* (January 1954).

Demachne, Georges. "Le Chemin de Fer Français d'Ethiopie." *Revue Française,* vol. 27 (1902).

Desaule, Philippe. *Djibouti.* Djibouti: Editions Chambre de Commerce de Djibouti, 1955.

Douteau, H. P. "Le Port de Commerce de Djibouti." *Marchés Tropicaux et Méditerranéens* (December 1965).

Dubois, Hubert Pierre. *Cheminot de Djibouti à Addis Abeba.* Paris: Perrin, 1959.

Gandillon, Pierre. *Djibouti, Questions Coloniales.* Paris: Société d'Etudes Economiques et Sociales, 1941.

———. "La Côte Française des Somalis." *L'Economie,* supplement no. 335 (January 31, 1952).

Getachew, Kinfe. "Jibuti, the Franco-Ethiopian Railway and the Ethiopian Hinterland." Master's thesis, Haile Selassie I University, Addis Ababa, 1969.

Grossmann, J. "Origines de l'Aéroport de Djibouti." *Revue du SGAC,* no. 148 (November 1973).

Harbeson, J. W. "Afar Pastoralists and Ethiopian Rural Development." *Rural Africana,* no. 28 (1975).

Hawkins, Clifford W. *Les Boutres. Derniers Voiliers de l'Océan Indien.* Lausanne: Edita, 1981.

Jouffrey, Roger. "La République de Djibouti et ses Activités Economiques." *Afrique Contemporaine,* no. 133 (1985): 33–42.

Lanthières, J. G. de la. "Les Débuts d'Air Djibouti." *Revue du SGAC,* no. 148 (November 1973).

Latrémoliere, Jacques. "Djibouti et l'Economie de Service." *Marchés Tropicaux et Méditerrannéens* (October 20, 1978).

Mayer, Pierre. *Investment in the French Territory of the Afar and the Issa.* Djibouti, 1972.

Olagnier, G., and A. Hesse. *La Concession du Chemin de Fer Franco-Ethiopien.* Paris: Librairie Générale de Droit et de Jurisprudence, 1921.

Pasques, G. "Une Immense Réserve de Sel: Le lac Assal en CFS." *Industries et Travaux d'Outre-Mer* (August 1959).

Perrot, Lieutenant Colonel. *Le Chemin de Fer Ethiopien et le Port de Djibouti.* Paris: P. Levé Imprimerie, 1917.

Pujo, Jean-Marie. "Les Boutres à Djibouti: Une Survivance de l'Age de la Voile." *Le Pount,* no. 2 (1967): 9–15.

Shiferaw Bekele. "The Railway Trade and Politics. A Historical Survey (1896–1935)." Master's thesis, Addis Ababa University, 1982.

Simon Mibrathu. "Le Problème de Surreffectif dans les Etablissements Publics de Djibouti: Le Cas du Port." Master's thesis, Université François Rabelais, Tours, 1989.

Souleiman Farah Lodon. "Le Rôle Economique du Port de Commerce de Djibouti. Master's thesis, Institut de Géographie, Nantes, 1969.

Stieltjes, Laurent. *Les Ressources Naturelles du TFAI.* Paris: BRGM, 1972.

Swift, Jeremy. "The Development of Livestock Trading in Nomad Pastoral Economy, the Somali Case." In *Pastoral Production and Society.* Cambridge: Cambridge University Press, 1979.

Terrier, Auguste. *La Concession du Chemin de Fer Franco-Ethiopien.* Paris: Dalloz, 1921.

Trampont, Jacques. "Le Chemin de Fer Djibouti-Addis Abeba." *Historia,* no. 379 (1978).

———. *Le CFE Hier et Aujourd'hui.* Djibouti, 1979.

Traore, Amadou. "Table Ronde: Le Long et Tortueux Chemin vers l'Ajustement Structurel." *Le Courrier,* no. 153 (September–October 1995): 27–28.

Tribunal Civil de la Seine. *La Concession du Chemin de Fer Franco-Ethiopien.* Paris: Librairie Générale de Droit et de Jurisprudence, 1924.

Tourism

Barrère, Pierre. *Un Port dans le Désert.* Paris: Larousse, 1975.

Delabergerie, Guy. *Fleuron de la Mer Rouge, le TFAI.* Boulogne: Delroisse, 1972.

Fontaine, P. "Au Carrefour de l'Enfer." *Connaissance du Monde,* no. 43 (June 1962).

Galves, Georges. *TFAI. Djibouti.* Boulogne: Delroisse, 1973.

———. *De Djibouti aux Comores.* Paris: Larousse, 1974.

Laurent, Alain, Ali M. Abdallah, and Baragoita S. Mohamed. "L'Ecotourisme par les 'Caravanes de Sel': Des Valeurs Partagées." *Les Cahiers Espaces,* spécial Tourisme et Environnement (February 1993): 239–250.

Rivals, René. *Le Guide de Djibouti.* Paris: Vilo, 1998

ANTHROPOLOGY, ETHNOLOGY, SOCIOLOGY

Abbadie, Antoine d'. "Les Somalis." In *Géographie de l'Ethiopie.* Paris: 1890.

Abdallah Mohamed Kamil. "Aspects Sociologiques de la Fi'ma." *Le Pount,* no. 3 (1967).

Abdulkader Moussa Ali. "Histoire Politico-Sociale des Afars du 12° au 16° Siècle." DEA thesis, Université Sorbonne-René Descartes, Paris, 1980.

Ahmed Dini Ahmed. "La Fi'ma. Différents Types d'Organisation et Fonctionnement." *Le Pount,* no. 3 (1967).

Ali Moussa Iye. *Le Verdict de l'Arbre.* Dubai: International Printing Press, 1990.

Aramis Houmed Soule. "Un Exemple du Pouvoir Traditionnel Afar: Le Sultanat de Tadjourah." *Le Pount,* no. 17 (1986).

———. "Le Fondement de l'Absuma chez les Afars." *La Nation* (February 1984).

———. "Sultanat de Tadjourah: La Succession Est Assurée." *La Nation* (April 1985).

———. "Les Rites Funèbres chez les Afars (Rabeyna)." *La Nation* (March 7, 1985).

———. "La *Qalla*: Solidarité et Art de Vivre." *La Nation* (February 20, 1986).

———. "La Procédure du Règlement d'un Crime de Sang chez les Afars." *Bulletin de l'ADEN,* no. 3 (February 1995).

Association Djiboutienne pour l'Equilibre et la Promotion de la Famille.

"Situation et Perspectives Juridiques, Politiques et Economiques de la Femme Djiboutienne." Report, Djibouti, June 1995.

Augustin, P. "Quelques Dénombrements de la Population du TFAI." *Le Pount,* no. 13 (1974) and no. 15 (1975).

Barton, J. "The Origins of the Galla and Somali Tribes." *JEANHS,* no. 19 (1924): 6–11.

Bernard, M. "Description de la Circoncision Dite *Moha.* Côte Française des Somalis." *JSA,* 4:1 (1934).

Bertin, Francine. "L'Ougas des Issas." *Le Pount,* no. 5 (1968).

———. "Quelques Signes de l'Arabisation des Noms Portés par les Issas." *Le Pount,* no. 3 (1967).

Bertin, Pierre. "La Division du Temps chez les Somalis." *Le Pount,* no. 9 (1971).

———. "Noms et Fractionnements chez les Populations de Langue Somalie." *Le Pount,* nos. 4-6 (1968).

Carette-Bouvet, Pierre. "Division de Somalis Issas." In *L'Anthropologie,* vol. 17 (1906).

Chailley, Marcel, Commander. *Chez les Danakils.* Paris: Cahiers de Foucauld, 1951.

Chauffard, Emile. "Les Populations Indigènes du Protectorat Français de la Côte de Somalis." *RIS* (1908).

Chedeville, Edouard. "Recueil de Prénoms Somalis et Danakils. Orthographe des Noms Somalis et Danakils." *Le Pount,* no. L (1966).

———. "La Transcription des Noms Propres Locaux et sa Réalisation en Côte Francaise des Somalis." *Le Pount,* no. 1 (1966).

———. "Quelques Faits sur l'Organisation Sociale des Afars." *Africa,* vol. 36, no. 2 (April 1966).

Cotigny, L. "Les Somalis." *La Revue Maritime et Coloniale* (1885).

Daoud A. Alwan, and Ali A. Houmed. *L'Artisanat Djiboutien, une Mosaïque de Traditions.* Djibouti: Iris Publications, 1996.

Dilleyta, Aden Mohamed. "Les Afars: La Fin du Nomadisme." *Politique Africaine,* no. 34 (1989): 51–63.

Dives, E. "Chez les Afars et les Issas." Thesis No. 261, CHEAM, Paris, 1963.

Erlich, Michel. *La Femme Blessée (Essai sur les Mutilations Sexuelles Féminines).* Paris: L'Harmattan, 1986.

Ferrand, Gabriel. "Notes sur la Situation Politique Commerciale et Religieuse du Pachalik de Harrar et Ses Dépendances." *BSGE,* vol. 8 (1886): 1–17, 23–44.

——. *Matériaux d'Études sur les Pays Musulmans: Les Somalis.* Paris: Leroux, 1903.

Ferry, Robert. "Esquisse d'une Etude Ethnique du Lycée de Djibouti en 1965." *Le Pount,* no.1 (1966)

——. "Esquisse d'une Etude Ethnique des Lignées de Djibouti en 1963–1964." *Le Pount,* no.1 (1966).

——. "Mémoire sur la Situation des Issas en CFS." Thesis, CHEAM, Paris, 1950.

Griaule, Marcel. *Les Flambeurs d'Hommes.* Paris: Calmann-Lévy, 1934.

Grignou, G. "Le Droit Coutumier et la Justice chez les Somalis." *RSGCP* (1912) and *L'Anthropologie,* vol. 24 (1913).

Guedda Mohamed Ahmed. "Etude Socio-Economique dans le Cadre de l'Aménagement Intégré de la Forêt du Day." *Revue de l'ISERST* (1987).

——. "La Question Nationale en Corne d'Afrique." Master's thesis, Université de Paris VIII, 1979.

——. *L'Organisation Sociale Afar.* Paris: EHESS, 1981.

——. "Les Approches de l'Organisation Sociales et Politique des Afars." Thesis, EHESS, Paris, 1994.

——. "Le Mariage Coutumier chez les Afars." *Revue de l'ISERST,* no. 2 (1989).

Guedda M. Ahmed, and J. Godet. "Le Pastoralisme en République de Djibouti: Données Générales." *Production Pastorale et Société, Revue de l'ISERST* (1984).

Helland, J. "An Analysis of Afar Pastoralism in the North-Eastern Rangelands of Ethiopia." *African Savannah Studies,* no. 20 (1980).

Hoffmann, Bernardin, Monseigneur. "Historique de la Mission de Djibouti." *Vivante Afrique,* no. 247 (1967).

Idriss Abdillahi Orah. "La Mortalité Infantile à Djibouti." Master's thesis in sociology, Université de Paris X-Nanterre, 1986.

——. "La Nuptialité et la Divortialité à Djibouti." DEA thesis in social sciences, EHESS, 1989.

——. "Les Mariages et les Divorces à Djibouti: Aperçu Socio-Démographique." *Revue des Etudes Djiboutiennes,* no. 1 (September 1994).

Ilmi Keddab, and E. Inbert. "La Légende des Issa." *Le Pount,* no. 12 (1973).

Hicks, Esther K. *Infibulation: Female Mutilation in Northeastern Africa.* New Brunswick, N.J.: Transaction, 1993.

Jousseaume, F. *Impressions de Voyage en Apharras (Afars).* 2 vols. Paris: Baqillere, 1914.

———. "Sur l'Infibulation ou Mutilation des Organes Génitaux de la Femme chez les Peuples de la Mer Rouge et du Golfe d'Aden." *Revue d'Anthropologie,* (1889).

———. "Réflexions Anthropologiques à propos des Tumulus et Silex Taillés des Somalis et Danakils." *L'Anthropologie,* vol. 6 (1985): 393–413.

Khayat, Jacqueline. *Rites et Mutilations Sexuels.* Paris: Authier, 1977.

Lacour, G. "L'Enseignement en Côte Française des Somalis." *Le Réveil de Djibouti* (October-November 1961).

———. "L'Enseignement et les Missions Catholiques au TFAI." *Vivante Afrique,* no. 247 (1967).

Lamy, Robert. "Le Destin des Somalis." In *Mer Rouge-Afrique Orientale.* Paris: J. Peyronnet, 1959.

Laurioz, Jacques. "Note sur les Pratiques Relatives aux Génies Zar en TFAI." *Le Pount,* no. 7 (1969).

Leiris, Michel. *L'Afrique Fantôme.* Paris: Gallimard, 1934.

Leroi-Gourhan, André, and J. Poirier. "La Somalie Française." In *Ethnologie de l'Union Française* (1953): 422–440.

Lewis, Ioan M. *Abaar: The Somali Drought.* London: International African Institute, 1975.

———. *Blood and Bone: The Call of Kinship in Somali Culture.* London: Haan Associates, 1993.

———. *Islam in Tropical Africa.* London: Haan Associates, 1966.

———. *Saints and Somalis: Popular Islam in a Clan-Based Society.* London: Haan Associates, 1998.

———. *Somali Culture, History and Social Institutions.* London: Haan Associates, 1981.

———. "The Somali Lineage System and the Total Genealogy: A General Introduction to Basic Principles of Somali Political Institutions." Report on C. D. and W scheme R.- 632, Anthropological Research, Hargeisa, April 1957.

Lucas, M. "Renseignements Ethnographiques et Linguistique sur les Danakils de Tadjourah." *JSA,* vol. 2 (1932): 181–203.

Mohamed Abdo. "Autour du Qat. Contribution à l'Etude de l'Usage du Qat en Afrique du Nord-Est." DEA Thesis, EHESS, Paris, 1994.

Mohamed Ali Sheik. "The Origin of the Isaq Peoples." *Somaliland Journal* 1:1 (December 1954): 22–25.

Mohammed-Moktar Bey. "Une Reconnaissance au Pays des Gadaboursis." *BSKG* (1880).

Muller, Robert, Captain. "Les Populations de la Côte Française des

Somalis." In *Mer Rouge. Afrique Orientale* (Cahiers de l'Afrique et l'Asie, V). Paris: J. Peyronet, 1959.

Nourrit, C., and W. Pruitt. *Musique Traditionnelle de l'Afrique Noire* (Djibouti No. 17). Paris: Radio France Internationale, 1983.

Oberlé, Philippe. "Des Haines Ataviques à la Coexistence." *RFEPA* (January 1973).

Pankhurst, Richard K. P. "Gabata and Related Board Games in Ethiopia and the Horn of Africa." *Ethiopian Observer,* 14:3 (1971).

Querillac, R. "L'Islamisme à la Côte Française des Somalis." *En Terre d'Islam* (1941).

Rayne, H. "Somal Tribal Law." *JAS* 20 (1920–1921): 1014.

———. "Somal Marriage." *JAS* 21 (1921–1922): 2530.

Revoil, Georges. "Rapport Ethnographique sur les Populations de Côte des Somalis." *Revue Coloniale* (1901): 206–238.

———. *Notes d'Archéologie et d'Ethnographie Recueillies dans le Çomal.* Paris: E. Leroux, 1884.

Rouaud, Alain. "Les Yéménites de Djibouti à la Veille de l'Indépendance." Typescript document, Table ronde d'histoire de l'Océan Indien, Sénanque, 1979.

Saint-Veran, A. *A Djibouti avec les Afars et les Issas.* Paris: Editions Tholomier, 1977.

Savard, Georges. "Cross-Cousin Marriage among the Patrilineal Afar." *Proceedings of the third ICES,* pp. 88-99. Addis Ababa: *ICES,* 1966.

———. "The Structure of Afar Society." Fieldwork report for the period January 19–September 7, 1963, IES, Addis Ababa.

Shehim, Kassim. "The Influence of Islam on the Afar." Ph.D. dissertation, University of Washington, 1982.

Sindzingre, Nicole. "Le Plus et le Moins: à Propos de l'Excision." *Commission Economique pour l'Afrique,* vol. 17, no. 65 (1977).

Villeneuve. "Etude sur une Coutume Somalie: Les Femmes Cousues." *JSA* (1937): 15–32.

CULTURE

Education, Language, Linguistics

Abraham, R. C., Major. *Somali-English Dictionary.* London: University Press, 1962.

Andrzejewski, B. W., and Ioan M. Lewis. *Somali Poetry.* Oxford: Clarendon, 1964.

Armstrong, Lillias E. "The Phonetic Structure of Somali." *Mitteilungen des Seminars für Orientalische Sprachen* 37, Teil III, 1934.

Bell, C. R. V. *The Somali Language.* London: Longmans, Green, 1953.

Bliese, L. F. *A Generative Grammar Study of Afar.* Dallas: Summer Institute of Linguistics, 1977.

Choukri M. Osman, and Ifrah S. Djama. *Lire et Ecrire en Somali.* Djibouti: Imprimerie Nationale, 1998.

Dimis, Ahmed Abdallah, and Jamaleddin Abdulkader Redo. *Qafar Afih Yabti-Rakiibo.* Paris: Imprimerie Parisienne de la Réunion, 1976.

———. *Qafar Afih Baritto.* Paris: Imprimerie Parisienne de la Réunion, 1976.

Duchenet, Edouard. *Histoires Somalies: La Malice des Primitifs.* Paris: Larose, 1936.

———. "Le Chant dans le Folklore Somali." *Revue du Folklore Français,* vol. 9 (1938).

Ferrand, Gabriel. *Notes de Grammaire Somalie.* Alger: P. Fontana, 1886.

Gamaledin, M., and R. J. Hayward. "Tolo Hanfare's Song of Accusation: An Afar Text." *Bulletin of the SOAS* 44-2 (1981).

Haan Associates. *English-Somali Dictionary.* London: 1994.

Hayward, R. J., and Ioan M. Lewis. "Voice and Power: The Culture of Language in Northeastern Africa. Essays in Honour to B. W. Andrzejewski." *African Languages Supplement* 3 (1996).

Hoffmann, Bernardin, Monseigneur. *Dictionnaire de la Langue Somalie.* 2 vols. Djibouti: Imprimerie de la Mission Catholique.

———. *Grammaire de la Langue Somalie.* Djibouti: Imprimerie de la Mission Catholique, 1968.

Kern, Luc. "Quelques Proverbes Afar." *Le Pount,* no. 4 (1968).

Lacour, G. "L'Enseignement en Côte Française des Somalis." *Le Réveil de Djibouti* (October–November 1961).

Laurence, Margaret. *A Tree for Poverty: Somali Poetry and Prose.* Shannon: Irish University Press, 1970.

Léon, Henri. *Essai de Vocabulaire Pratique Français-Issa.* Melun: Imprimerie Administrative, 1897.

Lucas, Maurice. "Renseignements Ethnographiques et Linguistiques sur les Danakils de Tadjourah." *JSA,* vol.5 (1938): 181–202.

Ministère de l'Education Nationale. *Rapport de la Commission Interministérielle Chargée de Superviser le Programme d'Arabisation.* Djibouti: July 1983.

———. *Rapport sur la Situation de la Langue Arabe à Djibouti.* Djibouti: 1987.

Morin, Didier. "Ports et Mouillages en République de Djibouti: Une Toponymie Ambigüe." In *Les Ports de l'Océan Indien au 19e et 20e Siècles*. Aix-en-Provence: IHPOM, 1981.

———. "Aspects du Multilinguisme en RDD." *Northeastern African Studies* 4:1 (1982).

———. "A Propos des Emprunts à l'Arabe et au Français en Afar et en Somali à Djibouti." In *Proceedings of the Second International Congress of Somali Studies*, vol. 1, pp. 277-286, edited by Thomas Labahn. University of Hamburg, August 1–6, 1983.

———. *Le Ginnili: Devin, Poète et Guerrier Afar*. Paris: Editions Peeters Selaf, 1991.

———. *Des Paroles Douces comme la Soie: Introduction aux Contes dans l'Aire Couchitique*. Paris: Editions Peeters Selaf, 1995.

———. *Poésie Traditionnelle des Afars*. Paris: Editions Peeters Selaf, 1997.

Orwin, Martin. *Colloquial Somali*. London: Routledge, 1995.

Parker, Enid, M. *An Afar-English-French Dictionary*. London: SOAS, 1985.

———. "Afar Stories, Riddles and Proverbs." *JES*, vol. 9, no. 2 (1971).

———. *An Afar-English Dictionary*. Addis Ababa: 1974.

Parker, E., and Margaret Munro. *An English-Afar Language Phrase Book*. London: SOAS, 1985).

Pénel, Jean-Dominique. *Documents pour une Histoire de l'Ecole à Djibouti*. Paris: Documentation Universitaire Fernando Pessoa, 1998.

Petracek, Karel. "Problèmes de Linguistique Couchitique." Colloque international sur les langues couchitiques et les peuples qui les parlent, CNRS, Paris, 1975.

Reinisch, Leo. *Die Afar Sprache*. Vienne: Carl Gerold's Sohn, 1885–1887.

Said Idriss Hassan. "Situation Linguistique de la République de Djibouti." Master's thesis in linguistics, Université de Paris, 1980.

Savard, Georges. "War Chants in Praise of Ancient Afar Heroes." *JES* 3:1 (1965).

William Johnson, John. *"Helloy" Modern Poetry and Songs of the Somali*. London: Haan Publishing, 1996.

Zaborski, Andrzj. *Arabic Loan-Words in Somali: Preliminary Survey*, vol. 5, pp. 125–175. Krakow: Folia Orientalia, 1967.

Literature

Abdi Ismael Abdi. *L'Enfance Eclatée*. Djibouti: CCFAR, 1996.

———. *Cris de Traverse*. Paris: L'Harmattan, 1998.

———. *Yeli Yelo ou le Retour du Faiseur de Miracles*. Unpublished drama.

Abdi Mohamed Farah. *Nomad, No Man's Land ou les Vers Volés à l'Instant.* Djibouti: CCFAR, 1998.

Abdourahman Waberi. *Le Pays sans Ombre.* Paris: Le Serpent à Plumes, 1994.

———. *Cahier Nomade.* Paris: Le Serpent à Plumes, 1996.

———. *Balbala.* Paris: Le Serpent à Plumes, 1997.

Ali Coubba. *L'Aleph-Ba-Ta.* Paris: L'Harmattan, 1998.

Ali Moussa Iye. "Bouh, un Nomade Urbain." *Autrement,* no. 21 (1987).

———. "Djibouti: Entre la Myrrhe et les Mythes." *Arabies* (1988).

———. *Le Chapelet des Destins.* Djibouti: CCFAR, 1998.

Chehem Watta. *Pèlerin d'Errance.* Paris: L'Harmattan, 1997.

———. *Sous les Soleils de Houroud.* Paris: L'Harmattan, 1998.

Daher Ahmed Farah. *Splendeur Ephémère.* Paris: L'Harmattan, 1993.

Diehl, Jean-Pierre. *Le Regard Colonial.* Paris: Regime DeForge, 1986.

Erouart, Siad Patrick. "Adieu aux Nostalgies Coloniales." *Autrement,* no. 21 (1987): 189–195.

Esme, Jean d'. "L'Homme des Sables." *La Nouvelle Revue Critique* (1930).

Idriss Youssouf Elmi. *Nostalgies ou le Joug du Verbe.* Paris: L'Harmattan, 1998.

———. *La Galaxie de l'Absurde.* Paris: L'Harmattan, 1997.

Kessel, Joseph. *Les Chasseurs d'Esclaves.* Djibouti, 1930; Paris: Editions de France, 1933.

———. *Tous n'Etaient pas des Anges.* Paris: Plon, 1963.

———. *Fortune Carrée.* Paris: Hachette, 1955.

Larminat, E. de. *Chroniques Irrévérencieuses.* Paris: Plon, 1962.

Londres, Albert. "Djibouti-la-Jolie." In *Pêcheurs de Perles.* Paris: UGE, 1975.

Monfreid, Henri de. *Sea Adventures.* London: 1937.

———. *Vers les Terres Hostiles d'Ethiopie.* Paris: Grasset, 1933.

———. *Hashish.* New York: Penguin Books, 1946.

———. *Les Derniers Jours de l'Arabie Heureuse.* Paris: Gallimard, 1935.

———. *Le Lépreux.* Paris: Grasset, 1935.

———. *L'Avion Noir.* Paris: Grasset, 1936.

———. *Les Guerriers de l'Ogaden.* Paris: Gallimard, 1936.

———. *Le Roi des Abeilles.* Paris: Gallimard, 1937.

———. *Le Serpent de Cheikh Hussein: Souvenirs et Légendes.* Paris: P. Elshe, 1937.

———. *Abdi, l'Homme à la Main Coupée.* Paris: Grasset, 1937.

———. *L'Enfant Sauvage.* Paris: Grasset, 1938.

———. *Secrets of the Red Sea.* London: Faber and Faber, 1934.

————. *Le Radeau de la Méduse, ou Comment Fut Sauvé Djibouti.* Paris: Edition Bernard Grasset, 1958.

Omar Youssouf Ali. *Bouti, l'Ogresse des Temps Anciens.* Djibouti: O. Y. Ali, 1997.

————. *Mon Frère, l'Hyène.* Djibouti: O. Y. Ali, 1998.

Pénel, Jean-Dominique. *Djibouti 70. Repères sur l'Émergence de la Littérature Djiboutienne en Français dans les Années 70.* Djibouti: CCFAR, 1997.

————. *Pays Gorge, Île dans la Terre.* Paris: L'Harmattan, 1997.

Ponchardier, Dominique. *La Dame de Tadjourah.* Paris: Gallimard, 1973.

Said Ahmed Warsama. *Hees Hawleeddo/Chanson de Travail Somaliennes.* Djibouti: ISERST/ACCT, 1987.

Syad, William. *Khamsin.* Paris: Présence Africaine, 1959.

————. *Naufragés du Destin.* Paris: Présence Africaine, 1978.

Sports

Burfoot, Amy. "The Desert Blooms." *Runner's World,* vol. 20 (December 1985).

Lidz, Franz. "Goats, Kat and Warrant Officers." *Sports Illustrated,* vol. 62 (May 6, 1985): 12.

Post, Marty. "Worlds Apart." *Runner's World,* vol. 20 (June 1985): 54.

SCIENCE

Archaeology, Geology, Paleonthology

Aubert de La Rue, Edgar. "Le Volcanisme en CFS." *Bulletin Volcanologique,* vol. 5 (1939).

————. "Rapport de la Mission Géologique à la Côte Française des Somalis." *Bulletin du Laboratoire de Géologie du Service des Mines de Madagascar* (1939).

Blanc, C., Paul Bouvier, and André Planes. "Monolithes Phalliformes et Pierres Levées en TFAI." *Le Pount,* no. 9 (1971).

Bouvier, Paul, and Serge Miche. "Enceintes. Tombes et Habitations Anciennes en TFAI." *Le Pount,* no.13 (1974).

Centre National de la Recherche Scientifique. "L'Afar." *RGPGD,* vol. 15 fas. (4) (1973): 346–490.

Chavaillon, J. "Un Siècle de Recherches Préhistoriques en République de Djibouti." *Revue de l'ISERST,* no. 3 (1990): 17–28.

Clark, J. Desmond. *The Prehistoric Cultures of the Horn of Africa.* Cambridge: Cambridge University Press, 1954.

Daoud A. Alwan, and Ali A. Houmed. *Lake Assal: A Salt Field, an Open Window on History.* Djibouti: Iris Publications, 1994.

Demange, J., and Laurent Stieltjes. "Géologie de la Région Sud-Ouest du TFAI." BRGM Report, series 2, section 4, no. 2 (1975): 83–119.

Dreyfuss, Maurice. "Etude de Géologie et de Géographie Physique sur la Côte Française des Somalis." *RGPGD,* vol. 4 (1932).

———. "Etude Géologique Sommaire de la Région Méridionale de la Côte Française des Somalis." *Mémoires de la Société de Géologie,* vol. 6 (1930).

Ferry, Robert, R. Grau, and Paul Bouvier. "La Préhistoire à Djibouti." *Archaeologia,* no. 159 (1981): 47–73.

Gasse, F., and A. Street. "Late Quaternary Lake Level and Environments in the Northern Rift Valley and Afar Region." *Palaeogeography, Palaeoclimatology, Palaeoecology,* vol. 24 (1978): 279–325.

Geraads, D., and M. Martin. "L'Homme Fossile de Djibouti." *Pour la Science* (April 1985): 8–9.

Haroun, T. "The Afar Triangle." *Scientific American,* vol. 22, no. 2 (February 1970).

Hentiger, R., and B. Stanudin. "Géothermie, Territoire Français des Afars et des Issas. Géophysique de la Rive Orientale du lac Abbe." BRGM report, Paris, 1974.

Joussaume, R. "Gravures Rupestres en République de Djibouti." *Revue de l'ISERST,* no. 2 (1989): 105–129.

Kern, Luc. "Le Site de Handoga." *Le Pount,* no. 6 (1968).

Lavigne, J., and M. Lopoukhine. "Reconnaissance Géothermique du TFAI." BRGM report, Paris, 1970.

Marinelli, G. "La Province Géothermique de la Dépression Dankali." *Annales des Mines* (May 1971).

Marinelli, G., and J. Varet. "Structure et Evolution du Sud du Horst Danakil." *CRAS,* vol. 276 (1973).

Nocairi, Mohamed. "Contribution à l'Etude de la Préhistoire de la République de Djibouti." Master's thesis, Université de Bordeaux I, 1986.

Stieltjes, Laurent. "Etude Géologique de la Région du Lac Assal." BRGM report, Paris, April 1973.

Valette, J. "Le Lac Abhe: Etude Morphologique et Géochimique." *Rapport du BRGM,* series 2, no. 2 (1975): 143–155.

Varet, J. "L'Afar, un Point Chaud de la Géophysique." *La Recherche,* vol. 6, no. 62 (1975): 1018–1026.

Vellutini, Pierre, and Patrick Piguet. *Itinéraires Géologiques*. Djibouti: Imprimerie Nationale, 1994.

Fauna, Flora

Aubert de La Rue, Edgar. "Les Forêts de la Côte Française des Somalis." *Sciences Naturelles,* vol.1 (1939).

Audru, J., J. César, G. Forgiarini, and J-P. Lebrun. *La Végétation et les Potentialités Pastorales de la République de Djibouti*. Paris: Maison-Alfort, IEMVT, 1987.

Beurier, J-P. *Les Problèmes Juridiques de l'Exploitation des Espèces à Djibouti*. Rome: FAO, 1992.

Blot, J. "Approche du Phénomène de Désertification dans les Massifs des Goddas." DEA thesis in tropical geography, Université de Bordeaux, 1986.

Chedeville, Edouard. *La Végétation du Territoire Français des Afars et des Issas*. Florence: Webbia, 1972.

Coulombel, Alain. *Coquillages de Djibouti*. Aix-en-Provence: Edisud, 1991.

Fischer-Piette, E. "Sur l'Intérêt de la Faune Malacologique Terrestre de la Région de Djibouti." *Le Pount,* no. 7 (1969).

Koechlin, J. *Végétation et Flore de la République de Djibouti*. Djibouti: CEGD, 1977.

Laurent, Alain. "Catalogue Commenté des Oiseaux de Djibouti." Typescript document, ONTA, Djibouti, 1990.

Radt, Charlotte. "Contribution à l'Etude Ethno-Botanique d'une Plante: Le Khat." *JATBA,* vol. 16 (1969).

Randall, John E. *Red Sea Fishes*. London: Immel Publishing, 1982.

Revoil, Georges. *Faune et Flore des Pays Somalis*. Paris: Challamel, 1882.

Robin, A. "Conchyliologie en TFAI." *Le Pount,* no. 11 (1973).

Rodinson, M. "Esquisse d'une Monographie du Khat." *Journal Asiatique,* no. 245 (1977).

Simonneau, Edmond-Louis. *Les Animaux du TFAI*. Djibouti: E. L. Simonneau, 1974.

Weinberg, Steven. *Découvrir la Mer Rouge et l'Océan Indien*. Paris: Nathan, 1996.

GEOGRAPHY, URBAN AREAS

Aden Hersi Mahamoud. "Les Fonctions Urbaines de Djibouti." Third-cycle thesis in geography, Université de Bordeaux III, 1984.

162 • BIBLIOGRAPHY

Amina Said Chire. "Les Problèmes Liés à la Croissance Urbaine à Djibouti et à Nouakchott." Master's thesis in physical planning, Université de Pau et des Pays de l'Adour, 1993.

———. "Sociétés, Aménagement et Développement Local. Université de Pau et des Pays de l'Adour." DEA thesis in physical planning, Université de Pau et des Pays de l'Adour, November 1994.

Barrère, Gil Seral. "Problèmes Urbains à Djibouti." CEGD Report, Djibouti, 1976.

Decoudras, Pierre-Marie. "Occupation de l'Espace Périphérique de la Ville de Djibouti." Cahiers d'Outre-Mer, no. 158 (1987): 93–110.

Gil, José. "Les Problèmes Urbains à Djibouti." Third-cycle thesis, Université de Bordeaux III, 1976.

Grolée, J. "Le Problème de l'Eau en Côte Française des Somalis." BCEOM (1961).

Hassan Omar Rayaleh. "L'Accès à l'Eau et les Inégalités Sociales dans la Ville de Djibouti." Master's thesis in geography, Université de Saint Etienne, 1995.

Idriss A. Doudoub. Esquisse Ethnique des Divers Groupes Autochtones de Djibouti. Thesis, ENFOM, Paris, 1962.

Kadar Ismael Guelleh. "La Structure des Anciens Quartiers de Djibouti." Master's thesis in geography and physical planning, Université d'Aix-Marseille II, 1989.

———. "Gestions Urbaines, Politiques Urbaines et Problèmes d'Urbanisme à Djibouti de sa Création à nos Jours: Nécessité d'une Municipalité." DEA thesis in geography and physical planning, Université d'Aix-Marseille II, 1990.

Son, Frédéric. Origine et Développement de Djibouti. Paris: Colonial, 1914.

Yasmine Ahmed Moussa. "Formation, Mutation Spatiale et Développement Urbain d'un Site: Balbala." Master's thesis in geography, Université de Provence, 1996.

Health, Medicine

Absieh, Ahmed. Le Khat, Toxique du TFAI. Bordeaux: Bergeret, 1973.

Charpin, Max. "Incidences Chirurgicales de la Consommation Habituelle du Khat." Le Pount, no. 6 (1968).

Courtois, D., and D. Gomart. "La Tuberculose en Territoire Français des Afars et des Issas." Revue d'Epidémiologie de Médecine Sociale et de Santé Publique, no. 21 (1973).

David, Alain. "L'Infibulation en République de Djibouti." Ph.D. dissertation in medical studies, Université de Bordeaux:, 1978.

Dufour, Sylvie. "Adaï, l'Arbre Brosse à Dents de la République de Djibouti." Ph.D. dissertation in pharmacy, Université de Picardie, 1995.

Erlich, Michel, and J. Poulet. "La Consommation du Khat à Djibouti et ses Conséquences." *La Vie Médicale,* no. 26 (November 1977).

Guedel, J. "Incidences Médico-Sociales de la Consommation du Kât en Côte Française des Somalis." *Le Pount,* no. 2 (1967).

———. "Incidences Médico-Sociales de la Consommation du Khat en TFAI." *Le Pount,* no. 3 (1967).

Le Bras, M. "Le Problème du Khat; Premiers Aperçus sur un Fléau Social." *Le Pount,* no. 2 (1967).

Lemordant D. *Le Problème du Khat en CFS.* Djibouti, 1962.

———. "Contribution à l'Etude du Khat." Ph.D. dissertation in medical studies, Université d'Aix-Marseille, 1959.

———. "Le Service de Santé en CFS. Historique et Organisation." *Le Réveil de Djibouti* (December 1959–February 1960).

Martin, Alice. "Women Pay Price for Drug Culture." *Guardian Weekly* (November 3, 1996).

Ministère de la Santé Publique et des Affaires Sociales. "Programme National de Lutte contre la Tuberculose." Report, Djibouti, December 1991.

Peters, G. "Gynécologie au Pays des Femmes Cousues." *Acta Chirurgica,* vol. 71 (1972): 173–193.

Stefani, B. "Aperçu de la Médecine Populaire à Djibouti." Master's thesis, Université Paul Sabatier, Toulouse, 1975.

About the Authors

DAOUD ABOUBAKER ALWAN was born and raised in Djibouti, where he currently works as a consultant for the U.N. Development Program. He has studied history and political science, and has worked as a journalist, a history teacher, and researcher at the Institut Supérieur d'Etude et de Recherche Scientifiques et Technologiques. He has published a number of articles on the history of Djibouti and the Horn of Africa.

YOHANIS MIBRATHU was born and raised in Djibouti. After studying English at the University of Provence, he taught both English and French at various public and private institutions in Djibouti, including the Centre de Formation Administrative and the Centre Régional Interlinguistique. He has also worked as an interpreter at the International Chamber of Commerce and Industry of Djibouti. He currently works as a continuing education coordinator at Dallas International School.